IN SICKNESS
AND IN HEALTH

IN SICKNESS AND IN HEALTH

The Mission of Voluntary Health Care Institutions

Edited by

J. David Seay, J.D.
Bruce C. Vladeck, Ph.D.

A United Hospital Fund Book

McGRAW-HILL BOOK COMPANY

New York St. Louis San Francisco Colorado Springs
Oklahoma City Auckland Bogotá Caracas Hamburg
Lisbon London Madrid Mexico Milan
Montreal New Delhi Panama Paris San Juan
São Paulo Singapore Sydney Tokyo Toronto

IN SICKNESS AND IN HEALTH
The Mission of Voluntary Health Care Institutions

1234567890 DOC DOC 8921098

ISBN 0-07-067532-5

This book was set in Optima by Digitype, Inc.; the sponsoring editor was Deborah Glazer; the production supervisor was Robert R. Laffler. The cover was designed by Alma Orenstein. Project supervision was done by Harriet Damon Shields & Associates.
R. R. Donnelley & Sons Company was printer and binder.

Library of Congress Catologing-in-Publication Data

In sickness and in health.

    "A United Hospital Fund Book."

    1. Hospitals, Voluntary — United States.   I. Seay,
J. David.   II. Vladeck, Bruce C.
RA981.A315   1988   362.1'1   88-2790
ISBN 0-07-067532-5

DEDICATION

This book is dedicated to the memory of Philip Bastedo, chairman of the board of directors of the United Hospital Fund of New York from 1978 to 1984, and an honorary director of the Fund at the time of his death in 1987. For more than 25 years, the United Hospital Fund and, in a real sense, all of New York benefited from his steadfast leadership and clear vision of the future.

Mr. Bastedo served for many years as president of one of New York City's not-for-profit hospitals and was deeply committed to the concept and practice of voluntarism in health care in America, and particularly in New York City where he lived and worked. As a lawyer and as a volunteer director and trustee of numerous charitable organizations, he was aware of the special contribution of concerned citizens to an organization and to society, and was also appreciative of professionals who likewise understood and nourished this most important and symbiotic American trait.

CONTENTS

FOREWORD

The evolution of the voluntary hospital in America closely reflects the medical, economic, cultural, and political history of this nation. What started as a response by ethnic and religious groups to help the "deserving poor" has evolved into the single largest component of our health care system. A number of very specific factors — the advent of anesthesia, the depression of the 1930s, World War II, the "Great Society," and current advances in medical technology — are all clearly reflected in, and were affected by, this evolution.

Throughout their history, voluntary institutions have not been static in terms of either their actual mission or in society's perceptions and expectations of them. To a great extent, at any given point, their success has been a function of how well they do respond to the demands and values of a particular time. In turn, their success is also either facilitated or impeded by the extant attitudes and actions of government. Ideally, only through a "synchronicity" of societal needs and expectations, public policy, and the hospitals' own activities can their mission be fulfilled.

It can be debated whether, historically, public policy has been responsibly developed with regard to how voluntary institutions can best fulfill their role — or whether these hospitals have been fully responsive to the needs of society. The question to be addressed now, however, is not one of analyzing this history. Rather, it concerns whether, given current societal needs and expectations, there is a unique role for voluntary hospitals and, if so, how public policy can both help define and facilitate that role.

Over the last decade, this role has been brought into question by a series of societal, economic, and political factors that, perhaps to a greater degree than in the past, may actually threaten the continued existence of the voluntary hospital. These factors are multiple and complex, but they can be summarized as follows:

• While the number of uninsured people has increased dramatically, many voluntary hospitals have not appeared willing to bear an increasing share of this burden. Some argue that voluntary hospitals, in the aggregate, in fact bear no more of this burden than their for-profit counterparts.

• In a political environment that preaches greater competition and less regulation in the health field, voluntary hospitals have often diversified into a number of enterprises that make it somewhat difficult to differentiate them from proprietary institutions. In addition, in a competitive environment, many hospitals feel that they cannot fulfill their charitable mission and still survive.

• At both the state and federal levels the tax-exempt status of voluntary hospitals has come into question. At least one state court has begun to restrict that status, and federal legislation has been discussed to remove or modify the current exemption.

• The growth in the federal budget deficit has brought into question the advisability of maintaining exemptions — which involve billions of dollars in lost revenues — granted to these institutions. A tax exemption has no less of an effect on the deficit than does an actual outlay of funds. Thus, at a time when expenditures are being cut and held to a rigorous test, some suggest that the same rules should be applied to such exemptions.

In this environment, a number of questions have thus arisen. Has the need for voluntary hospitals, which may have existed historically, disappeared? Is there a special role that voluntary hospitals can play in the future? Is their mission really different from that of their proprietary brethren? Can a hospital fulfill a charitable mission and still survive in a competitive marketplace? Can public policy be altered to define and assure that role? These are all questions that must be answered and answered soon. Their answers affect the future of the health care system as we know it, raise issues about voluntarism in general, and could have a broader impact on the nation's overall economy.

In a country that often acts best in crisis situations, the climate is right to address these questions. Whatever the appropriate way to achieve the "synchronicity" described earlier, any solution must first define more specifically what society's expectations are for the mission of voluntary hospitals, and then develop public policy that both reflects and facilitates the fulfillment of that mission. At the same time, the leaders of those voluntary institutions must also more specifically define — and publicly articulate — what their missions are for the benefit of society. It is in nobody's best interest to do otherwise.

JEFFREY MERRILL
Vice President
The Robert Wood Johnson Foundation
Princeton, New Jersey

PREFACE

Stating the case, in positive terms, for the continued existence and legitimacy of, as well as special treatment for, voluntary health care institutions is an important exercise if American society wishes to retain the major feature of our pluralistic health care system. It is an exercise that involves not only an empirical analysis of what voluntary health care institutions do for society in exchange for their special status and treatment but also a careful look at the intentions and motivations of the founding and governing individuals behind the institutions. Ultimately, making the case for the institution requires scrutiny of the institution's mission, a term that is inexorably intertwined with elements of intent and performance. It is not an easy exercise to accomplish.

This volume attempts, however, to do just that, and in doing so presents in its various chapters varying perspectives on this topic from differing disciplines. The first chapter, which we have prepared, and which has been separately published by the United Hospital Fund of New York, represents our best attempt in summarizing and synthesizing much of the thinking set forth in the other chapters of the book, while at the same time expressing some of our own views as well.

The second chapter, by Elizabeth Miller Guggenheimer, frames the issue in legal and policy terms, and suggests that a more substantive set of criteria be established under which the voluntary distinction should be granted. Chapter 3 provocatively outlines the tax exemption issue facing hospitals in today's environment. Carl Schramm suggests that the law merely mirrors public perceptions about voluntary health care institutions, and recommends that it is incumbent upon the governors and leaders of those institutions themselves to take actions to stem or reverse these trends.

In Chapter 4, David Rosner provides an important historical overview of voluntary hospitals in America and encourages health care leaders and policymakers not to lose sight of the origins and evolution of the voluntary health care institution as a vehicle for social policy implementation. The fifth chapter places the ethical question straightforwardly in inquiring whether or not the voluntary hospital has a unique moral mission. As Daniel Wikler points out, this question is not merely philosophical but has immediate and long-ranging practical implications and consequences as well, for if the voluntary form can be shown to be if not inherently superior, at least more likely than the other forms to forward the social and charitable goals of society, then a fairly sound policy case will have been made toward the continued support and approbation of these types of institutions.

The delicate balance of power and the interchange between the voluntary health care institution and its physicians is examined in the sixth chapter. Examining the not-for-profit health maintenance organization as a model, Merwyn Greenlick discusses the question of whether voluntary institutions have been, or can be, more successful in attempting to mediate the competing powers of professional autonomy in medicine and institutional imperatives of mission and community service. Chapter 7, by James McCormack, takes a number of these concepts even further, and explores the careful balancing that must be performed within mission-driven institutions in order to both serve and survive.

In the last chapter, Stanley Jones and Merlin Du Val return to the central theme of the book, in seeking to discover just what it is that distinguishes the voluntary health care institution in an increasingly commercial health care environment. This chapter strives to provide practical day-to-day guidelines and recommendations in order to assist hospital trustees and administrators in the increasingly difficult tasks of governing

and managing health care institutions that must not only have the forti-
tude to survive but also the conscience to serve.

Several of the chapters of this book, and a good deal of the work that
went into preparing it, were supported, in part, by Grant Number 10482
from the Robert Wood Johnson Foundation. Additional support was
provided by the United Hospital Fund of New York.

ACKNOWLEDGMENTS

In addition to the authors of the various chapters of this book — Merwyn
R. Greenlick, Elizabeth Miller Guggenheimer, Stanley B. Jones and Merlin K. Du Val, James J. McCormack, David Rosner, Carl J. Schramm, and
Daniel Wikler — to whom we owe a great debt of appreciation and
respect, we would like to acknowledge the many people who helped in
many ways during the course of the study which lead to this volume, as
well as during the development of the book itself.

Special gratitude is due to those advisors who attended a very helpful
session in New Orleans, in February of 1987: Nancy Barrand, Edward J.
Connors, Robert Cunningham, Jr., Msgr. Charles J. Fahey, Symond R.
Gottlieb, Bradford Gray, J. Rogers Hollingsworth, Anthony R. Kovner,
Maurice Lazarus, Linda B. Miller, Joseph M. Rees, Walter N. Rothschild,
Jr., Cecil G. Sheps, M.D., Sister Mary Caritas, Ronald C. Wacker, and
Charles H. White.

Also, many individuals assisted this project in many different ways, in
groups and individual meetings, by commenting on drafts of various
papers, in telephone conversations, and in correspondence. We want to
publicly thank them all for their assistance and thoughtful contributions:
Daniel Bourque, Lawrence Brown, Earl M. Collier, Norman Daniels,
Robert A. Derzon, William M. Evarts, Jr., Emily Friedman, Fred Goldman,
Rosalie Brown Greenberg, Henry Hansmann, William Jones, David
Kinzer, Lawrence S. Lewin, Carol M. McCarthy, Walter McClure, Walter
McNerney, Jeffrey Merrill, William H. Nelson, Scott Parker, Edmund
Pellegrino, M.D., De Witt Peterkin, Jr., Nora Piore, Marvin C. Reiter,
David Rothman, Gabriel Rudney, Robert M. Sigmond, Rosemary A.
Stevens, Peter Swords, and Dennis Young.

Special thanks are due to the United Hospital Fund staff who participated in these efforts, particularly Paula S. Kramer whose contributions

were immeasurable; also to Carol Ewig, David A. Gould, Sally J. Rogers, Judith Kunz, and Ramona Vega.

J. DAVID SEAY
Vice President, Secretary, and Counsel

BRUCE C. VLADECK
President
United Hospital Fund of New York

CONTRIBUTORS

Merlin K. Du Val, M.D., is president of the American Healthcare Institute, which represents the interests of not-for-profit health care systems. Dr. Du Val, a board-certified surgeon, was previously an assistant secretary for health of the Department of Health, Education and Welfare and was the founding dean of the University of Arizona College of Medicine. His extensive career in medical education and health policy has included several academic appointments, various honorary degrees, and memberships in numerous local and national health care organizations. Dr. Du Val received his M.D. from Cornell University Medical College.

Merwyn R. Greenlick, Ph.D., is a vice president of the Kaiser Foundation Hospitals and the director of the Center for Health Research, Kaiser Permanente, Northwest Region. He is a faculty member for the Oregon Program of the University of Southern California's School of Public Administration and chairman of its Oregon Advisory Committee, as well as an adjunct professor of sociology and social work at Portland State University. Dr. Greenlick has an M.S. from Wayne State University and a Ph.D. in medical care organization from the University of Michigan.

Elizabeth Miller Guggenheimer, J.D., M.P.A., is an associate at the law firm of Dewey, Ballantine, Bushby, Palmer and Wood. She holds a J.D. from New York University School of Law and an M.P.A. from the Woodrow Wilson School of Public Affairs at Princeton University.

Stanley B. Jones is president of the Consolidated Consulting Group, a firm specializing in health care payment techniques. He formerly served as staff director of the U.S. Senate Health Subcommittee and as vice president of the Blue Cross and Blue Shield Association, and he was a founding partner of Health Policy Alternatives. Mr. Jones is a member of the Institute of Medicine of the National Academy of Sciences.

James J. McCormack, Ph.D., M.P.H., is a visiting associate professor of social policy in the Graduate School of Social Services at Fordham University and a principal of Swan Management Consultants, Inc. Formerly, Dr. McCormack was the executive director of the New York State Health Planning Commission. He holds an M.S.W. from Boston College, an M.P.H. from Harvard University, and a Ph.D. in social welfare from Brandeis University.

David Rosner, Ph.D., M.P.H., is a professor of history at Baruch College and at the Graduate Center, City University of New York. Dr. Rosner has written extensively on the history of the American hospital and American medicine and is presently a Guggenheim Fellow. He received a Ph.D. in the history of science from Harvard University and an M.P.H. from the University of Massachusetts.

Carl J. Schramm, Ph.D., J.D., is president of the Health Insurance Association of America. He was formerly the director of the Johns Hopkins Center for Hospital Finance and Management at the Johns Hopkins University School of Hygiene and Public Health and was also a chairman of the Maryland Health Services Cost Review Commission. Dr. Schramm received a Ph.D. in economics from the University of Wisconsin and a J.D. from Georgetown University.

J. David Seay, J.D., is vice president, secretary, and counsel of the United Hospital Fund of New York. Previously, Mr. Seay worked for John Hancock Mutual Life Insurance Company; the Science and Health Communications Group, Inc.; the Center for Health Policy Studies of the National Planning Association; and the Cost of Living Council.

He holds an adjunct faculty appointment with the Graduate School of Management and Urban Professions at the New School for Social Research and has also taught at the Benjamin N. Cardozo Law School of Yeshiva University. He received his J.D. from the Columbus School of Law of the Catholic University of America.

Bruce C. Vladeck, Ph.D., is president of the United Hospital Fund of New York. He previously served as assistant vice president of the Robert Wood Johnson Foundation; assistant commissioner for Health Planning and Resources Development of the New Jersey State Department of Health; and associate professor of public health and political science at Columbia University. Dr. Vladeck is a director of the New York City Health and Hospitals Corporation, an adjunct professor of public administration at New York University, and a member of the Prospective Payment Assessment Commission, the Institute of Medicine of the National Academy of Sciences, and the editorial board of *Inquiry.* He received his Ph.D. in political science from the University of Michigan.

Daniel Wikler, Ph.D., is a professor in the Department of Philosophy at the University of Wisconsin and a professor in the Program in Medical Ethics at the University of Wisconsin Medical School. During 1980–1981, he was the staff philosopher for the President's Commission for the Study of Ethical Problems in Medicine. More recently, he was a member of the Committee on Implications of For-Profit Enterprise in Health Care of the Institute of Medicine of the National Academy of Sciences. Dr. Wikler received his Ph.D. in philosophy from the University of California at Los Angeles.

IN SICKNESS
AND IN HEALTH

CHAPTER 1

MISSION MATTERS

J. David Seay, J.D.
Bruce C. Vladeck, Ph.D.

THE DEBATE OVER THE VOLUNTARY
HEALTH CARE INSTITUTION

Voluntary — that is, private, not-for-profit — institutions are the predominant form through which health care services are provided in the United States, and through which the burdens of meeting the needs of communities and the special populations within them are shared with government.

This has long been the case. Throughout American history, most general hospital care, institutional outpatient services, and formal home care have been provided by nonprofit, nongovernmental organizations, yet the role and the legitimacy of nonprofit providers of health care have increasingly come under question, and often under attack.

Tax Attacks

The questions and attacks come from two directions. First, in a political climate concerned with economic growth and preoccupied with tax reform, questions are being raised about the legal treatment of all tax-exempt organizations, not just those providing health care. A recent report by the Small Business Administration, for example, alleged that tax preferences such as income and property tax exemptions and tax-exempt

1

financing create "unfair" competition between the voluntary, not-for-profit sector and the for-profit business sector.[1]

Similarly, the House Committee on Ways and Means has held hearings to reexamine the definition of "unrelated business income" earned by nonprofit institutions[2] while the Internal Revenue Service has proposed regulations that would define as "lobbying" almost all attempts by charitable organizations to participate in open discussion and debate on public policy issues.[3]

Second, while the legal status of all nonprofit institutions is being questioned in Washington, individual states have taken the lead in focusing specifically on nonprofit health care institutions. Taxing authorities or legislatures in at least nine states, in efforts to seek new sources of revenue, are currently considering removing or limiting the real property tax exemption for voluntary hospitals.[4]

Perhaps more significantly, in 1986 the Utah State Supreme Court upheld a county tax commission's challenge to the local property tax exemptions for two not-for-profit voluntary hospitals in that state.[5] The local tax commissioner argued, and the State Supreme Court agreed, that the hospitals no longer deserved such exemptions unless they could demonstrate that they provided free care to indigents in an amount at least equal to the value of the exemptions. The court implied, contrary to both case law and common law, that providing health care to the community at large did not by itself constitute charity, and that other, more narrow and quantifiable criteria should be utilized.[6] The Utah court provided a six-point test "which must be weighed in determining whether a particular institution is in fact using its property exclusively for charitable purposes."[7] These criteria include "(i) whether the stated purpose of the entity is to provide a significant service to others without immediate expectation of material reward; (ii) whether the entity is supported, and to what extent, by donations and gifts; (iii) whether the

[1] "A 'Growing Concern' of Small Business: Competition with Nonprofits: 'An Issue for the Eighties,'" *The Philanthropy Monthly* **17**(1):5–23 (January 1984); "Small Business Administration Challenges Nonprofit Competition," *Washington Social Legislation Bulletin* **29**(21):81–82 (November 11, 1985).

[2] Subcommittee on Oversight, Committee on Ways and Means, U.S. House of Representatives, Press Release No. 10 (June 3, 1987).

[3] *Federal Register* 40211-32 (November 5, 1986).

[4] "Special Report: Not-For-Profits Prepare to Battle Local Tax Assessor," *AHA News* **23**(16) (April 27, 1987).

[5] *Utah County v. Intermountain Health Care, Inc.*, S. Ct. Utah, No. 17699, Slip Op., June 26, 1985.

[6] Ibid. See especially the dissenting opinion for an excellent review of the history and case law of the tax treatment of voluntary, not-for-profit hospitals.

[7] Ibid.

recipients of the 'charity' are required to pay for the assistance received, in whole or in part; (iv) whether the income received from all sources (gifts, donations, and payment from recipients) produces a 'profit' to the entity in the sense that the income exceeds operating and long-term maintenance expenses; (v) whether the beneficiaries of the 'charity' are restricted or unrestricted, and, if restricted, whether the restriction bears a reasonable relationship to the entity's charitable objectives; and (vi) whether dividends or some other form of financial benefit, or assets upon dissolution, are available to private interest, and whether the entity is organized and operated so that any commercial activities are subordinate or incidental to charitable ones."

Immediately after pronouncing these criteria, the court stated that they are to be used only as "useful guidelines for our analysis of whether a charitable purpose or gift exists in any particular case." The court said that "each case must be decided on its facts, and the foregoing factors are not all of equal significance, nor must an institution always qualify under all six before it is eligible for an exemption." The practical result of this, at least in Utah, appears to be that the tax commissioners in each county are encouraged to challenge the exempt status of voluntary hospitals, thus creating in effect a presumption against the charitable purpose of such institutions. In each case the courts will have to decide, using a vague but clearly more rigid and conservative standard, whether each individual hospital continues to deserve a property tax exemption.

A subsequent statewide referendum to constitutionally exempt hospitals from real property taxes in Utah was defeated at the polls, which seems to indicate that the court's novel actions are not out of line with the mood of the people — at least not in the state of Utah. As pressures mount to locate new sources of revenue to make up for cuts in federal spending and to fund other needs, a number of states can be expected to consider Utah's example.

Reflections of a Broader Malaise

So far, the incursions into the legal status of voluntary health care institutions have been relatively modest, but they reflect a broader malaise in both popular and professional attitudes. The last decade's growth of large, national, publicly traded hospital, nursing home, and home care chains, even if their influence was more apparent than real, brought into the discourse on health policy the language of stock analysts, money managers, and new-issue underwriters whose concerns and priorities seemed infinitely more interesting than the humdrum routines of bedpans and catheters. And the current ascendancy of "pro-market," "competitive" theories in health policy gives short shrift to the noneconomic motivations of nonprofit institutions, while continuing concern with health care costs creates an almost irresistible temptation to villainize the largest and most expensive institutions.

A more subtle concern is whether the effects of competition in health care, urged on by law and public policy, will force a convergence of the previously distinct voluntary health sector with other types of institutions. This is a crucial point of departure, for a public policy designed to sustain the differences and maintain the benefits of a pluralistic approach to providing health care is quite different from a policy intended to force every institution to become more and more alike. If health care institutions do become indistinguishable from other types of institutions — both nonprofit and for-profit — as well as from one another, then it will be only logical to treat them all equally with regard to laws and tax policies as well as to, more subtly, expectations.

To some extent, and perhaps for some of the same reasons, the malaise exhibited toward nonprofit health care institutions has appeared in the institutions themselves. After two decades of unprecedented prosperity and success since the introduction of Medicare and Medicaid, voluntary institutions and the people who manage and govern them have not been extremely effective, in either practical or intellectual terms, in responding to attacks against them. A degree of self-satisfaction and self-righteousness is always a danger for successful institutions and is perhaps an occupational hazard in the nonprofit world. More importantly, it has been a long time since the nonprofit sector has come under such intensive pressure from the outside world — and the last time, the pressure was from the left rather than from the right. The world has changed since then, and American culture is notoriously weak in historical memory.

Restating the Case

It is time to restate the case for voluntary health care institutions, while explicitly recognizing that not every organization that calls itself not-for-profit deserves to be treated as such. This chapter identifies a rationale —indeed, a series of rationales— for the special role of voluntary, not-for-profit health care institutions. Most of what is said applies to all voluntary health care institutions, though some discussion is limited to hospitals. What emerges is an articulation of what the mission of these institutions should be, and of how they should behave in order to deserve the sanction of special treatment.

That every single voluntary institution is not living up to these ideals, however, is obvious. For leaders of such institutions, the challenge is to reawaken in themselves and in their boards the important spirit of voluntarism and to guide their institutions in a direction that is clearly consistent with this spirit. It is equally important for society and its policymakers to avoid the expectation that every institution can be all things and do all things for all people, including doing the many good works enumerated in the various rationales for their existence. There should be a much greater appreciation of the complex and delicate task of balancing a voluntary institution's mission to serve its community with its concomitant duty to preserve the assets of the institution so that it may survive into the future.

The clear articulation of a series of rationales and an appropriate sense of mission for voluntary health care institutions will have immediate and significant public policy implications. Because perhaps the greatest uncertainty about the contemporary purpose of voluntary health care institutions has arisen from, and prevails among, the leadership of the institutions themselves — who continue to have an almost reflexive belief in the inherent superiority of voluntary health care — there has been no effective articulation of what the special social role of such institutions is, or should be, in current circumstances. Financial pressures, combined with the rhetoric of "businesslike management" and, one suspects, not a little envy of the apparent success of the for-profit competition, have caused trustees and administrators of voluntary institutions to question whether they have a continuing purpose in the health care system. This chapter affirms that they do and shows why.

CONTINUING CHALLENGES: IS THE PAST PAST?

No attempt to predict the future should ignore the past. And the past, in terms of this nation's mix of hospital ownership, clearly reflects a preference for the voluntary, not-for-profit form.[8] This preference is substantiated by reasons that are as good today as they were when voluntary health care institutions became prominent — perhaps even more so — and that are not just a result of tradition or historical accident.

Fully 70 percent of hospital beds in the United States today are under voluntary ownership. In earlier years, voluntary hospitals were supplemented by a significant number of hospitals operated under governmental auspices, while more recently they have also coexisted with a relatively small percentage of hospital beds run by for-profit companies, as

---

[8] J. D. Seay, B. C. Vladeck, P. S. Kramer, D. A. Gould, and J. J. McCormack, "Holding Fast to the Good: The Future of the Voluntary Hospital," *Inquiry* **23:**253–260 (Fall 1986).

they continue to do today. While the growth of the for-profit form has largely been limited to certain sections of the country, predominantly the South and the West,[9] hospitals operated under voluntary and governmental auspices can be seen everywhere and in all types of communities: rural, suburban, and urban.

In addition to leading the hospital sector in terms of numbers of facilities, voluntary hospitals have consistently provided a different and broader range of services and activities. For example, the majority of the strides that have been achieved over the last century in health care technology, biomedical research, medical education and training, and individualized community service and outreach programs have occurred within the voluntary health care sector.[10]

Recent studies have shown that for-profit health care institutions neither operate more efficiently nor provide more charity care than voluntary institutions.[11] These findings are even more significant because those responsible for the studies did not have access to data that could test widely held suspicions that for-profit institutions both "cream" financially advantageous patients and "dump" nonpaying patients onto other institutions.[12] If these suspicions were confirmed, as many suspect they might be, the distinction between for-profit enterprises, on the one hand, and voluntary and government institutions, on the other, clearly would be greater.

Indeed, other reputable research efforts have shown that not-for-profit institutions provide more medical research, education, and community health care services than their for-profit counterparts,[13] are more efficient,[14] and deliver significantly more "unlucrative" health care services.[15] The only recent efforts to prove the contrary have suffered from

[9] Ibid.

[10] Ibid.

[11] B. H. Gray, ed., *For Profit Enterprise in Health Care*, Report of the Committee on Implications of For-Profit Enterprise in Health Care, Institute of Medicine, National Academy of Sciences, National Academy Press, Washington, D.C., 1986.

[12] Ibid.

[13] S. B. Jones and M. K. Du Val, "What Distinguishes the Voluntary Hospital in an Increasingly Commercial Health Care Environment?" (this volume); *No Room in the Marketplace: The Health Care of the Poor*, Final Report of the Catholic Health Association's Task Force on Health Care of the Poor, CHA, St. Louis, 1986.

[14] R. V. Pattison and H. M. Katz, "Investor-Owned and Not-For-Profit Hospitals: A Comparison Based on California Data," *New England Journal of Medicine* **309**(6):347–353 (August 11, 1983); R. V. Pattison, "Response to Financial Incentives Among Investor-Owned and Not-for-Profit Hospitals: An Analysis Based on California Data, 1978–1982," in *For Profit Enterprise in Health Care* (see footnote 11), pp. 290–302; A. S. Relman, "Investor-Owned Hospitals and Health Care Costs," *New England Journal of Medicine* **309**(6):370–372 (August 11, 1983).

[15] See footnote 13, *No Room in the Marketplace*.

serious methodological flaws, thinly veiled biases, and undocumented assumptions.[16] With the weight of the evidence in favor of the voluntary health care institution, as this chapter concludes, it really seems quite appropriate to ask if the past is really past.

The Myth of Competition

Despite these convincing arguments, however, juxtaposition of the rhetoric of competition and for-profit superiority in the current environment against the rich and decidedly different past of nonprofit institutions appears to be fostering conflicting and alarming changes in how the nonprofit organizations are perceived and how they perceive themselves, and subsequently, in their behavior and in the public policy created for them. For in the minds of most of the architects of the nation's public policy on health care over the past century, the provision of health care services, especially for those most vulnerable and least able to pay, was seen as existing alongside, but separate from, the marketplace within which other commodities and services were bought and sold.[17] The history of health care in this country reflects a clear preference for the allocation of health care services in a way different from markets that distribute services on the bases of wealth, income, and ability to pay. According to Mitchell T. Rabkin, president of Boston's Beth Israel Hospital, "Health care, once deemed a social good, now threatens transformation into a market economy with a return of two classes of care, for the 'haves' and 'have nots,' the very situation Medicare, Medicaid, and broadly applied health insurance for the working family were designed to eliminate."[18]

The myth of competition as a panacea for the nation's health care ills may be exploded in a number of ways, but perhaps its most insidious effects may be on the existence and future of voluntary health care institutions. These effects manifest themselves in various ways. Competition often, although not always, breeds imitative behavior, forcing previously differentiated providers of services to look more and more alike. Even when competitive pressures result in product or service differentiation, if the pressures for competition are primarily financially imposed,

---

[16] R. Herzlinger and W. S. Krasker, "Who Profits from Nonprofits?" *Harvard Business Review*, pp. 93–106 (January–February 1987).

[17] T. R. Marmor, M. Schlesinger, and R. W. Smithey, "A New Look at Nonprofits: Health Care Policy in a Competitive Age," *Yale Journal on Regulation* **3**(2):313–349 (1986); Jones and Du Val.

[18] M. T. Rabkin, "The Hospital as Organization: New Roles and Relationships," in *The Future of the Hospital* (forthcoming, 1988).

the dictates of the bottom line may take precedence over goals attributable to other values. Especially within the heady rhetoric of entrepreneurialism and competition, an obsession with the means (the operation of a health care institution) can obscure the ends — that is, providing a service, on the one hand, or seeking a profit, on the other.

As voluntary hospitals find themselves in an increasingly "monetarized"[19] and transformed sector,[20] one wonders whether this is just a temporary pendulum swing, during which, however, they run the risk of forfeiting their birthright. The public's perception of an institution is most often influenced by the institution's own articulation of mission, actions, service, and commitment, which are, in turn, shaped within a particular rhetorical and ideological climate. If voluntary hospital trustees and managers are indeed at risk of losing sight of the historical mission and societal *raison d'être* of their institutions, it is incumbent upon them to stop and take stock of what it means to be a voluntary institution, differentiated from other types of institutions. They should examine and understand why tax laws have traditionally favored and encouraged the growth of these types of institutions.

Thus, trustees and leaders, as well as the general public, need to know not only what the voluntary institution has been and what it is today, but also what it should be if it is to continue to be distinct and deserving of public support and special treatment. In this regard, how voluntary health care institutions are structured, who gains from them, what the ends are for which the institutions' operation is the means, and what the public or community can expect from them are relevant issues.

SOCIAL JUSTICE AND THE PLURALISTIC NATURE OF AMERICAN SOCIETY

Voluntarism and volunteering are bright threads in the social fabric of American life, and they are, if not unique, at least more pronounced here than they are in the European countries from which many of our social traditions came.[21] They represent strongly held values about helping

---

[19] E. Ginzburg, "The Monetarization of Medical Care," *New England Journal of Medicine* **310**(18):1162–1165 (May 3, 1984).

[20] P. Starr, *The Social Transformation of American Medicine*, Basic Books, New York, 1982.

[21] D. Rosner, "Heterogeneity and Uniformity: Historical Perspectives on the Voluntary Hospital" (this volume); R. A. Stevens, "Voluntary and Governmental Activity," *Health Matrix* **3**(1):26–31 (Spring 1985); R. Hollingsworth and E. J. Hollingsworth, "A Comparison of Nonprofit, For-Profit, and Public Hospitals in the United States, 1935 to the Present," Program on Nonprofit Organizations, Institution for Social and Policy Studies, Yale University, PONPO Working Paper No. 113 and ISPS Working Paper No. 2113 (June 1986); see Jones and Du Val.

one's neighbor and perceptions about the relative roles of government, business, and the community in serving human needs. This has been especially true in the fields of health and social services, notwithstanding the fact that hospitals from an early point in their history have received substantial support from government and have thus been viewed, at the same time, as both private and public in character.[22]

Community service and the promotion of social welfare are, in principle, the motivations behind organizations created voluntarily — that is, created at will, under no requirement, and with no expectation of personal gain. In these types of organizations, public good and civic betterment have been the goals, volunteering and helping neighbors in need have been the means, and, many times, communal spirit and community solidarity have been the results.

Often, voluntary enterprises have emerged as private alternatives, or additions, to public efforts to fairly and equitably distribute social justice — in this case, through the availability of health care and its provision to those who need it. The creation of voluntary health care institutions can be seen as an attempt to address the perceived inability of a market economy to recognize any priorities of claim to health care other than wealth or income. Conversely, voluntary institutions have embodied the traditional American reluctance to grant too much of a role to government, preferring instead localized initiatives, self-reliance, and private approaches.

Service through Diversity

Voluntary health care institutions can also be seen as both an expression of and a vehicle for addressing the needs of a pluralistic society such as our own. These institutions, which fundamentally are social charities as well as providers of medical services, have attempted to deal with the social and health care needs of a society characterized by cultural heterogeneity, ethnic diversity, and geographic distinctiveness. The many community, religious, and other private charitable organizations that exist have served to address the unique and varying needs of particular communities in particular locations.

Specifically, the pluralism of American society has been reflected in the formation of many of its service institutions. As hospitals began to proliferate toward the end of the nineteenth century and into the beginning of the twentieth century, great numbers of them, especially in the

[22] R. A. Stevens, "A Poor Sort of Memory: Voluntary Hospitals and Government before the Depression," *Milbank Memorial Fund Quarterly* **60**(4):551–584 (1982).

eastern and midwestern states, were sectarian and ethnically sponsored.[23] Catholic and Jewish facilities stand out as stark examples, perhaps mainly because they represented minority populations in a predominantly Protestant country; but hospitals under denominational Protestant sponsorship were also abundant.[24] Other voluntary human service institutions were similarly ethnic, sectarian, and fraternal in origin and sponsorship, including old age homes, rest homes, and nursing homes. They were as similar in purpose as they were diverse in their sponsorship, having been created not only to make a special gift to American society, but also to provide an environment of medical refuge and treatment that was at the same time homogeneous, familiar, and intimate for patients from these particular ethnic and religious communities and backgrounds.[25] Indeed, specific doctrinal concerns for health care are expressed in many Catholic, Jewish, and Protestant traditions.

Public Trust and Public Policy

Tax law, as an instrument of public policy, has traditionally encouraged voluntary health care institutions and has fostered their growth in a number of ways. For example, these organizations have been described in both the law and the literature as providing a community service for which compensation was not otherwise offered.[26] They also have been identified as holding, in public trust, contributed assets which, if not deemed owned on behalf of the community, would be otherwise unowned.[27] This is particularly true where the law has prescribed the special duties and responsibilities of voluntary trustees as governors or stewards of communal assets.

In different cases, the courts have identified a unique role for nonpro-

---

[23] D. J. Rothman, "The Hospital as Caretaker: The Almshouse Past and the Intensive Care Future," in *The Future of the Hospital* (forthcoming, 1988).

[24] Ibid.

[25] Ibid.

[26] R. M. Sigmond, "Re-examining the Role of the Community Hospital in a Competitive Environment," 1985 Michael M. Davis Lecture, Center for Health Administration Studies, Graduate School of Business, Division of Biological Sciences, University of Chicago (May 10, 1985); R. M. Sigmond, "Old and New Roles for the Community Hospital," William B. Woods Memorial Lecture, Park Ridge Hospital and Rochester Area Hospitals' Corporation, Rochester, New York (October 22, 1981); see footnote 5, J. Stewart dissenting; Jones and Du Val; Stevens, "A Poor Sort of Memory," pp. 578–579.

[27] J. J. McMahon, "Judicial Review of Internal Policy Decisions of Private Non-profit Hospitals: A Common Law Approach," *American Journal of Law and Medicine* 3:164–165 (1977); R. S. Bromberg, "Public Charity Status: Can the Organization Pass the Test?" *Healthcare Financial Management* 40(11):70–78 (November 1986); S. Levey and D. D. Hesse, "Sounding Board: Bottom-Line Health Care?" *New England Journal of Medicine* 312(10):644–647 (March 7, 1985).

fit organizations in relieving the burdens that would otherwise fall on government, especially in the delivery of health care services to those who cannot pay. This same concept has also been identified in other cases and by other commentators to be a "charitable gift" to the community as a quid pro quo for tax exemption and other policy considerations.[28]

The existence of so many justifications for tax exemption might also appear to be consistent with the broad permissiveness of the Internal Revenue Service and the Internal Revenue Code[29] toward nonprofit providers of health care. More realistically, however, it can be said to reflect the broader public attitude of approbation and support for such institutions over the years. That all nonprofit hospitals and similar organizations should be tax exempt is something that tax policy long took for granted.

We now live, however, in more skeptical, if not cynical, times. Policymakers, and increasingly the general public as well, increasingly expect not only the profession of good intentions and laudable purposes but also explicit demonstrations of performance. Benefits are no longer granted; they must, at least in principle, be earned.

DISTINGUISHING CHARACTERISTICS

To respond to the issues described in the previous section, voluntary health care leaders need to cultivate those characteristics that precisely identify and define the voluntary health care institution. From these characteristics, certain behavioral prescriptions will follow. What will result, in turn, is a set of expectations in the form of a series of behaviors that, if reaffirmed and followed by the trustees and managers of voluntary institutions, will keep the voluntary distinction alive.

In particular, five "themes," or general sets of concepts, clearly define voluntary health care institutions, both today and in the past. These include

- values
- governance and accountability
- long-term commitment
- physician – hospital relationship and
- institutional voluntarism

Understanding these five differentiating characteristics is a prerequi-

---

[28]See footnotes 6, 13, 21 (R. A. Stevens), and 26 (R. M. Sigmond).
[29]U.S. Internal Revenue Code, U.S.C.A. Sections 501–528.

site to being able to lead a voluntary health care institution in the right direction—toward "virtue." As Daniel Wikler, Professor of Philosophy with the Program in Medical Ethics at the University of Wisconsin Medical School, has noted, "what is needed is an account of the 'virtuous hospital': a portrait of the ideal, or of an approximation to it, to which voluntary hospitals worthy of the name should aspire. This ideal consists of both a list of virtues and a standard for judging how close an approximation to the ideal is 'enough.' "[30] In the rest of this section, the former is presented, and in the following section, the latter.

Values

The provision of health care is an inherently value-laden enterprise. No matter how monetarized health care has become or how transformed the American system of providing it appears to be, there are still very personal and very human aspects of the relationship between a medical practitioner and a patient, and between a health care institution and a patient, that cannot be quantified, analyzed in economic terms, or adequately explained by means of regression analyses.

Since early in this century, medical care has been viewed largely as a scientific enterprise.[31] The advent of aseptic surgery, the introduction of antibiotics and other "wonder drugs," and the proliferation of highly technological diagnostic and therapeutic interventions confirmed popular faith in the scientific method, and in the concepts of uniformity and standardization that grew out of this method. More recently, however, many observers—more than a few of them patients—have come to realize that medical care involves much more than technical science. These interested observers have much broader personal and social expectations of the health care enterprise.

Furthermore, the heterogeneous and pluralistic nature of America's communities has given rise to a set of institutions that are often quite particularistic and closely rooted in specific communities. These have included not only ethnically and religiously based hospitals and nursing homes, but also health care facilities sponsored by unions and employee groups, fraternal associations, and others. Each reflects, in a uniquely

[30] D. Wikler, "The Virtuous Hospital: Do Nonprofit Institutions Have a Distinctive Moral Mission?" (this volume).

[31] A. Flexner, *Medical Education in the United States and Canada: A Report to the Carnegie Foundation for the Advancement of Teaching,* Carnegie Foundation, New York, 1910.

tailored way, the particular community values and needs shared by the institutions' founders.

Voluntary health care institutions that have their roots deeply set in their communities, whether in geographical communities or affiliational ones, and that have community trustees who are charged with managing the institutions in the public interest, have always more closely reflected — and, indeed, have always been the primary focal points and repositories for — community values, in the broad sense of "community." Embodiment of those values in institutional performance occurs both at the level of policy, as in deciding which service will be emphasized, and at the less tangible level of "organizational culture," in terms of shared orientations of hospitality and service. Sometimes, shared cultures even extend literally to a common language.

In a pluralistic, secular society such as the United States, maintaining particularistic cultural or community values in complex institutions that are heavily reliant on public support creates significant, but often fruitful, tensions. Hospitals operated under religious auspices, for example, must constantly balance fidelity to denominational principles with openness to patients and staff from other traditions. Rural institutions must balance the resources and preferences of their communities with regulatory pressures toward standardization and uniformity. Given the limitations of government — arising both from constitutional constraint and bureaucratic incapacity — to promote what are essentially more compelling and intimate human values, voluntary health care institutions provide the only plausible mechanism for melding the particularistic with the universal, linking local or cultural values with service to the public at large.

Local Responsiveness The formal governance structure of voluntary institutions also promotes their role as repositories for "local" values. Most boards of trustees are dominated by representatives of the local community, again in the broad sense of "community." The choice not to make a profit or receive any personal gain, the "nondistribution constraint,"[32] serves to unfetter the actions of voluntary trustees. Relieved from the burden of paying dividends to shareholders or maximizing quarterly results, voluntary trustees can keep their attention and funds focused on local needs and concerns as they, and the various "communities" that the hospitals serve, change and shift over time.

In that sense, it is the very absence of uniformity and standardization

[32] H. B. Hansmann, "The Role of Nonprofit Enterprise," *Yale Law Journal* **89**(5):835–901 (April 1980).

— hallmarks of large national businesses — that gives local voluntary institutions the flexibility to serve the health care needs of specific communities that may differ from those of other areas or groups. This, of course, raises the question of whether the complex, corporate organizational forms that are more common today[33] — such as the multi-institution holding company and subsidiary arrangement used by proprietary companies and some not-for-profit health care chains — are really consistent with the voluntary form. Two observations provide a response to that question. First, some "communities," such as those served by certain religious orders, are not specifically bound to a given geographical location and thus need mechanisms to coordinate services and policy across different localities. More importantly, however, new forms of corporate organization do pose serious problems for institutional trustees, who must balance the possible advantages of such arrangements against the need to maintain an identity consonant with the community's expectations and values. Such a balance is not achieved easily, if it is achieved at all.

The role of voluntary health care institutions as repositories of values is not only a question of the styles of particular facilities. For example, if society desires part of the private — that is, nongovernmental — sector to be involved in the process of ensuring social justice in health care, a distinction based upon values is important. The public cannot expect the for-profit part of the private sector to do this job without being paid extra, but public expectations of voluntary, not-for-profit organizations are, and should be, different.

This is not to argue that the not-for-profit health care organization can be expected to provide all things to all people, but to suggest that if we reject government as the sole guarantor of just results in society — and in this case, in particular, as the sole distributor of health care services — other mechanisms will be needed to supplement the government's role. For those who believe that the distribution of social justice is purely within the domain of government, the involvement of the voluntary, not-for-profit sector in this regard may be seen as a "second best" approach.[34] Historically, however, the attempt to mesh government and the voluntary, not-for-profit sector in sharing responsibility for the distribution of social justice in health care has been the distinctively American approach, the success of which is, of course, open to constant reassessment and debate. The alternatives — a government monopoly of service

[33]C. J. Schramm, "The Legal Identity of the Modern Hospital: A Story of Evolving Values" (this volume).
[34]Wikler.

provision or a universal public underwriting of service providers — have their own drawbacks, including problems of political feasibility.

Governance and Accountability

The critical linkage between the values of particular communities and the day-to-day operations of a complex health care organization is provided by the governing body of a voluntary institution. Institutional trustees are accountable to a standard of fiduciary stewardship that embodies the complex set of expectations communities have toward health care and that at the same time requires a constant balancing of competing pressures. This form of governance, when properly observed, constitutes in itself a principal strength of the voluntary sector.

Fiduciary Stewardship The duties and responsibilities of the trustees of a public charity are derived mainly from the law of trusts, and thus the specific duties of a trustee of a charitable trust resemble those of a trustee of a private trust.[35] These duties have been interpreted by the law as caring for and managing the property of the trust.[36] The corpus, or principle of the trust, should be carefully guarded and protected so that the charitable intent of the donor or donors will be carried out and so that the trust property will not be depleted by being used for purposes not intended.[37] Specifically, a charitable trust has been defined as a fiduciary relationship with respect to property, arising as a result of an intention to create it, and subjecting the person or persons by whom the property is held to what the law calls "equitable duties" to deal with the property for a charitable purpose.[38] Those charged with the responsibility of operating and governing a public charity must operate it for the charitable purposes intended, but, in the absence of charter limitations, may exercise reasonable discretion as to the manner and the means by which its purposes are accomplished.[39]

Trustees of public charities — just like trustees of private trusts — must depend primarily upon the terms and conditions under which the trust or institution was established in an effort to interpret the mission or

[35] *Gbur v. Cohen,* 93 Cal. App. 3d. 296; 155 Cal. Rptr. 407 (1979).
[36] *Trustees of Dartmouth College v. Woodward,* 17 U.S. 518; 4 L. Ed. 629.
[37] *Hinckley v. Beardsley,* 28 Ill. App. 2d. 379; 171 N.E. 2d. 401; 89 A.L.R. 2d. 686; *Ranken-Jordan Home for Convalescent Crippled Children v. Drury College,* 449 S.W. 2d. 161.
[38] Restatement of Trusts Second, Section 348.
[39] See footnote 37, *Ranken-Jordan Home for Convalescent Crippled Children v. Drury College.*

intent to be followed. In the case of a voluntary, not-for-profit hospital that was established a number of years ago, and that has been the recipient of countless donations in the intervening years, the institution's trustees have a unique obligation to ascertain just what the purposes of the institution are in contemporary terms. Trustees of a charitable corporation need to comply with strict trust principles in the performance of their duties, and while these trustees may be exempt from personal liability for the debts, liabilities, or obligations of a corporation, they are not immune from personal liability for their own fraud, bad faith, negligent acts, or other breaches of duty.[40]

In addition to being responsible for interpreting and pursuing the intent and purposes of the charitable institution, trustees have a duty to conserve the assets and property of that institution in a prudent, fiduciary manner. In a broad sense, these assets include not only the charitable funds and the bricks, mortar, and equipment of the institution, but also the human, social, and political capital wrapped up in the institution. Conservatorship and stewardship over these assets are quite different from duties and responsibilities in other forms. For example, while the directors of a for-profit corporation may owe their shareholders a duty to seek financial gain — including risking capital in the short term for long-term gain — the trustees of a charitable organization are strictly bound to see that the institution's assets are not depleted in the short run in pursuit of the institution's mission at the expense of its longevity.

Voluntary trustees therefore owe a high — indeed, a fiduciary — standard or duty of care to the institutions they govern and, in turn, to the communities they were created to serve. The process through which they carry out these obligations thus constitutes a special kind of social decision making, in which individuals without immediate prospect of tangible personal gain are obligated to try to figure out how best to advance some important social purposes.

Part of the distinctive role of the voluntary trustee is to continually attempt to ascertain the institution's best response to the often vague or general expectations of its community or communities. These questions are not always easy to answer, yet there is something profoundly distinct about the nature of voluntary trustee governance that arises out of the tension created by the dual — and sometimes conflicting — obligations of service to the community, on the one hand, and conservation of resources to assure the future of the institution, on the other.[41]

[40] *Lynch v. John M. Redfield Foundation*, 9 Cal. App. 3d. 293; 88 Cal. Rptr. 86; 51 A.L.R. 3d. 1284.

[41] J. J. McCormack, "Hospital Strategy and Public Policy: Seeking the Just Right Balance" (this volume).

James J. McCormack, Visiting Professor in the School of Social Services at Fordham University, has observed that "short-term responses to fiscal pressures, acceptable for commercial enterprises in adapting to changing market circumstances, are not behaviors desired of permanent institutions whose contract with the community includes long-term resource maintenance through periods both good and bad."[42] Thus, for example, Professor McCormack notes, "a balance must be struck on when to press a competitive advantage and when to refrain from an action in the interest of the institution's essential identity — that is, in recognition of its obligation as well as its opportunities."[43] It seems fair to propose that one key area of threat to a modern voluntary hospital may be its own enthusiasm for commercial initiatives.

Such motivations and circumstances are far more complex than the duty owed by a for-profit board member to the shareholders of a corporation. Trustees of voluntary health care institutions are obliged to seek the "just right balance" between service and caring that is the purpose of the institution, and the conservation of resources that is its continuance.[44]

Long-Term Commitment

Society at large, and any community in particular, is better served in the long run by a hospital or other health service institution that is organized to operate and plan its future on a long-term rather than a short-term horizon. While for-profit hospitals, and some voluntaries, are market-sensitive and exit as nimbly as they enter, the more geographically bound and community-responsive voluntary institutions provide a continuing presence and continuity of readiness, service capability, and capacity, thus giving patients and the community a hospital or institution that will exist tomorrow as well as today — over time as well as during a profitable fad.

Trustees of charitable institutions, as previously noted, have a clear obligation to consider the long-term picture as opposed to risking capital in pursuit of short-term gains. Although the latter may sometimes be necessary to sustain operations over the long term, trustees of charitable organizations must be extremely careful not to abuse their discretion in balancing caring and conservation. If an institution is predominantly

---

[42] Ibid.
[43] Ibid.
[44] Ibid.

market-driven, it is really obligated to try to stay one step ahead of the current fad, since competitive pressures force similar goals and promote imitative behavior and convergence. However, the economic language of the efficient production of services for health care is not everything; it may be an issue, but it is not *the* issue. It has not always been and will not always be economically rewarding to do the right thing in health care, and, conversely, to do what is appropriate, from the perspective of community need, is not always profitable.

In this sense, the very inertia of voluntary institutions, often viewed pejoratively in other contexts, is clearly a very good thing. This is not to ignore or downplay the other costs usually attributed to institutional inertia, such as perpetuation of some unneeded facilities and services and failure to respond quickly enough to real changes in community needs. But it is to suggest that in this context, the community clearly benefits from the social stability, and the long-term commitment, made possible by voluntary institutions.

If health care is a vital community service, then there is considerable value in the simple fact of a health care institution being in the community and staying in the community. Moreover, the importance of a health care institution to its community is not contained entirely in the services it provides. Not only are health care institutions employers and generators of economic and community activity, but as repositories of values and embodiments of community purposes, they are valued themselves. In many inner-city neighborhoods and many small towns, the supermarkets have closed, the banks are long gone, and most other retail businesses are shuttered, but the hospital is still there. In these cases, then, it may not be going too far to suggest that inertia is a virtue.

Many not-for-profit institutions are considered to be charitable or donative entities, not just in the sense that they are recipients of charitable donations. Perhaps more importantly, they are charitable and donative because they contribute and provide to the community the general availability of certain services such as 24-hour, seven-day-a-week emergency rooms, health education and research activities, and other services that may not always be profitable, irrespective of the fact that they may do so for a fee to many users. The institutions' very presence and readiness to serve are donative and charitable services, especially where the "market" would not ordinarily reward a for-profit organization doing likewise. Call it inertia or "nonmarket responsiveness," but in many communities, this aspect of a not-for-profit health care institution alone may be part and parcel of what it means to be a fiduciary steward of the community's assets over the long term.

Physician–Hospital Relationship

Perhaps the most difficult and complex aspect of voluntary health care institutions, particularly voluntary hospitals, is their potential for creating a special environment for and relationship with physicians, thus managing the problem of professional autonomy in medicine and cultivating a tradition of caring. Patients and the community are better served by hospitals that are more than just a doctors' workshop. Voluntary hospitals' management and trustee leadership have long worked in partnership with physicians, and in the most successful instances, they have created a delicate but vital balance between institutional imperatives and professional independence.

There are really two aspects to this special relationship between the voluntary institution and its medical professionals. First is the formal governance and control mechanisms through which the board of trustees and the medical staff operate in tandem to further the mission of the hospital. The boards of hospitals generally oversee and certainly always have ultimate responsibility for the effective implementation of professional credentials, quality assurance, and medical staff bylaws and contractual relationships. In voluntary hospitals, this basic legal responsibility is often expanded to include self-imposed and nonobligatory responsibilities to do something beneficial for the community — a public good. Uncompensated clinic service and supervision of physicians in training have long been the paradigms of such activity; in our increasingly bureaucratic world, participation on one or another committee may more often be an expression of service. As the supply of physicians continues to increase and as different types of economic relationships emerge between health care institutions and physicians, boards of trustees of voluntary institutions may well find new opportunities to be innovative in ways that serve the community's and the public's best interest, while at the same time maintaining fiscally viable institutions and providing physicians with socially as well as financially gratifying environments within which to practice medicine.

A second and extremely important aspect of the special relationship between the voluntary institution and its medical professionals lies in the institution's "corporate culture."[45] Expectations of medical staff as well as other staff are influenced by the values and mission articulated and implemented by the institution. Physician behavior can be affected positively and to the betterment of the community through the existence of a

[45] M. R. Greenlick, "Profit and Nonprofit Organizations in Health Care: A Sociological Perspective" (this volume).

corporate culture of caring. Also, the needs of the community can be well served by an organization dedicated to balancing professional practice and community concerns.

Merwyn R. Greenlick, Vice President for Research of the Kaiser Foundation Hospitals and Director of Kaiser Permanente's Center for Health Research in Portland, Oregon, has argued that up to now, "the interest of the patient has been protected in our society by the professionalization of the medical practitioner. The socialization of the physician is totally geared to instilling the social control mechanism as an internalized component of the practicing professional. All the social control mechanisms of the profession work to create group norms to protect patients' interests and the social pressure mechanisms to enforce these norms. The system works relatively well in Western society, considering the significant pressures medical practice puts on the situation, as long as physicians practice alone or in small social groupings and make critical decisions in an environment where the pressures are for conformity to professional norms that protect the patients."[46] In the environment of a large, complex organization such as a not-for-profit health care institution, the attempt is to balance the natural push toward professional autonomy with the equally important goal of responsible community service.[47]

The perceptions of physicians themselves seem to bear out the theory that the quality of care for patients in not-for-profit hospitals is superior to that received in for-profit or public hospitals. According to an Institute of Medicine report, using data from an American Medical Association survey conducted in 1984, "32 percent of physicians surveyed believed that not-for-profit hospitals provide better quality of care than do for-profit hospitals, while only 5 percent believed the opposite to be true."[48] Even when the physicians surveyed had staff privileges at for-profit hospitals, 24 percent felt that the quality of patient care was better in not-for-profit hospitals, while only 8 percent felt that care was superior in their own for-profit hospitals.[49]

Institutional Voluntarism

Recent survey research has shown that the phenomenon of volunteering is very much alive and well in America. Approximately 84 million Ameri-

[46] Ibid.
[47] See McCormack.
[48] Gray, p. 131.
[49] Ibid.

cans, 52 percent of the adult population, volunteer at least 8.4 billion hours each year with organizations and causes, health care — and hospitals in particular — predominant among them.[50]

Volunteering has been, and apparently continues to be, a source of civic betterment, community improvement, and social solidarity. Institutions and organizations that are natural objects of, or outlets for, volunteers, and that serve as a locus for these important social resources, have an important part in this process. Voluntary hospitals in particular, and other voluntary health care institutions in general, have long been — and mostly continue to be — primary focal points of this sort of institutional embodiment of voluntarism, and of the values held by those who volunteer.

These characteristics of voluntary institutions, together with the often forgotten fact that the institutions' trustees themselves are volunteers, go a long way toward creating the environment or "culture of caring" that so importantly extends and objectifies the founding values and mission of the institution. Regardless of an organization's motives or mission — be it profit, community service, or whatever — its values can, and most often do, determine how it is structured, what types of services it provides, and what the overall environment within which it makes decisions is. For these reasons, qualitatively different products or outcomes result from organizations dedicated to and structured around voluntary, charitable values.

The Value of Voluntarism There is something special about the relationship between the voluntary institution and its volunteers. To begin with, there is almost always a mutuality of expectations and benefits. The institutions obviously benefit from the volunteered time itself and from the local social and community support that comes with it. The volunteers, in turn, expect that they and their community will benefit by their acts of service and charity, which free up the time of professionals and other hospital workers, thus allowing the voluntary institution to pursue a broader range of services. Volunteers also feel that their volunteered time contributes to the quality of care in the institution, making it a warmer, more humane, and more comfortable and familiar place for their families and neighbors — who are, after all, the institution's patients. A community served by this type of institution — one created for the rich and the poor alike, and by the community as well as for the community — is a decidedly better and richer community as a result.

[50]*Americans Volunteer*, a survey conducted by the Gallup Organization, Inc., for Independent Sector, Washington, D. C. (June 1981); and "The 1983 Gallup Survey on Volunteering," in *Voluntary Action Leadership* (Winter 1984).

The influence of philanthropy, once the primary hallmark of the voluntary endeavor, cannot be ignored either. Although philanthropic support has declined dramatically in recent years as a percentage of total health care revenues,[51] philanthropic support of hospitals still amounts to several billion dollars per year,[52] not including earnings on assets donated in the past. Moreover, as every fund raiser knows, the relationship between donor and recipient is more than a unilateral economic transaction. Philanthropy represents another, often especially tangible, way in which institutions and communities bind themselves to one another.

Indeed, there is something terribly significant about the fact that great numbers of people donate both their time and their money to voluntary causes and institutions in health care. Voluntary organizations that measure up to the model or ideal outlined here can be a positive force for social good, and those that do measure up should in fact be rewarded, or at least not hindered, by public policy. The fact that there are business aspects to the provision of health care services, even perhaps increasingly so, does not make voluntary health care institutions functionally indistinguishable from businesses, so long as, and to the extent that, they also can be identified by these other characteristics.

IMPLICATIONS FOR DAY-TO-DAY DECISION MAKING

The five characteristics discussed previously — a repository for community values, fiduciary governance and accountability to the community, a special environment for and relationship to physicians, a long-term commitment to the community, and the institutional embodiment of voluntarism — taken together, define the essence of the voluntary health care institution. That definition, it must be emphasized, is both descriptive and prescriptive. What voluntary institutions are, moreover, is less important than what they should be, and the prescriptive definition suggests certain sets of behaviors to which voluntary institutions should aspire; the successful pursuit of these behaviors can, in fact, result in a "virtuous" institution.

But these five characteristics themselves don't clearly dictate specific behaviors; they must be examined and extrapolated. A voluntary trustee or manager might appropriately ask what these five attributes mean for day-to-day decisions in governing a complex and changing institution. A

[51] J. D. Seay, "Making A Stronger Case for Health Care Philanthropy," Fund Raising Management 15(8):34–40 (October 1984); "Giving U.S.A.," Annual Report of the American Association of Fund Raising Counsel, Inc., New York, selected years.
[52] Ibid.

trustee also needs to understand how knowledge of these five characteristics can assist in determining whether a hospital striving to be virtuous should also compete vigorously with rival organizations for patients and dollars, whether the hospital's affiliation with a national system can be undertaken in a way consistent with fidelity to the organization's original mission, and, moreover, just who the hospital's community is in a changing environment.

In addition, there is another set of questions that must be addressed concerning the issue of charity care and its rightful place in the definition of a voluntary mission. For what purposes should the institution's assets and resources be used? What are the means and what are the ends in pricing behavior and accumulation of assets? Is there a "right" amount of charity? In the constellation of issues surrounding the identity of voluntary institutions, those having to do with charity care may not be singularly important, but they appear to have been attached such an importance in much of the public discourse about the role of nonprofit institutions.

What makes voluntary management and trusteeship both interesting and frustrating is that although all of these questions are important, there are no quick answers or easy solutions to any of them. At best, what voluntary health care leaders can hope to do if they wish to continue the voluntary distinction is to set in motion a process or a series of processes that is designed to lead decisions — and, therefore, the institutions making those decisions — in the direction of the desired ends — the mission, or community service, of the institution — rather than toward an entanglement with the means. Mechanisms should foster operational decisions made with regard to the end results rather than reflexive responses to the pressures of an increasingly confusing environment brought on by the reality of operating a health care institution. Merely aping the behavior of one's business competitors will not help to distinguish the ends from the means; in most cases, in fact, it will simply result in substituting the latter for the former.

In attempting to address these issues, it is clear that process is very important. What institutions do matters, but so does how they decide what they are going to do. What follows is an illustrative list, one meant to be neither exhaustive nor engraved in stone, but categorized for the purpose of discussion into "mission," "methods," and "policy."

Mission

"Mission" refers to the philosophical tenets that underlie an institution's commitment to serve. These reasons for being provide the basis for determining the institution's strategic plan, and hence, its future. Clarity, differentiation, volition, organizational culture, and social compact are important aspects of an institution's mission.

Clarity As conventional management theory suggests, leaders of voluntary health care institutions, like leaders of other enterprises, must strive for clarity of purpose. They need to make sure that there is a current and clear mission statement for the institution, and that it is fully understood by all members of the board of trustees and of the administration. Further, an understanding of this mission and a commitment to it should be instilled in as many hospital employees and volunteers as possible. Ambiguity of mission cannot contribute positively to an understanding of what the institution is supposed to be and to achieve.

The challenge of creating clarity of purpose grows with the size and complexity of the enterprise, in such a way that conceptual clarity of purpose is most important for large and intricate academic medical centers and for hospitals that are parts of chains or that are involved in other complex corporate structures. And as Professor McCormack has noted, the greatest share of responsibility for keeping the institution true to its service mission lies with its trustees and its senior administrative personnel, aided by medical and other professional staff.[53]

Differentiation Voluntary health care institutions should accentuate the differences between the voluntary institution and other types of organizations. When the trustee and management interpretation of the mission statement results in choices — such as determining the mix of services, the admissions policy, and the like — that are different from the choices made by other types of organizations, this difference should be emphasized and given high public, professional, and institutional visibility. If there is virtue in the voluntary form of governance and operation, as there does seem to be, then it makes little sense to blur the distinction with other types of institutions, and it makes all the sense in the world for the leadership of voluntary institutions to clearly and publicly enunciate the crucial differences.

Volition The board of trustees must reaffirm the nonobligatory choice to serve. For trustees and managers of voluntary organizations, this means that governance decisions should be guided by the service ethic rather than by the statutory mandates or profit incentives that are the motives for the existence of other kinds of institutions. In short, we

[53] See McCormack.

must rediscover what it truly means to volunteer. And, in this context, it is important to remember that what has made nonprofit hospitals so special throughout their history has been the apparent motive, in the creation of these organizations, of a nonobligatory joining together of people to accomplish a communal good.[54]

As Professor McCormack has observed, "In all of these instances a choice was made to assume a responsibility — not for the risks of a commercial concern, but for acts of service. These positive acts of service can be seen as defining the essential character of nonprofit voluntary hospitals in the United States. The conscious act to fulfill the needs of others is the foundation of the voluntary hospital — its essence and the rationale for its existence. That this is a simple and unselfish idea should not obscure the uncomplicated reality."[55]

Organizational Culture   Voluntary health care administration and management must continue to create an internal environment that encourages "virtue" and a culture of caring. IBM does not have a monopoly on corporate culture. The discussion of mission, and all it entails, should not be confined to the boardroom but, rather, should permeate the institution and infuse the management and medical practice environments with its flavor.

The culture of caring should be continually cultivated at all levels within the institution, such that its patients and the community feel it and know it no less than do its trustees, administrators, and employees. An active commitment to an organizational culture of caring and service can become a self-fulfilling prophecy for the good of both the institution and the community and can facilitate the prudent discharge of the trustees' fiduciary responsibilities.

Social Compact   The leadership of voluntary health care institutions should make public promises about mission. Going public with commitments to mission and values can have the specific effect of self-imposing certain external expectations that serve to keep the institution accountable to itself.

The relationship between a voluntary health care institution and its community depends on a careful process that endeavors to balance the community's and the institution's needs. Specifically, the community's expectations of the institution and its health needs must be balanced with a realistic and fiscally prudent interpretation of the extent to which

[54] See footnote 26 (R. M. Sigmond) and McCormack.
[55] See McCormack.

the institution's assets can be expended in the short term while being, at the same time, maintained for the long term. This balancing process in turn depends on the dialogue and personal interaction of representatives of the community with those of the institution.

Methods

"Methods" are, quite literally, the strategies by which an institution seeks to pursue its mission and to achieve its goals. These can be both operative, in the sense that they are specific steps to be undertaken, and symbolic, in that, often, the tone, public stature, and culture of the institution can affect the institution's success. Community service, innovation, fiscal focus, organizational purpose, and interinstitutional planning are key elements of an institution's methods.

Community Service An organization dedicated to community service will make a systematic effort to ascertain and address, to the extent possible, the most pressing health care needs identified in the community. Whether the community's needs are related to the AIDS epidemic, teenage pregnancy, geriatric medicine, the availability of postacute care resources for patients needing a continuing level of care, or, indeed, all of the above, it is voluntary institutions, and to a decreasing degree government, to which communities can turn to address those problems that are least desirable to work with, not as glamorous to tout, and inherently unprofitable.

The process of identifying and assessing community needs has a special and complex relationship to the identity of voluntary health care institutions. On the one hand, to the extent that they are mission-driven, rather than purely market-driven, voluntary institutions cannot simply equate public opinion or consumer preference with community needs without violating the importance of internally set priorities. On the other hand, the very idea of service implies a responsiveness to those being served — and, perhaps more importantly, to those going unserved or underserved who need help. A self-righteous indifference to those being served is a failing to which voluntary institutions may have been all too prone in the past.

Once again, the critical issue is the extent of mutuality and reciprocity in the institution's relationship to its community or communities. People expect voluntary institutions to make the right decision — to do the right thing — with the public's interest in mind. Voluntary institutions, however, may violate such expectations whenever they are either too sensitive to short-term perturbations of the public pulse or too concerned with institutional self-aggrandizement at the expense of community needs.

Innovation   As demographic patterns shift within hospitals' communities, as technology changes, and as other health care providers enter and exit the market, the definition of what it means to provide charity and community service may also vary considerably. Because of this, a community service organization will continually strive to keep current its definition of charity and its commitment to community service.

Innovation and resourcefulness are crucial traits for the leadership of voluntary health care institutions, as they are for the leadership of other institutions. Just as voluntary hospital leadership was — and, indeed, had to be — innovative in the period following the Great Depression when this leadership helped create the private, nonprofit insurance mechanism to assist both patients and hospitals, so must today's leaders of voluntary institutions recognize that they are not always — and, in fact, rarely have been — the passive "victims" of the changing economic, regulatory, and reimbursement environments. One of the greatest threats to voluntary health care is the danger that its leaders — both trustees and administrators — will throw up their hands in despair in the face of perceived "uncontrollable" fiscal incentives and pressures. Their fiduciary obligations require them, on the contrary, to respond to new external forces with new internal adaptations.

Fiscal Focus   In an increasingly monetarized and commercialized health care sector, where the apparent social approbation attached to entrepreneurialism is great, pressures to diversify will arise both within and outside the immediate service mission of the institution.

Although various sources of related, and unrelated, business income may be attractive in an effort to bolster the fiscal position of the institution, or even to underwrite and support charitable activities, branching out into areas not related to the mission of the institution can be detrimental, not only in terms of public relations and public perception but also in terms of public policy. There certainly is nothing wrong with unrelated business income per se; where such income is earned, it should be taxed, as the law now requires. However, a health care organization that gets too heavily involved in too many of these unrelated business activities may run the risk of blurring its own image in the perception of the public and of policymakers.

How an institution raises its revenues can be as important as why they are raised, especially when certain types of revenue-producing activities blur the community's perception of the mission and purpose of the organization. Where the mission and purpose remain crystal clear in the fiscal focus of the institution — and where that mission remains predominantly community service — legislators and regulators will be hard-pressed to rationally articulate, and receive the public's support for, policies and actions detrimental to the institution.

Organizational Purpose Operating a modern health care institution requires businesslike behavior to achieve operating efficiencies in furtherance of its goals. However, businesslike behavior does not necessarily require converting the institution to a business.[56] Indeed, the latter is a particularly delicate trap to avoid, especially given the prevailing ideological climate and the changing nature of health administration education and training in this country.[57] Once again, the danger exists of supplanting the ends of the enterprise with the means: that is, promoting institutional imperatives over and to the exclusion of fidelity to mission and community service.

The fiduciary obligations of voluntary trustees extend to the most rational and efficient use of the institution's, and the community's, resources. If "businesslike" means being "rational" or "efficient," or using sophisticated managerial tools, voluntary institutions are obliged to be businesslike. But having too narrow a set of goals, a concern with profit over people, a preoccupation with means over ends, or a short-term outlook is quite another thing. For if "businesslike" behavior requires substitution of the voluntary institution's value set with that of the profit-maximizing corporation, policymakers and legislators would be quite right in treating voluntary institutions no differently than they do these corporations. A proper interpretation of "businesslike" behavior thus allows the voluntary institution to remain true to its mission while utilizing the most current and sophisticated managerial tools and techniques from the business world in pursuit of its goals.

Interinstitutional Planning Cooperation with other health care providers in the community in an effort to achieve the proper level and mix of services may no longer be fashionable and may even be viewed as "anticompetitive." However, to the extent that this sort of cooperative behavior is antithetical to competitive marketplace behaviors, it may also

---

[56] R. S. Bromberg, "Can a Joint Venture Threaten the Hospital's Tax-Exempt Status?" *Healthcare Financial Management* **40**(11):76–85 (December 1986); M. P. Squires, "Corporate Restructuring of Tax-Exempt Hospitals: The Bastardization of the Tax-Exempt Concept," *Law, Medicine, and Health Care* **14**(2):66–76 (1986).

[57] See Rosner.

be an indicator of the extent to which a hospital or an institution can be called voluntary.

The very concept of community service implies — indeed, requires — a relationship to the community and the community's needs, the proper appreciation of which cannot be achieved merely by introspective, intra-institutional planning but, rather, cries out for rational and cooperative needs assessment and planning among the various community providers of service.

Policy

"Policy" recommendations refer to public issues that an institution's leadership must address in pursuing its goals and objectives. Voluntary leadership must recognize that hospitals and other health care institutions do not operate in a vacuum; they have immediate and specific effects on issues of public policy and public concern. Community services, quality of medical care, public expectations, criteria, community integration, and participation are all crucial to creating situations in which health care institutions can, and should, affect the public good.

Community Services   In order to retain a legitimate role in the community, voluntary institutions must formulate and maintain rational policies toward charitable service. It is no longer defensible to take the position that the mere process of providing health care suffices to demonstrate an institution's charitable intent. Community requirements and institutional missions do differ, creating concomitant differences in communities' needs for charitable services.

A few basic principles should, however, be widely observed. Voluntary institutions are obligated to provide all the charitable services they can afford. They should turn away no one they are equipped to care for, although equipped in this sense implies financial as well as technical capability. Perhaps more importantly, the mandate of community service, as noted, requires true efforts to identify unmet community needs and to seek to meet them.

Being charitable has another, more subtle dimension. Even in an increasingly competitive and price-sensitive health care environment, the essential character of many health services affords the providers of those services substantial freedom to set prices. While Augustinian notions of a "just price" have long since been discredited, it is reasonable to expect that voluntary institutions will set their prices in a way consistent with economic cost and institutional preservation but far short of profit maximization. The empirical evidence indeed demonstrates that voluntary institutions have long priced that way.[58]

Charity also begins at home. While it is at least theoretically possible for an institution to behave charitably toward its community without being charitable toward its own employees, volunteers, and other constituents, it is hardly desirable. As a practical matter, employees and volunteers frequently are, and should be, members of the communities the institutions are striving to serve.

Quality of Medical Care As a legal and, far more importantly, philosophical matter, voluntary institutions and their medical staffs must continuously work to improve the quality of the services they provide. The oversight of medical care is far too important to be either enforced through the arbitrary, unilateral actions of hospital boards and managers or blindly delegated to the medical staff. Finding mechanisms that appropriately recognize both the obligations of trustees and the unique claims of competent physicians is a difficult challenge, the substance of which changes over time as medical knowledge, patterns of physician organization, and legal constraints change.

The key here, again, is reciprocity and mutuality, although now the relationships are trifold — encompassing physicians as well as institutions and communities — and thus still more complicated. But communities and their individual members, quite appropriately, look to institutions and physicians to provide checks and balances between them that protect consumers, while institutions must figure out how best to serve their communities at the same time as they serve their physicians.

Public Expectations Communities expect different services and different behaviors from voluntary, government, and for-profit hospitals. To the extent that there are different expectations for voluntary institutions, a public enunciation of those expectations should be encouraged as a vehicle of both differentiation and accountability.

Differentiation will occur when it is clear that the public expects a special set of obligations and services from voluntary institutions. The clearer and more explicit the expectations are, the better defined the standards for success in meeting them will be.

Accountability will occur when the public enunciation of these expectations is clear and unequivocal. The establishment of the social compact between the institution and the community results in certain duties and responsibilities on each side: The voluntary institution agrees to serve and benefit the community, and the community agrees to

[58] See footnote 14.

accord the voluntary institution relief from the burden of certain taxes and other market-related responsibilities.

Criteria   There ought to be clearly articulated standards for what it means to deserve the special voluntary designation. Those who work within and advocate for voluntary institutions in health care should take the lead in developing and urging compliance with such standards. Voluntary institutions may be near the crucial point at which, if they do not, they will lose the voluntary distinction altogether. It would be both regrettable and illogical for all voluntary institutions to suffer a penalty that should, perhaps, be incurred by only a minority of them.

Some have suggested that these criteria be sponsored by the hospital industry and implemented by a private mechanism, such as the Joint Commission on the Accreditation of Hospitals.[59] Others have argued that the Internal Revenue Service or another governmental body should enforce such rules,[60] while still others have suggested that the industry simply police itself.[61] It has also been suggested by Robert Sigmond, Scholar in Residence in the School of Business of Temple University, a long-time observer of and participant in the voluntary health care scene, that in all likelihood, all three types of control probably will, or should, coexist at different levels of specificity and rigidity, with the voluntary institutions themselves self-imposing the highest standards of quality and excellence.[62]

While the argument for one particular form of enforcement over another is beyond the scope of this chapter, it is strongly suggested that since those voluntary, not-for-profit health care institutions deserving of the appellation can indeed be clearly defined and identified, such definition and identification take place before it is too late. It is becoming clear that failure to define clearly and articulate standards for what it means to be a voluntary health care institution may result in tossing the baby — the voluntary health care institution as a distinct entity — out with the bath water — those institutions that either no longer care about voluntary ideals or have hopelessly lost their way.

Community Integration   As Professor McCormack has observed, "The current atmosphere of unbridled self-realization and economic Darwinism has supplanted an earlier focus on integrative strategies to

[59] R. M. Sigmond, unpublished interview, Philadelphia (1986).
[60] See Schramm.
[61] T. Citrin, "Sounding Board: Trustees at the Focal Point," *New England Journal of Medicine* **313**(19):1223–1226 (November 7, 1985).
[62] R. M. Sigmond, interview, correspondence, 1987.

achieve a health system ideal of adequacy, equity, and equality."[63] The divisiveness that accompanies the market segmentation and product-line orientation of the competitive model neither is consonant with nor bodes well for voluntary institutions and their communities, especially those communities that do not recognize the important distinctions and challenges that differentiate the voluntary institution. Voluntary institutions thus have an obligation to oppose fads in public policy or administrative theory that contain implications inimical to the values these institutions were created to promote. In particular, they also need to work to restore a legal and political environment hospitable to voluntary community planning.

Participation Leaders of voluntary health care facilities must participate actively in public policy formulation. A detachment from the policy-making process could hinder the institution's pursuit of its broader mission and goals. Furthermore, as mentioned earlier, there is a great danger in presuming that voluntary health care institutions are merely buffeted about by the winds of change concerning reimbursement policy and other regulatory issues, including tax and capital financing policies. It should instead be obvious that as a matter of process, the voluntary health care institution is, and should be, a full, active participant in any public policy debate.

The fact should not be lost that voluntary health care leaders themselves largely designed the health insurance plans in this century in response to a not-too-distant national fiscal crisis, and that they more recently served as architects, along with government, of Medicare and Medicaid reimbursement principles. Voluntary health care leaders should not abdicate their rightful role and responsibility in helping to shape our nation's health care policy, and moreover, they should understand how powerful and effective an influence on public policy they have had and can continue to have.

Creativity in the public policy arena has served voluntary health care institutions, and the nation as a whole, well in the past, and there is no reason that it should not in the future.[64] To do so, there must be capable leaders on both the national and the state levels who can speak clearly and unequivocally on behalf of such institutions. It is important, however, to keep in mind that the voluntary health care sector did not achieve many of the successes it has had with leadership and spokespeople whose allegiances were dissipated over a diffuse and competitive

[63] See McCormack.
[64] B. C. Vladeck, "Hospitals and the Public Purse," in *The Future of the Hospital* (forthcoming, 1988).

sector. Perhaps the most significant challenge for the not-for-profit voluntary health care sector, then, is to rediscover its collective voice.

CONCLUSION: MISSION MATTERS

The end of cost-based reimbursement, together with the deterioration of private insurance coverage for many people and the effects of new federal budgetary reductions, is progressively driving the profits out of the general acute care hospital business. The boom days of the late 1960s and the 1970s have passed, and the hospital sector is returning to its historically prevailing condition of fiscal stringency and financial risk. The chances for private investors to achieve short-term gains are diminishing, and overall, the national chains are disinvesting in the general hospital business, seeking higher returns elsewhere.[65] In short, as inpatient acute general hospital care loses its recent lucrative appeal and once again becomes a "nonmarket" enterprise — characterized by stringent fiscal constraints and scarce capital, as it has been for most of its history — its provision will be dominated by voluntary institutions. When the dust clears, the future of health care in America will be the future of the voluntary hospital.[66]

For these reasons, it is critical that the trustees and managers of voluntary institutions rediscover their mission and set their sights at the level of the values that were behind the founding of their institutions. The voluntary distinction is still valid and positive, so long as the unique characteristics and behaviors of voluntary institutions can be preserved. Public policy that chills these behaviors and characteristics is decidedly bad public policy and should be reoriented. And perhaps inevitably, public policy, whether in the form of the Internal Revenue Code, local tax authorities, or others, must eventually deal with the issue of setting explicit definitions, limits, and boundaries of what it means to be a voluntary institution worthy of both public approbation and special placement in our society. Voluntary trustees and managers should see this point of departure quite early and clearly, and they should act upon it in a manner that lives up to the voluntary ideal. Likewise, those who make public policy should understand the importance of this distinction and not revoke it while dealing with those institutions that do not measure up.

Both in hospital and institutional behavior and in public policy formulation, voluntary health care leaders should not confuse the means —

---

[65] B.C. Vladeck, "The Future of Voluntary Hospitals," *President's Letter*, United Hospital Fund, New York, October 1986.
[66] See footnote 8.

operating a health care institution — with the ends — community service. Finding the "just right balance" in understanding the means and the ends is an important goal, to be sure; but the very process of attempting to do so may well ultimately be definitive.

Even more to the point, *mission matters*. Mission matters in at least two ways. First, mission is essential to effective organizational performance. Students of corporate management, notably those most concerned with the apparent capacity of Japanese corporations to outperform their American counterparts, are rediscovering a simple truth: that a commitment to performing the organization's basic task — whether that task is serving hamburgers, building automobiles, or providing health care services — in the highest quality way is a prerequisite to success. The "pursuit of excellence" produces excellent competitive results in the marketplace. Further, clarity of mission promotes employee morale, loyalty to the organization, and internal teamwork. It is also essential to effective planning. You can't figure out how to get somewhere unless you know where it is you want to go.

Second, mission matters because the well-being of any nonprofit institution providing human services ultimately hinges on the relationship between that institution and the broader community. Economics are important, but not autonomous. Hospitals can survive while continually losing money if there is a strong and well-rooted base of community support, expressed variously through volunteer efforts, social approbation, philanthropic donations, and even — or especially — political assistance. However great any one year's profits may be, on the other hand, hospitals will not survive, over time, without this base of community confidence and support. We live in a social and political economy, not a textbook one.

In short, effective hospital management requires a clear articulation and understanding of an organization's purpose. As times get tougher, lack of a sense of mission can lead to short-term overreaction, organizational disarray, and even panic. It is a positive sign, then, that many hospital trustees and managers today are devoting the considerable time and energy required to undertake this type of redefinition, reaffirmation, and rededication of their institutional mission. Nothing could be more important to their institutions' futures. In stormy seas, one needs a rudder even more than a sail, and a compass as well as a chart.

CHAPTER 2

MAKING THE CASE FOR VOLUNTARY HEALTH CARE INSTITUTIONS: POLICY THEORIES AND LEGAL APPROACHES

Elizabeth Miller Guggenheimer, J.D., M.P.A.

A NEED TO PLAY POLICY CATCH-UP

The voluntary — that is, private, not-for-profit — form of organization has long been predominant among providers of general hospital care. Today's voluntary health care institutions have diverse roots, but they share a form traditionally associated with service, charity, and community involvement. Law and literature pertaining to health care institutions have reinforced the belief that, as a matter of public policy, voluntary providers should be encouraged. During the past several decades, voluntary health care institutions have received political, moral, and economic support through favorable treatment under tax laws. In particular, voluntary providers are eligible for exemptions from federal and state income taxes, exemptions from state and local property taxes, tax-deductible contributions, and tax-exempt financing for capital projects.

Recently, however, courts, legislatures, and commentators have begun to question whether such tax advantages are justified in an increasingly competitive health care environment. Hospital care has undergone major changes over the past few decades, especially in terms of services provided, institutions providing them, and means of financing. As the entire health care industry has confronted these changes, some of the differences between not-for-profit and for-profit institutions have blurred. Consequently, the role, and, in turn, the privileged tax status, of voluntary health care institutions is in a confused and uncertain state.

This chapter suggests that the not-for-profit form, in itself, is necessary but no longer sufficient assurance that individual providers will exhibit tendencies expected of tax-exempt health care institutions. There are strong policy justifications for the continued preferential tax treatment of voluntary health care institutions. These justifications draw upon the positive values and behaviors associated with the voluntary form, including purpose, service, admissions, charity, volunteerism, community, and governance. Thus, many important characteristics and distinctions among voluntary providers relate less to their form and structure than to their objectives and functions. Clearer, substantive guidelines, from law and within the health care industry, would help to ensure that the tax treatment of individual providers is consistent with public policy goals.

The first part of this chapter outlines various public policy theories for supporting voluntary hospitals and other health-related organizations. The second section examines existing legal approaches for characterizing and distinguishing voluntary providers. Law pertaining to not-for-profit institutions, charities, trusts, and taxation adds insight into why and how voluntary health care institutions have received public appropriation and support. The third part discusses the need for improved, substantive criteria to guide the tax treatment of health care providers. And finally, this chapter concludes that, while the not-for-profit form is a necessary prerequisite, tax status determinations should also be based on factors indicative of community service.

PUBLIC POLICY THEORIES: THE CASE FOR VOLUNTARY HEALTH CARE INSTITUTIONS

Central to the continued support and reliance on voluntary health care institutions is the belief that private, not-for-profit hospitals provide benefits to society that are not adequately provided by the government and for-profit sectors. As policymakers and providers grapple with a changing health care environment, they must dive under the turbulent surface and reexamine the positive rationales for distinguishing voluntary health care institutions from other organizations. Otherwise, individual health care providers that do deserve preferential tax treatment stand to lose it in the shuffle and doubt surrounding those that do not.

This section categorizes rationales for the existence of voluntary health care institutions into six public policy theories for advancing the role and mission of voluntary institutions. Clearly, some theories have more current vitality than others, but all have been articulated repeatedly and merit consideration. Moreover, they are not necessarily mutually exclusive. The positive theories must be underscored in efforts to formulate guidelines and standards for preferential tax treatment of voluntary providers.

Relief of Government Burden

A commonly advanced theory is that voluntary health care institutions undertake a variety of functions that the government would otherwise have to assume.[1] The implication is that if voluntary hospitals discontinued many of their activities and services, particularly those inconsistent with an economic bottom line, then the costs to the government would increase.

One version of the government burden theory portrays voluntary providers as responding to heterogeneous, unmet health care needs that the government has avoided or abandoned.[2] For example, voluntary hospitals lessen government burdens by rendering medical services to the indigent and by making health resource allocation decisions. Some commentators and courts have described such activity as providing a "charitable gift" to the community.[3] This line of reasoning has appeal today when millions of Americans are uninsured and underinsured, and when all levels of government are trying to limit health care expenditures.

Another version of the relief of government burden theory argues that Americans prefer the government to delegate certain health care activities to voluntary institutions, rather than to carry these activities out itself.[4] This preference stems from a societal and cultural bias toward decentralization of public functions as well as from ideas about economic efficiency. Private organizations are not as constrained by wage rates, procurement procedures, and other rules imposed on public insti-

[1]W. R. Ginsberg, "The Real Property Tax Exemption of Nonprofit Organizations: A Perspective," *Temple Law Quarterly* **53:**291, 307 (1980); S. B. Jones and M. K. Du Val, "What Distinguishes the Voluntary Hospital in an Increasingly Commercial Health Care Industry?" (this volume).

[2]S. G. Yoder, "Economic Theories of For-Profit and Not-For-Profit Organizations," in B. H. Gray, ed., *For-Profit Enterprise in Health Care*, Report of the Committee on Implications of For-Profit Enterprise in Health Care, Institute of Medicine, National Academy of Sciences, National Academy Press, Washington, D.C., 1986, p. 21; D. A. Stewart, "The History and Status of Proprietary Hospitals," *Blue Cross Reports Research Series* **9:**2,5 (March 1973).

[3]*Utah County v. Intermountain Health Care, Inc.*, 709 P.2d 265, 269 (Utah 1985); R. S. Bromberg, "The Charitable Hospital," *Catholic University Law Review* **20:**237, 241–244 (1970); Jones and Du Val.

[4]Ginsberg, p. 311; Yoder, in Gray, p. 21.

tutions. Thus, voluntary hospitals are assumed to provide more efficient services because they are less bogged down by regulations than government hospitals. As the government increasingly relies on the voluntary sector to discharge health care and other functions, this perspective has particular vitality.

Pluralism

According to the pluralism theory, voluntary health care institutions are an important expression of the pluralism in hospital care and in American society. Today's voluntary hospitals have diverse roots and histories. Many originated in connection with religious missions. Some began in urban centers, whereas others developed in rural or suburban areas. The varied origins of voluntary providers reflect the heterogeneous and evolving medical, social, economic, religious, and cultural needs and priorities in American society.[5]

One application of the pluralism theory focuses on the variety of hospitals in the modern health care system. The United States benefits from a mix of health care institutions and individuals that includes public and private, sectarian and nonsectarian, and voluntary and proprietary.[6] Although today's hospitals have diverse roots, there are three chief forms of organization: proprietary, voluntary, and governmental.

The contemporary mix, with a strong and predominant voluntary sector, reflects continued public support of voluntary health care institutions. Voluntary institutions are welcomed as a valuable alternative between government provision of hospital services and marketplace distortions.[7] They are also a locus for employees, volunteers, and patients who are interested in delivering or receiving care in a private yet not-for-profit setting.[8]

Another use of the pluralism theory is in reference to the diversity of activities and services in which health care institutions engage. The theory supports a hospital system that is responsive to the multitude of medical problems and the heterogeneous patient populations in Ameri-

[5] D. Rosner, "Heterogenity and Uniformity: Historical Perspectives on the Voluntary Hospital" (this volume).

[6] M. Doody, "Looks Like a Duck? Not Necessarily So," *Healthcare Financial Management*, p. 12 (February 1986); E. Ginzberg, "The Grand Illusion of Competition in Health Care," *Journal of the American Medical Association* **249**:1857, 1859 (1983); Jones and Du Val.

[7] *Comprehensive Tax Reform: Hearings Before the House Committee on Ways and Means* [hereinafter *Hearings*], 99th Cong., 1st Sess. 5855 (1985) (testimony of G. C. Phillips, Jr.); R. Stevens, "Voluntary and Governmental Activity," *Health Matrix* **3**:26, 29 (1985).

[8] Jones and Du Val.

can society. Voluntary providers are valuable institutions for providing a range of medically important services to a variety of patient populations, in part because their historical development has been linked to the needs of their communities.

Public Trust

The third theory depicts voluntary health care institutions as holding assets in public trust for the benefit of the institutions and, in turn, the communities served. While private in the sense that they are not under government control, voluntaries have several characteristics and responsibilities that are public-oriented. The traditional nineteenth century hospital was public in the sense that it was "for the public," regardless of whether it was run by a private charity or the government.[9] Contemporary voluntary hospitals are deemed to benefit the public interest by pursuing broad societal goals.

In particular, voluntary trustees are charged with two major roles which may, but need not, be antagonistic. First is their responsibility as stewards over assets, which are to be used in pursuit of the purposes for which their institution was created. Second is their obligation to discharge their institution's community service role.[10] In exchange for tax exemptions and other legal benefits, voluntary hospitals and their trustees are expected to serve broad societal interests. The trustees have a duty to serve the public, as opposed to the private interests of those who own or control the institution.

Accountability

A fourth policy consideration emphasizes the unique context in which voluntary health care institutions make decisions. Unlike their for-profit counterparts, voluntary providers are not ultimately accountable to investors who seek a financial return on their equity. Voluntary health care organizations have a legal obligation to fulfill a stated purpose, such as delivering health services. Their charters or organizational form ban the distribution of any net earnings to any individual who owns or controls

[9] R. Stevens, "'A Poor Sort of Memory:' Voluntary Hospitals and Government before the Depression," *Milbank Memorial Fund Quarterly* **60**:551, 555–556 (1982). *

[10] T. Citrin, "Sounding Board: Trustees at the Focal Point," *New England Journal of Medicine* **313**:1223–1226 (1985); S. Levey and D. D. Hesse, "Sounding Board: Bottom-Line Health Care?," *New England Journal of Medicine* **312**:644–647 (1985); J. J. McMahon, "Judicial Review of Internal Policy Decisions of Private Nonprofit Hospitals: A Common Law Approach," *American Journal of Law and Medicine* **3**:149, 164–165 (1977).

them—the so-called "nondistribution constraint."[11] Instead, surplus earnings, if any, are to be directed toward furthering the nonpecuniary purpose for which the institutions were formed.

The accountability theory assumes that positive behavior consequences flow from the nondistribution restraint. Voluntary health care institutions are deemed responsive to local and community needs, accountable for contributions, and involved with community leaders and volunteers. Because profit-making is not a primary incentive, voluntary health care institutions are expected to play a vital role in rendering important, but not necessarily profitable, health care services to the communities they were created to serve.[12] Positive notions of admissions, charity, and patient mix also flow from this theory. In proprietary hospitals, investors often monitor the economic bottom line. For not-for-profit hospitals, the tax law and other public policies remain valuable mechanisms for monitoring the behavior of voluntary hospitals.

Community Service

The fifth theory portrays voluntary health care institutions as providing a range of health and social benefits to the general community, for which they do not receive full compensation. This theory is broader than the relief of government burden theory because it encompasses activities that might not otherwise fall to the government. Several community service features are identified in the law and literature, including provision of care to disadvantaged groups, cooperation with other providers to promote access and continuity of care, medical research, education, and provision of valuable although not necessarily profitable services.[13] Given the diversity among institutions and communities, the community service orientation of individual providers varies depending on the populations and localities involved.

[11] H. B. Hansmann, "The Role of Nonprofit Enterprise," *Yale Law Journal* **89**:835, 838, 845 (1980); see also Gray, p. 8.
[12] See *Hearings*, p. 5865 (testimony of B. Brooks); Citrin, p. 1225; Jones and Du Val; Stewart, pp. 5–7. The New York Public Health Council enumerated several of these issues in late 1985 when it recommended continuation of the state law prohibiting corporate ownership of hospitals in New York. See New York State Public Health Council, "Corporate Ownership of Stock in Institutional Health Services," Draft for Council Review, December 20, 1985.
[13] This list is far from exhaustive. See generally Jones and Du Val; R. M. Sigmond, "Reexamining the Role of the Community Hospital in a Competitive Environment," 1985 Michael M. Davis Lecture, Center for Health Administration Studies, Graduate School of Business, Division of Biological Sciences, University of Chicago (May 10, 1985); "Small Business Administration Challenges Nonprofit Corporation," *Washington Social Legislation Bulletin* **29**:81, 82 (1985).

The view that voluntary hospitals serve important community functions is deeply rooted in history. Hospitals originated in the eighteenth and early nineteenth centuries as institutions that benefited the entire community by keeping certain ill populations off the street. By the mid-nineteenth century, hospitals began to focus on offering humane care to their patients, most of whom were poor. By the early twentieth century, voluntary hospitals emerged as the major center of health care for all patients, not just the poor, and they have continued as a dominant and adapting force.[14] In this vein, the community service theory implies that, with the appropriate public policy support, voluntary health care institutions stand to be a valuable resource for community-oriented hospital services in the future.

Response to Information Failure

While the theories discussed above explain the existence of voluntary health care institutions in positive terms, the sixth theory is relatively negative. This theory notes that patients often lack the technical information or flexibility to shop for medical services on the basis of quality or cost. Because of the asymmetry of information between patients and providers, ordinary market devices for policing providers of consumer goods are often inappropriate for health care — the so-called contract-failure problem.[15] The information theory assumes that patients are less likely to be exploited in a voluntary setting than one operated with unequivocal goals of pecuniary gain.[16] As one commentator wrote, the "lack of confidence in the ability of profitable enterprises to maintain quality care has helped maintain domination by nonprofit hospitals."[17]

Because pessimism and controversy currently surround the information theory, its use in making a positive case for voluntary hospitals is limited. Debate exists as to the degree to which voluntary hospitals actually fit the information theory. On one hand, because of their non-pecuniary purpose and structure, voluntary hospitals offer a potential

---

[14] C. W. Bays, "Patterns of Hospital Growth: The Case of Profit Hospitals," *Medical Care* **21:**850–851 (1983); R. M. Sigmond, "Old and New Roles for the Community Hospital," William B. Woods Memorial Lecture, Park Ridge Hospital and Rochester Area Hospitals Corporation, Rochester, New York, October 22, 1981; R. Stevens, "A Poor Sort of Memory," pp. 578–580.

[15] Hansmann, pp. 843–845.

[16] See Yoder, in Gray, p. 20; Ginzberg, p. 1857. For an enunciation and then rebuttal of this view, see R. C. Clark, "Does the Nonprofit Form Fit the Hospital Industry?," *Harvard Law Review* **93:**1416 (1980).

[17] Stewart, p. 5.

mechanism for protecting patients from information problems.[18] On the other hand, there is little affirmative evidence that the voluntary form reduces the basic asymmetry of information problem.[19] Commentators have suggested that historical factors and values play a larger role than contract failure in explaining the presence of not-for-profit hospitals.[20]

Policy Theories Revisited

The strength of these six public policy theories stems largely from historical and normative perspectives. First of all, many of the positive qualities illuminated in the theories are generalizations about what has been — or should be — the role of voluntary providers, not necessary or inherent characteristics of the voluntary form. These qualities include notions of community, governance, charity, service, and volunteerism. The theories tend to group voluntary health care institutions together, despite differences among them.

Second, when applied to the case for tax exemption, not just the question of voluntary status, the public policy theories rest heavily on the assumption that the social benefits of voluntary providers are well worth the losses in tax revenues from any privileged tax status. But rarely have attempts been made to quantify exactly the social benefits, so this assumption remains more of a value judgment than an economic one.[21] Benefits are far more difficult to calculate than taxes, and debate continues as to whether social gains should have a price tag.

Thus, the importance of these theories is their articulation of beliefs and ideals for a general group of providers, not assurance that individual providers will behave as desired. The theories imply that if voluntary health care institutions are to retain their valued features, then they must have the requisite public policy support to do so. Today's voluntary health care institutions face multiple, often conflicting, goals and pressures. On one hand are positive values such as service, community, mission, and volunteerism that are embodied in the community service and other theories. On the other hand, hospitals often must consider and follow businesslike practices in order to survive in a competitive health care environment. The theories provide a strong foundation for public

[18] M. R. Greenlick, "On the Nature of Nonprofit Institutions in Health Care: A Sociological Perspective" (this volume).

[19] C. W. Bays, "Why Most Private Hospitals Are Nonprofit," *Journal of Policy Analysis and Management* **2:**366, 369 (1983); M. Pauly and M. Redisch, "The Not-For-Profit Hospital as a Physician's Cooperative," *American Economic Review* **63:**87 (1973).

[20] E.g., Hansmann, pp. 866–867.

[21] Ginsberg, p. 308.

policy support of voluntary health care institutions that exhibit the values, activities, and tendencies deemed to be fostered by the voluntary form.

VOLUNTARY HEALTH CARE INSTITUTIONS AND THE LAW

Voluntary health care institutions derive their legal identity from several, not always consistent, areas of the law, including the law of not-for-profit hospitals, charities, trusts, corporations, and taxes. Expectations about voluntary hospitals and other health care institutions stem in large part from their legal characteristics.

When the determination is one of tax status, the result depends both on the tax statutes involved and on perceptions about a provider's behavior given other aspects of its legal identity. The courts and taxing authorities have drawn upon public policy theories in determining eligibility for tax exemptions. Tax law has tended to follow, not lead, the changes in structure, financing, and activities occurring in health care.[22] Today the tax law is not fully developed when it comes to distinguishing among voluntary providers.

This section reviews the current legal status of voluntary health care institutions. First, it discusses issues separate from, but with implications for, tax law. Then it focuses on preferential tax treatment itself.

The Not-For-Profit Field

Voluntary health care institutions share certain inherent characteristics because of their not-for-profit form, although the specific requirements for not-for-profit status depend on the state laws under which the institutions are incorporated. As not-for-profit organizations, voluntary hospitals cannot distribute earnings to directors, trustees, members, or any other private individual who controls their operations, except as reasonable compensation for services rendered. Moreover, upon dissolution, they cannot distribute assets to benefit any private individual.

Not-for-profit institutions are to be formed and operated for nonpecuniary purposes. Modern state incorporation statutes tend to be lenient regarding what constitutes a qualifying purpose for not-for-profit status, and the provision of medical services generally is sufficient. The test for hospitals is not whether fees are charged, income received, or profits (often called "surpluses") earned but whether funds and efforts are

[22]C. J. Schramm, "The Legal Identity of the Modern Hospital: A Story of Evolving Values" (this volume).

directed toward financing and production of hospital services. Voluntary health care institutions can therefore retain their not-for-profit status even if they charge fees or otherwise receive compensation for services rendered.[23]

The not-for-profit field clearly draws from and contributes to the accountability theory of public policy. Not-for-profit hospitals must use surpluses and assets in furtherance of their not-for-profit purpose. In contrast, proprietary hospitals are organized with the intention of earning profits to be distributed to benefit private investors. Beyond a definition stage, however, there is little unified law governing not-for-profit organizations. Although the voluntary sector dominates the hospital industry, it must look beyond its not-for-profit structure to develop more fully its legal identity.

Definition of a Charity

Law and literature pertaining to voluntary health care institutions frequently describe them as eleemosynary or charitable entities. Because tax exemptions and other legal benefits are available to charitable entities, designation as a legal charity has important implications for voluntary providers. Courts and commentators have noted that to some extent a legal charity "has its roots in the law of trusts, to some extent in the law of corporations; to some extent it may partake of both or indeed be *sui generis*."[24]

The weight of legal authority takes a broad approach in defining charities and charitable purposes. The concept of a legal charity is not limited to relief of the poor and destitute. It encompasses a broad range of organizations that are first, private; second, not-for-profit; and third, "devoted to serving the general welfare — not simply the welfare of their members or supporters."[25] The last requirement, the so-called charitable purpose, adds more flavor than the not-for-profit field by putting emphasis on objectives and missions rather than form. Courts and commentators have noted that "[t]he scope of charity and the standards under

---

[23] E. L. Fisch, D. J. Freed, and E. R. Schachter, *Charities and Charitable Foundations* [hereinafter Fisch et al.], Lond Publications, Pomona, New York, 1974 and supplement 1986, secs. 393–396; see, e.g., *Darsie v. Duke Univ.*, 48 N.C. App. 20, 28–29, 268 S.E.2d 554, 559 (1980); *Evangelical Lutheran Good Samaritan Soc'y v. Bd. of County Comm'rs*, 219 N.W.2d 900, 907 (N.D. 1974).

[24] E.g., *Paterson v. Paterson Gen. Hosp.*, 97 N.J. Super. 514, 518, 235 A.2d 487, 489 (1967); N. D. Ward, "The Charitable Fiduciary Liability Question," *Real Property, Probate, and Trust Journal* **17**:700 (1982).

[25] W. Nielsen, *The Endangered Sector*, Columbia University Press, New York, 1979, quoted in Ward, pp. 703–704.

which it is administered are not frozen by the past, but keep pace with the times and the new conditions and wants of society."[26]

For decades, courts have classified voluntary hospitals as charities when they are organized and operated to benefit the public at large, and when they use their revenues for such nonpecuniary purposes.[27]

Voluntary health care institutions generally do not lose their identity as a charity because they charge for services or because there is little or no evidence of free care.[28] Nor do they lose it by earning profits.[29] Rather, one key factor has been whether or not hospitals have a policy or practice against turning away people who are not able to pay. Some courts have been less likely to deem as charitable those hospitals who make financial ability to pay a condition of medical care.[30] Nevertheless, cases throughout the twentieth century have reaffirmed that the fact that most of its patients pay for their care does not deprive a hospital of its charitable character.[31] That is, the amount of free care has not been a basis for designation as a legal charity.

Many courts and commentators have recognized that a broad concept of charity is necessary in the modern hospital system. The increased demand and costs for medical services, along with the growth of insurance and government programs, have prompted several to note expressly that the traditional image of charities devoted to almsgiving is no longer appropriate. For example, commenting on the development of Medicaid and Medicare, the Supreme Court of Nebraska said in *Evangelical Lutheran Good Samaritan Society v. County of Gage*:

> Formerly all institutions furnishing services of this nature, including both hospitals and nursing homes, were providing care for many patients without compensation and extended charity in the sense of alms-giving or free services to the poor. With the advent of social security and welfare programs,

[26] E.g., *Bozeman Deaconess Found. v. Ford*, 151 Mont. 143, 149, 439 P.2d 915, 918, 37 A.L.R.3d 558, 563 (1968), quoted in Ward, p. 700.

[27] 15 Am. Jur. 2d, *Charities*, sec. 183 (1976); see, e.g., *Southern Methodist Hosp. and Sanatorium of Tucson v. Wilson*, 51 Ariz. 424, 429–431, 77 P.2d 458, 461–462 (1938); *Evangelical Lutheran Good Samaritan Soc'y v. County of Gage*, 181 Neb. 831, 836, 151 N.W.2d 446, 449–450 (1967).

[28] *Evangelical Lutheran Good Samaritan Soc'y v. County of Gage*, 181 Neb. at 837, 151 N.W.2d at 450; *Evangelical Lutheran Good Samaritan Soc'y v. Bd. of County Comm'rs*, 219 N.W.2d at 908–909.

[29] *Evangelical Lutheran Good Samaritan Society v. Bd. of County Comm'rs.*, 219 N.W.2d at 907.

[30] Compare *Iowa Methodist Hosp. v. Bd. of Review*, 252 N.W.2d 390, 392 (Iowa 1977) (people turned away who cannot pay; not a charitable use of property) with *Evangelical Lutheran Good Samaritan Soc'y v. Bd. of County Comm'rs*, 219 N.W.2d at 908 (policy against discharging people who are unable to pay; charitable use of property).

[31] See Annotation, *Receipt of Pay from Beneficiaries as Affecting Tax Exemption of Charitable Institutions*, 37 A.L.R.3d 1191, 1199 (1971).

this type of charity is not often found because assistance is available to the poor under these programs.[32]

Quoting from a 1921 decision, the court added:

[T]he courts have defined "charity" to be something more than mere alms-giving or the relief of poverty and distress, and have given it significance broad enough to include practical enterprises for the good of humanity operated at a moderate cost to those who receive the benefits.[33]

In a more recent decision involving a not-for-profit, prepaid health plan, *Harvard Community Health Plan, Inc. v. Board of Assessors of Cambridge,* a Massachusetts court commented:

[W]e recognize too that major changes in the area of health care, especially in the modes of operation and financing, have necessitated changes as well in definitional predicates. The term "charitable," as applied to health care facilities, has been broadened since earlier times, when it was limited mainly to almshouses for the poor. As a result, the promotion of health, whether through the provision of health care or through medical education and research, is today generally seen as a charitable purpose.[34]

Commentators have also pointed out that the strict view of charity as almsgiving never completely applied to hospitals because hospitals historically looked to paying patients and government funds, not merely large endowments, to help cover expenses.[35]

However, a recent Utah Supreme Court decision threw the well-established definition of a legal charity, as applied to health care institutions, into a confused and uncertain state. In *Utah County v. Intermountain Health Care, Inc.,*[36] the court held that two not-for-profit voluntary hospitals were not "charitable" institutions for purposes of property tax exemption because they did not provide a sufficient "gift" to the community. The court applied a rigid analysis, looking for an imbalance in the exchange between the value of "free" services provided and the tax benefits received. In reaching its decision, the court applied a vague but narrow six-point test. Finding against the hospitals, the court gave substantial weight to the fact that voluntary hospitals are "market institu-

---

[32] *Evangelical Lutheran Good Samaritan Soc'y v. County of Gage,* 181 Neb. at 836, 151 N.W.2d at 449.

[33] *Evangelical Lutheran Good Samaritan Soc'y v. County of Gage,* 181 Neb. at 836, 151 N.W.2d at 449 (quoting *Young Men's Christian Ass'n of Lincoln v. Lancaster County,* 106 Neb. 105, 111, 182 N.W. 593, 595, 34 A.L.R. 1060, 1064–1065 (1921)).

[34] *Harvard Community Health Plan, Inc. v. Bd. of Assessors of Cambridge,* 384 Mass. 536, 542–543, 427 N.E.2d 1159, 1163 (1971).

[35] See Stevens, "Voluntary and Governmental Activity," p. 28.

[36] 709 P.2d 265 (Utah 1985).

tions,"[37] not traditional charities, but instead similar to for-profit companies in many respects. As the dissenters noted, the majority opinion in *Utah County* contains reasoning directly contrary to well-established common law of charities as well as state and federal tax laws.[38]

Although the specific analysis in *Utah County* has limited applicability, because few states require an element of gift for every charity, the case has important implications for the identity and objectives of voluntary health care institutions. The decision signals that courts, tax assessors, and the public are questioning the continued tax-exempt status of voluntary hospitals which, to some, are not behaving as expected given their tax benefits. The result in *Utah County* may have been appropriate on the facts, for example, if the hospitals had an excessive record of turning away nonpaying patients. However, in the absence of clear legal guidelines for differentiating voluntary hospitals, the struggling Utah court pronounced extreme yet vague criteria. Thus, it is clearly time for policymakers and providers to participate in the development of useful legal standards that do not confuse the definition of a legal charity with the separate, although often related, definition of a tax-exempt organization.

Trusts and Governance

Additional legal features of modern voluntary hospitals and health-related organizations arise from the law of trusts. In particular, the law often equates voluntary hospitals with charitable trusts, and voluntary hospital boards thus have governance and stewardship responsibilities.

According to the Restatement (Second) of Trusts, it is generally agreed that "the promotion of health . . . [is] of such social interest to the community as to fall within the concept of charity."[39] Although trusts for the promotion of health may also be trusts to relieve poverty, they need not be devoted to the poor to be charitable. A leading trusts treatise supports this view:

> A trust for the promotion of health, however, is nonetheless charitable although the benefits are not limited to the poor. Thus a trust to establish a hospital for all persons whether rich or poor is charitable. Most hospitals, indeed, are of this character.[40]

Rather, a trust for the promotion of health is charitable as long as it is not

---

[37] Id., at 270 (quoting P. Starr, *The Social Transformation of American Medicine*, Basic Books, Inc., New York, 1982, p. 146).
[38] Id., at 279 (Stewart, J., dissenting).
[39] *Restatement (Second) of Trusts*, sec. 368, comment b (1959).
[40] IV *Scott on Trusts*, sec. 372 (3d ed. 1967 and supplement 1985).

run for the private gain or profits of any individual, and the beneficiaries are a sufficiently large class so that the community is interested in enforcing the trust.[41]

Members of the governing boards of voluntary health care institutions, frequently called trustees, are responsible for managing and supervising the institutions' operations. Some of the traditional privileges accorded voluntary trustees have eroded, such as the charitable immunity doctrine which insulated charities from tort liability. Increasingly, courts are requiring governing boards to take an active role in the affairs of the institutions.

First of all, trustees of a charitable trust or charitable corporation must act faithfully in furtherance of the purposes for which the charity was created. In contrast to directors of a for-profit organization, who have duties to shareholders, voluntary trustees must pursue the nonpecuniary intent of the institution.[42] In the event that specific intent is not evident from the donors or charter, or it is impractical, trustees must manage the institution and its funds as they deem best to accomplish the charter's aims.[43]

Second, trustees of voluntary health care institutions owe a duty of due care and loyalty to the institutions. This duty includes preservation of assets: the buildings, equipment, finances, and other human and financial investments that are invested in an institution. One way to breach this duty is by self-dealing or imprudent investments. Another way is by mismanaging or not managing those to whom investment decisions are delegated. If the governing board delegates investment activities to committees or individuals, all of the board members retain responsibility for supervising their work.[44] In investing assets, the trustee of a charitable trust has a duty similar to that of the trustee of a private trust — namely, to preserve them and make them productive.[45]

Third, in addition to owing duties to the institution, trustees of voluntary hospitals have responsibilities to the community at large. Courts have recognized that voluntary hospital boards have a "fiduciary" relationship with the public. This relationship stems from the fact that,

---

[41] Id., secs. 368 and 372.

[42] *Hinckley v. Beardsley,* 28 Ill. App. 2d 379, 384, 171 N.E.2d 401, 403, 89 A.L.R.2d 686, 689 (1961); see also Fisch et al., sec. 513.

[43] *Burr v. Brooks,* 83 Ill. 2d 488, 500, 416 N.E.2d 231, 234 (1981); see also Fisch et al., sec. 518.

[44] *Stern v. Lucy Webb Hayes Nat'l Training School for Deaconesses and Missionaries,* 381 F.Supp. 1003 (D.D.C. 1974).

[45] *Lynch v. John M. Redfield Found.,* 9 Cal. App. 3d 293, 298, 88 Cal. Rptr. 86, 89, 51 A.L.R.3d 1284, 1288 (1970); see also Fisch et al., sec. 517.

although private in the sense of being nongovernmental, voluntary providers have several quasi-public features: they exist to deliver vital health care; payments come through Medicare and other publicly supported programs; they are eligible for tax exemptions; and the health field is heavily regulated. As one court observed:

> A non-profit hospital serving the public generally is a quasi-public institution whose obligation to serve the public is the linchpin of its public trust and the fiduciary relationship which arises out of the management of that trust.[46]

Thus, some cases have expressly supported the view that voluntary hospitals exercise their health care powers and activities as a "public trust."

The primary context in which courts have enunciated this fiduciary relationship is in reviewing decisions of voluntary hospital boards, particularly regarding the selection of medical staff. Although the granting or denying of physician privileges at voluntary hospitals is within a board's discretion, such action is not completely discretionary. A growing number of jurisdictions support some degree of judicial review, not as strict as that applicable to governmental agencies, on the ground that physician selection decisions have a direct impact upon patient and community needs. For courts ascribing to this view, a voluntary hospital's power to appoint medical staff is "deeply imbedded in public aspects" and therefore among those powers that are "fiduciary" in nature.[47]

Another area in which courts have considered the quasi-public features of voluntary hospitals involves state legislation about citizen representation on hospital boards. The Fourth Circuit recently upheld a West Virginia statute requiring that the governing boards of not-for-profit and local government hospitals contain consumer representatives.[48] In an effort to control rising health care costs, the state legislature prescribed hospital boards that were "representative of the communities they serve." The West Virginia district court, with which the appeals court agreed, allowed the statute to apply to voluntary hospitals, and not proprietary hospitals, in part because the former "are entitled to preferential treatment and tax benefits."[49]

---

[46]*Garrow v. Elizabeth Gen. Hosp. and Dispensary,* 79 N.J. 549, 557, 401 A.2d 533, 537 (1979).

[47]*Greisman v. Newcomb Hosp.,* 40 N.J. 389, 402–404, 192 A.2d 817, 824 (1963); see also *Silver v. Castle Memorial Hosp.,* 53 Haw. 475, 479, 497 P.2d 564, 568 (1971), *cert. denied,* 409 U.S. 1048 (1972); *Berman v. Valley Hosp.,* 103 N.J. 100, 106, 510 A.2d 673, 676 (1986).

[48]*American Hosp. Ass'n v. Hansbarger,* 783 F.2d 1184 (4th Cir.), *cert. denied,* 107 S. Ct. 85 (1986).

[49]*American Hosp. Ass'n v. Hansbarger,* 600 F. Supp. 465, 473 (N.D.W.V. 1984), *aff'd,* 783 F.2d. 1184 (4th Cir.), *cert. denied,* 107 S. Ct. 85 (1986).

Federal Tax Exemption

Exemption from federal income tax is a valuable legal characteristic for those voluntary health care institutions that qualify. In the case of hospitals, income tax exemptions are available not because they are necessary for a proper definition of income, but instead as a matter of public policy — and health policy. When the question is one of tax status, the specific requirements of the Internal Revenue Code (the "Code") are determinative, but other legal characteristics of voluntary providers are intertwined. In applying the Code to voluntary health care institutions, courts and the Internal Revenue Service (IRS) have drawn loosely upon the policy justifications for tax exempt status.

Of the various provisions of the Code that grant tax exemptions, 26 U.S.C. Section 501(c)(3) is the most important for voluntary hospitals and health-related organizations. In pertinent part, Section 501 states:

(a) EXEMPTION FROM TAXATION. — An organization described in subsection (c) . . . shall be exempt from taxation under this subtitle . . .

(c) LIST OF EXEMPT ORGANIZATIONS. . . .
(3) Corporations, and any community chest, fund, or foundation, organized and operated exclusively for religious, *charitable*, scientific testing for public safety, literary, or educational purposes, . . . *no part of the net earnings of which inures* to the benefit of any private shareholder or individual, no substantial part of the activities of which is carrying on propaganda, or otherwise attempting, to influence legislation . . . [emphasis added]

One of the more ambiguous, yet powerful, elements of this section involves identification of an appropriate purpose. In addition to meeting the requirement of charitable purpose, a voluntary organization must be organized and operated exclusively for such a purpose.[50] The second key element is the prohibition against private inurement.

A second exemption provision applicable to voluntary providers is Section 501(c)(4), which covers not-for-profit "civic" organizations that are "operating exclusively for the promotion of social welfare." Designation under Section 501(c)(4) and not under Section 501(c)(3) means that an entity will not be eligible for various benefits, such as tax deductible contributions, available to those falling within Section 501(c)(3).

---

[50]The "organizational" test looks at the articles of incorporation and bylaws for the proper structure and designated purpose. For example, the IRS will require provisions about the distribution of assets upon dissolution. Treas. Reg. 1.501(c)(3)-1(b)(4). The "operational" test is met if the institution is engaged "primarily" in activities that further the exempt purposes. For example, the IRS will look at the distribution of earnings. Treas. Reg. 1.501(c)(3)-1(c)(2).

Charitable Purpose   Because Section 501(c)(3) does not mention the provision of medical services, voluntary hospitals and other health-related organizations generally seek classification under the "charitable" rubric. The regulations that accompany the Code do not specify that the term "charitable" includes the provision of hospital care, but they do prescribe that "'charitable' is used in Section 501(c)(3) in its generally accepted legal sense."[51] Meanwhile, the Supreme Court has held that all entities deemed "charitable" under Section 501(c)(3) or Section 170, the charitable deduction provision, must meet certain common law standards of charity. In particular, they must "serve a public purpose and not be contrary to established public policy."[52]

Drawing on charitable trusts law, the IRS and courts have interpreted the tax regulations to mean that the promotion of health is a charitable end for Section 501(c)(3) purposes. This has been the view of the IRS since at least 1969, when it explicitly announced Revenue Ruling 69-545, stating "the promotion of health is considered to be a charitable purpose."[53] The Court of Appeals for the District of Columbia upheld this position in 1974 in *Eastern Kentucky Welfare Rights Organization v. Simon* (*EKWRO*).[54] This court concluded that Congress intended the term "charitable" in the Code to "be broadly interpreted as was done in Revenue Ruling 69-545," not restricted to the relief of the poor.[55] Although the Supreme Court reversed the appeals court on standing grounds,[56] it did not rule on the merits, so Revenue Ruling 69-545 remains in force.

The IRS has not always followed this broad approach toward voluntary health care organizations. Revenue Ruling 56-185, published in 1956, included the following criterion for a hospital to be charitable under Section 501(c)(3):

> It must be operated to the extent of its financial ability for those not able to pay for the services rendered and not exclusively for those who are able and expected to pay.[57]

This earlier ruling, with its emphasis on free or below-cost care to the indigent, was premised on an image of hospitals long outdated. Hospitals

---

[51] Treas. Reg. 1.501(c)(3)-1(d)(2).

[52] *Bob Jones Univ. v. United States*, 461 U.S. 574, 586 (1983).

[53] Rev. Ruling 69-545, 1969–2 C.B. 117, 118; see also Rev. Ruling 73-313, 1973-2 C.B. 174.

[54] *Eastern Kentucky Welfare Rights Org. v. Simon* [hereinafter *EKWRO*], 506 F.2d 1278, 1287 (D.C. Cir. 1974), *vacated on other grounds*, 426 U.S. 26, 46 (1976).

[55] Id. at 1287.

[56] *Simon v. Eastern Kentucky Welfare Rights Org.*, 426 U.S. 26, 46 (1976).

[57] Rev. Ruling 56–185, 1956–1 C.B. 202, 203.

of the early nineteenth century were often almshouses, financed largely by philanthropy and government funds, as opposed to paying patients. In the 1950s, when the relief of government burden theory was the primary justification for tax benefits,[58] charities were associated with visions of the original, custodial-oriented hospitals.

With Revenue Ruling 69-185, the hospital community succeeded in insisting that the historical and theoretical bases for Revenue Ruling 56-185 had long eroded.[59] The appeals court in *EKWRO* noted that such a limited, "inflexible construction fails to recognize the changing economic, social, and technological precepts and values of contemporary society."[60] The development of Medicare and Medicaid and the rapid growth in private insurance altered hospital financing. Thus, caring for paying patients has become a vital concern of modern voluntary hospitals.[61]

Revenue Ruling 69-545 modified, rather than revoked, Revenue Ruling 56-185. The later ruling removed "the requirements relating to caring for patients without charge or at rates below cost."[62] A hospital may still qualify as charitable under the financial ability standard of Revenue Ruling 56-185, but it has a broader, modern alternative with Revenue Ruling 69-545.

In addition to adopting charitable trust notions, Revenue Ruling 69-545 compares two hypothetical, not-for-profit hospitals. Hospital A is described as a 250-bed community hospital, with a board of trustees composed of civic leaders. The hospital maintained an open medical staff policy. It operated a full-time emergency room, which served everyone needing emergency care. Admissions ordinarily were granted to those who could pay the cost of their hospital care. The hospital usually had an annual surplus, which it used to expand facilities, improve patient care, and advance medical training, education, and research. The IRS held that these facts indicated that Hospital A was operated "in furtherance of its exempt purposes," and therefore eligible for federal tax exemption.[63]

In contrast, Hospital B was a 60-bed general hospital. It originated as a proprietary institution owned by five doctors. When the hospital became not-for-profit, these five doctors continued to make up the medical

[58] See Note, "Exemption of Educational, Philanthropic, and Religious Institutions from State Real Property Taxes," *Harvard Law Review* **64**:288 (1950).
[59] Bromberg, pp. 241–251; see also *Sound Health Ass'n. v. Comm'r*, 71 T.C. 158, 177–180 (1978).
[60] *EKWRO*, 506 F.2d at 1288.
[61] See id.; *Sound Health Ass'n*, 71 T.C. at 180.
[62] Rev. Ruling 69-545, at 119.
[63] Id. at 118.

selection committee and, with their accountant and lawyer, the board of trustees. They limited the number of doctors admitted to the medical staff. There was an emergency room, but it was relatively inactive and primarily used for patients of staff doctors. The IRS held that these facts indicated "that the hospital is operated for the private benefit of its original owners, rather than for the exclusive benefit of the public," and in turn the IRS concluded that Hospital B was not exempt.[64]

Revenue Ruling 69-545 suggests that various public policy theories have influenced the IRS. First, the ruling employs a variant of the community service theory in defining charitable purpose. Several of the distinguishing characteristics of Hospital A, in comparison to Hospital B, relate to its community orientation. Such an approach represents a delayed response to changing perceptions about the hospital industry and the types of benefits the voluntary sector provides. Second, the ruling draws on both public trust and governance theories in contrasting Hospital A and Hospital B. The dichotomy between the two hospitals reveals two premises related to these theories. One is that tax-exempt hospitals should operate for the benefit of the community at large. A second belief is that the governing body of a tax-exempt health care organization should be representative of and accountable to the community, as opposed to a small group with private stakes in the organization.

Most significantly, by discussing different factors, the IRS indicates its desire for positive (although primarily qualitative) evidence of benefit to the community. Several commentators and courts have labelled this the "community benefit" approach.[65] In this vein, Revenue Ruling 69-545 identifies several features of Hospital A that suggest a strong community commitment: services to all those able to pay, whether through third-party payments or otherwise; an active emergency room open to all; and control by civic leaders. It is the combination of factors that counts. For example, Revenue Ruling 83-157 reviewed a situation analogous to Hospital A except that there was no emergency room "because the state health planning agency [had] made an independent determination that this operation would be unnecessary and duplicative."[66] The IRS concluded that the other significant factors indicated that the hospital was operating "exclusively to benefit the community" so as to warrant tax sively to benefit the community" so as to warrant tax exemption.[67]

Still unresolved is what role free and below-cost care should play in the community benefit analysis. Public interest groups have tried unsuc-

[64] Id.
[65] E.g., *Sound Health Ass'n.*, 71 T.C. at 181; Bromberg, pp. 241, 248–251.
[66] Rev. Ruling 83–157, 1983–2 C.B. 94 (1983).
[67] Id. at 95.

cessfully to overrule the proposition of Revenue Ruling 69-545 that indigent care is not a precondition for Section 501(c)(3) status. Challengers have repeatedly lost for lack of standing, not on the merits.[68] The IRS has considered indigent care in determining whether a voluntary hospital was operated "exclusively" in furtherance of a charitable purpose. In one instance the Sixth Circuit upheld the revocation of tax exempt status when one of five factors of concern was a low percentage of free or below-cost medical services to the poor.[69] Nevertheless, no clear guidelines exist for how policies and practices regarding free care should weigh in determinations of federal income tax status.

Although Revenue Ruling 69-545 suggests that several factors should be considered, in practice the IRS has been reluctant to rule against voluntary hospitals as long as the central purpose and activity is the provision of hospital care.[70]

No Private Profit The reluctance to rule against voluntary health care institutions in these matters is also evident for the prohibition against private inurement, the second key component of Section 501(c)(3) status. The notion that tax exempt providers should benefit the community at large suggests, as its corollary, that they should not be operated for the private or pecuniary advantage of individuals. The Treasury Regulations include the following requirement for tax exemption:

> It is necessary for an organization to establish that it is not organized or operated for the benefit of private interests such as designated individuals, the creator or his family, shareholders of the organization, or persons controlled, directly or indirectly, by such private interests.[71]

Physicians, administrators, and other "insiders" at health care organizations are entitled to reasonable compensation for services rendered. However, the regulations bar them from abusing their relationship with an organization for private benefit.

Commentators have listed a range of factors that are indicative of private inurement: control by a small group of doctors, excessive compensation for services, equity distribution, below market loans, inexpensive office space, exclusive admissions privileges, joint ventures, and low free care record.[72]

---

[68] E.g., *Simon v. Eastern Kentucky Welfare Rights Org.*, 426 U.S. 26 (1976); *Lugo v. Miller*, 640 F.2d 823 (6th Cir. 1980); *Lugo v. Simon*, 453 F. Supp. 677 (N.D. Ohio 1978).

[69] *Harding Hosp., Inc. v. United States*, 505 F.2d 1068 (6th Cir. 1974).

[70] See Schramm.

[71] Treas. Reg. 1.501(c)(3)-1(d)(1)(ii).

[72] Bromberg, pp. 252–253; B. R. Hopkins and E. J. Beckwith, "The Federal Tax Law of Hospitals: Basic Principles and Current Developments," *Duquesne Law Review* **24**:691 701–704 (1986).

Nevertheless, the critical issue is not one item in itself, but how the balance of factors play out in terms of benefits to the hospital and community versus benefits to individuals. The IRS emphasized this point in Revenue Ruling 69-545, where it stated:

> In considering whether a nonprofit hospital claiming such exemption is operated to serve a private benefit, the Service will weigh all of the relevant facts and circumstances in each case. The absence of particular factors set forth above or the presence of other factors will not necessarily be determinative.[73]

In that ruling, Hospital B operated largely to benefit the five physicians who founded it and dominated its operations. Thus, while there are no clear-cut rules, there is limited IRS guidance and a variety of case law pertaining to particular situations.

One illustrative case, *Sonora Community Hospital v. Commissioner,*[74] involved a hospital similar to Hospital B. In that case, the five founding doctors of a proprietary hospital remained in control when it became not-for-profit. They and their associates accounted for 90 percent of the hospital's patients, and the charity record was poor. Moreover, they received a percentage of the receipts of the laboratory and x-ray departments, although they did not provide services in those areas. The court concluded, based on the overall facts, that this was a clear case of private benefit and upheld revocation of the hospital's federal income tax exemption.[75]

A later case demonstrated that private inurement may occur in ways other than the distribution of equity and dividends. In *Harding Hospital, Inc. v. United States,*[76] physicians in an association rented equipment and office space from the hospital at below market rates, received excessive payments including an annual sum for hospital supervision, and treated 90 to 95 percent of the patients. These were among the factors that led the court to deny a federal income tax exemption.[77]

Generally all but the clearly private and entrepreneurial activities of voluntary providers have been permitted without loss of tax exempt status.[78] Just as some factors indicate private inurement, others suggest the opposite. For example, reasonable rental rates, reasonable and arms-length compensation, and privileges to all qualified physicians are evidence of charitable operation. Moreover, characteristics of private in-

---

[73] Rev. Ruling 69-545, at 118.
[74] 46 T.C. 519 (1966).
[75] Id. at 526.
[76] 505 F.2d 1068 (6th Cir. 1974).
[77] Id. at 1078.
[78] See Bromberg, pp. 252–253; Hopkins and Beckwith, pp. 701–704; Schramm.

urement are balanced against evidence of community benefit so, in themselves, are not determinative of tax status.

Property Tax Exemption

Voluntary health care institutions frequently qualify for property tax exemptions authorized by state statutes and constitutions. However, the wording and application of provisions vary from state to state.

Many states exempt property of voluntary hospitals when such property is actually used for "hospital purposes." This may be labeled an "organizational standard" because it singles out hospitals with a not-for-profit form. A second common, but not necessarily separate, approach is to exempt property of voluntary hospitals that is actually used for "charitable purposes." This may be deemed a "substantive standard" because it looks beyond a hospital's not-for-profit form to its charitable purposes. In practice, this distinction blurs because most states accept the common law notion that the promotion of health is a charitable purpose in and of itself.[79] Nevertheless, the *Utah County* decision implies that some taxing authorities are prepared to scrutinize the alleged purposes more closely before granting voluntary providers a property tax exemption.

Much of the case law regarding the property tax exemption deals not with the exempt purposes of the owning entity, but with whether the property in question is used to advance those purposes. Most states require the property to be devoted "exclusively" to the specified exempt objectives, with the term "exclusively" open to interpretation. The determining issue ordinarily will be whether a certain use is sufficiently related to the primary objectives of the hospital.[80] Depending on the circumstances, states have exempted property used for housing for residents and nurses, noncommercial rentals, cafeterias, and parking areas for hospital patients and staff. Taxing authorities have looked less favorably on parking for private patients, offices for private practice, and commercial rentals.[81]

Two public policy theories are prominent in case law and commentaries dealing with property tax exemptions.[82] First, there is the notion that property used for public functions should not be taxed. Because voluntary health care institutions provide medical services that would

---

[79] E.g., *West Allegheny Hosp. v. Bd. of Property Assessment*, 500 Pa. 236, 239, 455 A.2d 1170, 1171 (1982).

[80] See, e.g., *Barnes Hosp. v. Leggett*, 646 S.W.2d 889, 893 (Mo. App. 1983).

[81] R. D. Miller, *Problems in Hospital Law*, 4th ed., Aspen Systems Corporation, Rockville, MD, 1983, pp. 88–91.

[82] See Fisch et al., sec. 787; Ginsberg, p. 307.

otherwise fall to the government, they are deemed to be relieving the government of a burden. This theory has particular strength in communities where there is a relatively large indigent population but limited municipal hospital services.[83]

The second rationale is that organizations furthering socially desirable objectives should be encouraged. According to one court, "[t]he policy underlying the statute is to encourage charitable organizations."[84] Voluntary hospitals are perceived as using their property to undertake activities that provide social benefits to the community at large. This concept is a version of the community service theory. It incorporates the issue of whether a voluntary hospital serves a large enough segment of the population to qualify for exemption.[85]

Because of differing property tax statutes, and differing assumptions underlying the development and application of the statutes, there is not uniformity of taxation. Equally disconcerting for health care providers and tax assessors is that the guidelines for exempt status are not necessarily clear and organized. Thus, states courts like that in *Utah County* end up with unsupported reasoning in order to reach a locally desired result.

TOWARD NEW GUIDELINES

Despite the policy, historical, and legal bases for the existence of voluntary health care institutions, uncertainty and confusion loom over their preferential tax treatment. Several recent flares signal discontent with the current state of tax exemptions for voluntary providers. The *Utah County* decision is evidence that standards are being questioned at the state level. In Congress, there have been proposals to reduce tax-exempt bond authority of voluntary organizations and to reform the unrelated business income tax. Congress recently removed the income tax exemption for most Blue Cross and Blue Shield plans. Meanwhile, the business and for-profit communities have expressed concern that tax-exempt providers are competing in the same activities as tax-paying ones, and that their tax exemptions give them an unfair and unjustified competitive edge. The signs and sources of dissatisfaction have not been so dramatic as to undermine policy rationales for preferential tax treatment. What

[83] E.g., *Lamb County Appraisal District v. South Plains Hosp.-Clinic*, 688 S.W.2d 896, 906 (Tex. App. 1985); *Barnes*, 646 S.W.2d at 893.

[84] *Barnes*, 646 S.W.2d at 893.

[85] See, e.g. *Harvard Community Health Plan, Inc.*, 427 N.E.2d at 1163.

they do, however, is confirm the need to reassess hospital missions and legal standards in light of contemporary health care realities.

Policymakers must not sell voluntary health care institutions short. Overzealous legislative activity based on the idea that voluntary hospitals are behaving more and more like businesses will force them to become so. Instead, public policy must be directed toward encouraging voluntary providers to behave in socially desirable ways. Clearly, voluntary health care institutions that are tax-exempt should be expected and obligated to discharge certain social responsibilities in exchange for their tax status. However, because of changes in the perceptions, structure, and financing of the health care industry, the current standards for determining taxation are inadequate. Substantive guidelines regarding such responsibilities are needed as voluntary providers confront a changing health care environment and reformulate their mission and role.

The community service theory is a valuable starting point for enunciating guidelines because it incorporates elements of the other public policy theories but adds to them a sense of current vitality. For example, while the government burden theory is too narrow, especially when hospitals are not devoted to the relief of poverty, medical care to the poor and the performance of other public or quasi-public functions may be subsumed within notions of community service. The pluralism theory is advanced if voluntary hospitals are encouraged to exist and thrive in a diverse hospital system. The trustee and governance theory suggests useful indicia concerning which institutions are serving community interests, as opposed to the private interests of those in control. The accountability theory encourages not-for-profit status to remain a necessary element for exemption. Meanwhile, the information theory is more likely to be advanced than negated under a community service scheme. Thus, if enhanced by affirmative criteria, the community service theory is an important tool.

This section of the chapter focuses on three main issues that must be addressed in developing standards for tax exemption: What is meant by the term community? What is meant by the term service? And, what elements should be included among indicia of community service? Included within the third question is the issue of what role the not-for-profit form should play in tax exemption determinations. The factors of community service to be discussed are not intended to be a checklist, but rather a starting set of considerations while actual standards are formulated.

The Community

The issue of what constitutes the appropriate community for tax purposes is increasingly complicated as voluntary providers engage in activities that reach beyond their traditional or "local community." For example, many voluntary hospitals have affiliated with other health care organizations, for-profit as well as not-for-profit, as part of the growth of multicorporate enterprises. Meanwhile, many voluntary health care institutions provide specialized services and in turn attract patients from outside their immediate geographic area.

The critical question, which is supported by legal doctrines, is whether the group of beneficiaries is sufficiently large so as to constitute a community. In the case of general care, the community service theory is strongest when it emphasizes the importance of the local community in which a health care organization operates. While evidence of service to a community beyond the local one should weigh favorably in the analysis, inattention to local community needs should be a negative factor. Moreover, as demographics shift and other health care providers enter and exit the hospital industry, the relevant community will change in scope and composition.

Three principal factors should be considered in assessing the relevant community. One is the purpose for which the institution was created, in particular whether the intended beneficiaries are limited and if so how. A second factor is whether other hospitals exist in the geographic area. The concept of community should include a consideration of relationships among providers. Cooperation among providers is essential for quality, access, and continuity of care. Third is the different population groups seeking health services from an institution, for patient subclasses vary in their illnesses, incomes, and needs.

The Services

Another important issue is what constitutes socially desirable benefits to be deemed a service for tax exemption purposes. The promotion of health, although recognized as charitable in the common law of charity, is in itself a vague guideline. More informative is the corollary that the primary focus should be human need, rather than business or financial opportunity.

There are a variety of important medical and social services — innovative as well as traditional — which, although not necessarily profitable, advance the mission and priority of meeting human need. Among potential indicia of service are low-volume and high-cost care, medical education and research, volunteerism, care to the indigent, and standby capacity. Most importantly, it must be remembered that voluntary health care institutions should be allowed — and even encouraged — to discharge their social responsibilities in a variety of ways. The services provided by one voluntary hospital may be quite different from those of another, yet both hospitals may deserve to qualify for tax exemptions.

Factors of Community Service

If community-oriented behavior is to be encouraged through preferential tax treatment, then taxing authorities, courts, and voluntary providers need better guidance as to what constitutes community service for tax exemption purposes. With the exception of not-for-profit status, which is a necessary but not sufficient condition, the determinative elements of community service will vary depending on the communities and institutions involved. Nevertheless, there are several areas in which substantive standards should be articulated and particular factors considered. The discussion below focuses on factors in three important areas: governance, admissions, and range of services.

Not-for-Profit Status as a Prerequisite The organizational standard provides an important first check on health care institutions. First of all, the not-for-profit form imposes constraints on the distribution of earnings and assets. Thus, those in control are driven by motives other than private gain. In this vein, accountability concerns support continuation of the not-for-profit form as a prerequisite for preferential tax treatment. Second, not-for-profit health care institutions are to be operated for specific nonpecuniary purposes, such as to provide health care services or to sponsor medical research and education. The organizational standard requires that not-for-profit hospitals direct their funds and efforts toward such nonpecuniary purposes, as opposed to toward private benefit. In turn, the fiscal savings from preferential tax treatment will be used for further financing and provision of health care services.

While the not-for-profit form does not guarantee community service, its absence makes community service far less likely. For-profit health care organizations are organized and operated with the intention of making a financial return for investors and private individuals. The community service theory supports making tax benefits contingent on community-oriented performance. Meeting community needs often entails providing services and serving patients that are not profitable. Therefore, the not-for-profit form is an important floor for ensuring that motives and obligations broader than the economic bottom line influence the behavior of tax-exempt providers.

Governance The community service theory demands that those controlling the operations of tax-exempt providers be well attuned to the community service role of their institutions. In the contemporary health care environment, hospital governance is becoming more and more complex. The trustees and managers of voluntary institutions are confronted with multiple goals. On one hand is their social responsibility to serve the community at large, and on the other are concerns about the financial viability of their institutions. Additional pressures are imposed by the increase in corporate reorganization and the expansion of multi-hospital systems.[86] As board members confront the changing health care environment, the composition and activities of governing boards are useful indicia of community service.

In particular, taxing authorities should give weight to whether governing boards are representative of and responsive to the community at large. An important factor is the extent to which board members are civic leaders, rather than persons with personal or pecuniary motives. For example, physicians can play a vital role on hospital boards because of their health care expertise. However, their participation will be less harmonious with community service if they represent the special interests of medical staff or if a small group of physicians control hospital operations. A similar issue arises in regard to board members with business experience. Their business sense is valuable when directed toward further financing and production of hospital services, but becomes questionable when used for private gain.

In addition, law regarding trusts and governance indicates that voluntary hospital boards are accountable to their institutions and, in turn, their communities. When the issue is one of tax exemption, not duty, taxing authorities should look for affirmative evidence that the boards have a fiduciary relationship with the community they serve. The activities and decisions of governing boards, in areas from physician selection to capital expenditures, can contribute to the overall configuration of community service.

Admissions Patterns and policies regarding admissions are also telling of community service. In particular, admissions practices can shed light on the extent to which health care providers are open and accessible to the community at large. Given that millions of Americans are uninsured or underinsured, and that medically needy patients are not necessarily profitable ones, those health care institutions with community-oriented admissions patterns are providing important benefits to the

[86]See H. J. Anderson, "Changes in Board Composition, Size Are Occurring Very Slowly," *Modern Healthcare*, pp. 30–31 (January 30, 1987); C. M. Ewell, "Boards Face Governance Gridlock," *Modern Healthcare*, p. 36 (January 30, 1987).

community. Taxing authorities should therefore be entitled to consider admissions as one of several factors in making tax exemption determinations.

Admissions practices must be viewed in light of providers' resources and, very importantly, their role in the community. Where a hospital is located and whether there are other providers in the area both bear on who should be included among the class of admittees.

Two aspects of admissions should be considered. First are policies and practices involving those unable to pay for their medical services. In many situations, policies emphasizing the availability, not the quantity, of free care should be recognized. The provision of uncompensated care has long been rejected as a condition for tax-exempt status, given the trends and demands of the modern hospital system. In some localities there will be a large number of people who cannot pay, whereas in others that number will be much lower. Nevertheless, the fact that a voluntary health care institution delivers a significant amount of free and below-cost care should help to justify its preferential tax treatment.

The second aspect is whether the voluntary health care institution ordinarily admits patients who are able to pay. One factor is whether the provider limits admissions to patients of certain physicians, rather than being easily accessible to members from the general community. Another factor is the provider's admissions practices toward patients with illnesses that are complicated or expensive to cure. The concern from the standpoint of public policy, and health policy, is that certain subclasses of patients will be denied admission or receive inadequate medical treatment because they generally are not profitable. In contrast, an open and easily accessible hospital system will score higher in the admissions area of community service.

Range of Services The community service theory supports a hospital system that offers a broad range of medical services, without being duplicative. Many health care services are valuable from the standpoint of human need, but not necessarily from that of the economic balance sheet. For example, some services such as burn units may require large investments for a relatively small number of patients. Some, such as emergency rooms, obstetrical services, and many outpatient clinics, may lose money because many of the patients are commonly uninsured. Still others, such as some ambulatory care services, may actually reduce hospital revenues by decreasing the inpatient census. Whether services are profitable or not depends on a variety of conditions, such as admissions patterns and the needs of the particular community.

In carrying out their social responsibilities, tax-exempt health care institutions will be expected to offer services important to their community, rather than only the profitable ones. Data from the American Hospital Association indicate that, while most hospitals have a set of basic services, there is a large group of services that are more common in not-for-profit hospitals than in the investor-owned chain hospitals.[87] For tax purposes, however, the key is not merely the number of services but what the services consist of and how well they satisfy needs in the community. In this vein, the particular community is relevant in terms of relationships among providers and services already available in the locality.

Therefore, taxing authorities should consider the overall range of services and activities offered by voluntary providers, including unprofitable ones. In many instances, services will lose money because they are expensive or because they attract large numbers of uninsured and underinsured patients. Because such services will often be important, if not essential, the provision of unprofitable services is a way voluntary health care institutions can benefit the community in exchange for tax exemptions.

A DISTINCTION WORTH SAVING

The preferential tax treatment of voluntary health care institutions continues to have strong policy justifications. The major theme running through these justifications is that voluntary institutions provide important public service functions in exchange for their tax exemptions. As a start, the not-for-profit form, with its limits on the distribution and use of income and assets, requires voluntary health care institutions to be organized and operated for nonpecuniary purposes.

Going beyond inherent form and structure, the community service theory emphasizes the key role of voluntary health care institutions in generating a range of health and social benefits to the general community, for which they may not receive full compensation. The United States health care system relies heavily on the willingness of voluntary providers to treat patients and offer services that are not necessarily profitable. However, expenses and feasibility problems impose limits on the ability and proclivity of providers to deliver all needed care to

---

[87] At hospitals with 100 or more beds, these services are premature nursery, dental, hospice, outpatient department, home care, hospital auxiliary, health promotion, family planning, radioisotope implants, radiation therapy, and therapeutic radioisotopes. Gray, p. 108. See "Appendix to Chapter 5: Data on Hospital Services and Facilities," in Gray, pp. 121–126 for a compilation of data provided by Hospital Data Center, American Hospital Association, Illinois, 1985.

patients in the community. Therefore, public policy support, through tax benefits and otherwise, is vital to ensure that voluntary hospitals continue, to the best of their fiscal abilities, to meet individual and community needs.

The complexities and turbulence of the contemporary health care environment demand that additional guidelines be developed to ensure that tax-exempt providers exhibit tendencies expected given their tax benefits. In particular, for tax-exemption purposes, hospitals should be held to standards that focus on their substantive contributions to the community, not just their form. Case law and IRS revenue rulings have suggested that affirmative evidence of community benefit and community service should be considered in tax status determinations. However, they have been lax in developing and employing discerning standards.

This chapter identifies public policy rationales and legal characteristics from which clearer, substantive criteria should be drawn. Moreover, it begins to outline areas where guidelines should be created to assist voluntary health care organizations and taxing authorities concerned with preferential tax treatment. Governance, admissions, and range of services are all indicative of community orientation, but by no means are an all-inclusive list. Tax-exempt health care institutions should be encouraged to provide benefits to the community in a variety of ways. For this reason, they all need not score equally high on the same factors of community service. While specific factors can and should be identified, it must be remembered that it is the combination of factors that counts.

CHAPTER 3

THE LEGAL IDENTITY OF THE MODERN HOSPITAL: A STORY OF EVOLVING VALUES

Carl J. Schramm, Ph.D., J.D.

THE TRAILING ART

Just as music is often said to be the trailing art, the law reflects advances in social thought once they are in hand. While the law may be among the first places that the changed view is expressly articulated and perhaps where society first becomes conscious of (often alarmed at) its realization, the law seldom operates as the prime mover of social reform.

The law pertaining to hospitals has undergone radical change in the last 20 years. The hospital has been recast in the eyes of the law, reflecting a changed concept of what the essence of the hospital is as a social institution in contemporary terms. Indeed, the vision of the hospital as it is seen in recent common law is altogether different from the traditional conception of the hospital throughout its early history, and through the late nineteenth and early twentieth centuries.

This chapter describes the changing nature of the hospital as seen in the eyes of the law. Special emphasis is placed on the importance of legal doctrine regarding the tax liability of hospitals. It is the premise of this approach that the tax treatment of the hospital is key to understanding how society has come to view the hospital as an institution. Tax statutes reflect social views, via legislatures, toward the hospital, just as tax rulings call on judges to articulate the basis for determining a hospital's tax liability under the statutes. In both cases, widely shared values regarding the hospital are the fundamental basis on which the law relies. In what philosophers might refer to as a phenomenological approach, tax laws can be seen as having the particular analytic property of forcing lawmakers to determine the implicit social value of the hospital, since every decision relating to it is ultimately tested in terms of its impact on the public fisc.

ORIGINS OF SPECIAL TREATMENT

The social and organizational history of the hospital recently has received increased attention.[1] The American hospital was established first as a social institution designed to attend to the sick poor without other means of support. Its medical identity developed later, really within the last 100 years, when the hospital seemed to be the most likely institution in which to center the investment in medical science and expensive technology. The hospital was the natural place where society could rationalize the complex mix of skills necessary to develop the modern, machine-based therapeutic practice of medicine.

The earliest hospitals were nondenominational, though they often had a decidedly Protestant identity,[2] and were often established by voluntary associations with aid from local government.[3] In some older cities, a municipal hospital was founded in large part to deal with immigrants whom the voluntary hospitals would not admit. In addition to the municipal hospitals, ethnic hospitals were established for various groups of immigrants, notably Catholics and Jews, who were discriminated against as patients. Ethnic hospitals also gave physicians of similar backgrounds, who were often denied access to other hospitals, a place in which to conduct an inpatient medical practice. Physician-owned hospitals were a significant phenomenon in certain places, most importantly in the post-bellum South, where social spending was limited.

Hospitals, with the exception of those privately owned, historically have benefited from supportive tax treatment. Like churches, universities and colleges, museums, symphonies, and such charities as the Red Cross and the Salvation Army, hospitals have been protected from the

---

[1] See generally E. Freidson (ed.), *The Hospital in Modern Society*, Collier-Macmillan Ltd., London, 1963; P. Starr, *The Social Transformation of American Medicine*, Basic Books, New York, 1982; F. Hanckel, "American Hospitals in 1910," unpublished thesis, Johns Hopkins University, Baltimore, Maryland, 1985.

[2] See Starr, *The Social Transformation of American Medicine*, p. 175.

[3] See W. Knowlton and R. Zeckhauser (eds.), *American Society: Public and Private Responsibilities*, Ballinger Publishing, Cambridge, Massachusetts, 1986, p. 23.

burden of taxation. The hospital's exemption from support of the economic burden of government is perhaps more fully developed in the eyes of the law than any of the other institutions, with the possible exception of the university, because of the hospital's level of economic activity, its sizable real property holdings, the presence of significant endowment funds and investment income, its relatively well-paid labor force, and its complex organizational structure that often involves ties to universities as well as to individuals and organizations that are decidedly profit driven.

RATIONALES FOR TAX EXEMPTIONS

The hospital's principal identity from the perspective of taxation is defined in relation to three obligations: (1) income taxes levied by federal and state governments, (2) *ad valorem* or property taxes assessed by the state or its subdivisions, and (3) the treatment of the hospital as a public use for the purpose of permitting hospitals access to capital funds by issuing revenue bonds that are tax exempt in the hands of the holder.[4] In each instance, the law is generally quite clear that the hospital is exempt from the obligations of other organizations or individuals to participate in the cost of supporting government. What follows is a brief discussion of the status of the law as regards each area of taxation. In particular, the apparent change in the law of tax exemption is examined in some detail, since it may well be reflective of a much larger dynamic of how society has come to view the hospital.

Income Taxation[5]

The hospital is treated as a tax-exempt charity in the eyes of the federal government. This treatment arises from the ancient common law treatment of the hospital as a charitable trust where preservation of the donors' intent was the supreme consideration.[6] Under the common law,

---

[4] Federal law provides two additional tax exemptions for hospitals as charitable organizations. They are allowed to receive tax-deductible contributions under Section 501(c)(3) of the Internal Revenue Code (hereinafter referred to as the I.R.C.), and they are not subject to unemployment taxes on wages paid employees under I.R.C. Sec. 3306(c)(8).

[5] The discussion here is limited to federal tax law. Virtually all of the states treat hospitals as exempt entities for income tax purposes. However, as is seen below, this is an area of law where the states, as a result of changing treatment of the hospital for property tax purposes, may rely on rules fashioned on local rationales rather than bowing to federal justifications for the exemption.

[6] *Restatement of Trusts, 2d*, sec. 368 and sec. 372, as cited in Internal Revenue Service Revenue Ruling (hereinafter cited as Rev. Rul.) 69-545, 1969-2 C.B. 117.

the interpretation of the donor's intent was always that the exclusive permitted use of his grant was for charitable purposes and *not* for paying taxes.

With the passage of the Internal Revenue Act, Congress intended that charitable institutions be exempt from federal income tax.[7] Throughout its history, the commissioner of the Internal Revenue Service (IRS) has leniently applied the statute in issuing Revenue Rulings, the regulatory interpretations of tax questions, in deciding questions about the activities of charitable institutions. The contemporary status of federal tax law relating to the hospital may be thought of as resting on principles and broad rules of reason that have emerged over time, through examining specific questions.

A general presumption exists that all nonprofit providers of health care qualify for exemption from federal income tax, provided that the entity, at the time of its formation, meets four fundamental standards that the IRS applies each time an institution seeks to qualify as a Section 501(c)(3) entity. (1) It must above all, be organized as a charity *and* operated for a charitable purpose. To qualify under Treasury Regulations a hospital must be organized only to render care to inpatients and otherwise promote health in the community.[8] In addition to examining the hospital's charter and bylaws, the IRS looks to the actual performance of the institution to determine whether it operationally fits the exemption. Thus, (2), the hospital will qualify if it is "primarily" focused on inpatient care,[9] and no more than an "insubstantial" part of its activities are unrelated to the primary purpose qualifying it for exemption.[10] (3) The hospital as an exempt entity must also serve a clearly established public interest.[11] (4) The hospital must not be a direct conduit of monies to private hands. Such private benefit, or inurement, as it is called in the

---

[7] See Section 501(c), which provides for tax-exempt status for charitable organizations. See *Bob Jones University v. United States*, 461 U.S. 574 (1983), which reviews the principle.

[8] See Treasury Regulations (hereinafter Treas. Reg.) Sec. 1.501(c)(3)–1(b)(1)(i)(b).

[9] Treas. Reg. Sec. 1.501(c)(3)–1(c)(1).

[10] Loc. cit.; see also *Better Business Bureau v. United States*, 326 U.S. 283 (1945).

[11] The test seems to be service of any public. The hospital need not benefit all members of the public. The exemption has been found to not be conditioned upon the hospital's serving specific subgroups of the population, such as the poor or others seeking care under other federally imposed standards such as Hill-Burton. See *Simon v. Eastern Kentucky Welfare Rights Organization*, 426 U.S. 26 (1976), where the Supreme Court stated: "The promotion of health, like the relief of poverty and the advancement of education and religion, is one of the purposes in the general law of charity that is deemed beneficial to the community as a whole even though the class of beneficiaries eligible to receive a direct benefit from its activities does not include all members of the community, such as indigent members of the community, provided that the class is not so small that its relief is not of benefit to the community." While this finding rested on the hospital's having an emer-

law, is offensive, since it suggests that the nonprofit vehicle is being manipulated or abused for private gain.[12]

Situations relating to health care organizations are analyzed with these four guidelines in mind. In general, all but those activities of the nonprofit hospital that are clearly entrepreneurial and without any arguable connection to the principal activity of the hospital are permitted.[13] Examples of the application of the rules to hospital cases illustrate how far the IRS has gone in finding a hospital's affairs beyond tax liability.

One of the first areas where the tax exemption question arose related to the now common practice of office buildings being built by hospitals for physicians. Generally, hospitals sought to increase the likelihood of admissions by housing the private practices of physicians in office facilities adjacent to the hospital. Hospitals sometimes required physicians to locate in these buildings as a condition of privileges. More often, however, physicians enjoyed lower-than-market rents. Notwithstanding physicians' ability to compel the hospital to certain behavior in their economic interests, the IRS found that the below-market-value rental to physicians was within the contemplation of the exemption, provided that the hospital's need to have physicians close at hand was met and that the physicians' economic status was not unduly enhanced.[14]

A similar issue arises in cases where physicians are given below-market-rate loans as an "inducement" to join the staff of a hospital. Again, such behavior could seem questionable, since it could be argued that it results in an implicit subsidy of private individuals who are directly

---

gency room that served all people who presented themselves, a subsequent ruling found that even the emergency room was not necessary to preserve the exemption. See Rev. Rul. 83-157, 1983-2 C.B. 94.

[12]One test of the "privateness" of the entity is what happens to the assets of the institution upon dissolution. Truly charitable organizations are identified by the absence of a private interest to whom property eventually devolves. In one case involving a physician practice plan in a university teaching hospital, the plan was found taxable because its assets, upon dissolution, would revert to individuals. [(See University of Maryland Physicians v. Commissioner, 41 T.C.M. 732 (1981).] Another test of the private nature of the institution relates to how the managers of the hospital benefit from the services the hospital provides. Individuals who can control the institution's assets are generally barred from receiving funds other than reasonable salaries from the organization. [See IRS "Exempt Organizations Handbook" (IRM 7751) sec. - 342.1(3).]

Also see, regarding excessive payment to persons connected to the management of the institution, Harding Hospital v. United States, 505 F.2d 1068 (6th Cir., 1974).

[13]Small businesses have been a persistent source of agitation to circumscribe hospitals' permissible limit of tax-exempt activity, arguing that the exemption acts as a subsidy to competitors. See the U.S. Small Business Administration, Office of Advocacy, "Unfair Competition by Nonprofit Organizations with Small Business: An Issue for the 1980s" (November 1983).

[14]See Olney v. Commissioner, 17 T.C.M. 982 (1958).

benefiting from the charitable institution. Nevertheless, the IRS has found that hospitals do not risk their tax exempt status in running certain kinds of special loan programs for doctors.[15] And, of course, hospitals are permitted to engage in otherwise profit-making businesses, provided that they are related to the main purpose of the institution. This test has been construed to include as tax exempt such areas as parking garages (because they encourage patient visitors),[16] gift shops (including sales to staff because they improve staff morale),[17] and pharmacies (provided no other pharmacies are proximate to the patients).[18]

Only in recent years has the apparent leniency of the IRS regarding hospital tax exemption been tested. The subject is the entrepreneurial behavior of hospitals seeking to diversify and develop a multiorganizational framework through corporate restructuring. Typically motivated by an impulse to maximize government reimbursement for patient care, hospitals have set up several new corporations around the inpatient hospital organization.[19] These corporations generally include a foundation for the receipt of certain non-patient-related monies, such as those earned by the hospital's endowment funds; a corporation for ancillary services, such as parking garages and gift shops;[20] a separate corporation for inpatient hospital care (the hospital itself); and other entities.

The rise of these multiple firms around the hospital has caused some to complain that the hospital is really just competing in more traditional markets, and should not enjoy the indirect subsidy afforded by the tax exemption. The IRS continues to hold that as long as the central business of the newly reconstituted corporate group is the provision of inpatient care, the existence of subsidiaries, including even for-profit entities, does not call the exemption into question. The IRS expressly believes that the

[15] See Bruce R. Hopkins and Edward J. Beckwith, "The Federal Tax Law of Hospitals: Basic Principles and Current Developments," *Duquesne Law Review* **24**:703 (Winter, 1985).

[16] Rev. Rul. 69-269, 1969-1 C.B. 160.

[17] Rev. Rul. 69-267, 1969-1 C.B. 160.

[18] See Hopkins and Beckwith, footnote 15, p. 725. These authors cite a number of other related business activities of the hospital that have been found to be protected, including drug testing by a teaching hospital, the sale of silver by-product from X-ray film, the operation of a community health club, the provision of CAT scanners to unrelated health care providers, collection services for radiologists, the operation of condominium residences for patients, and the rental of pagers to staff physicians.

[19] Under Medicare reimbursement rules, government payment was offset for the proportionate amount of non-patient-related revenues in any accounting period. Thus, hospitals successfully confining inpatient income and expenses to the same corporate entity may keep Medicare inpatient payments at the highest possible level.

[20] Ancillary service profits, under reimbursement rules, are also used to offset expenses for inpatient care.

organization of for-profit business is permissible, provided that the charitable entity is the ultimate beneficiary.[21] The IRS suggests that such new firms represent "investments" by the hospital.

The only real constraint on the reorganizing hospital to preserve its tax exemption is that it must control all of the spin-off corporations rather tightly. In other words, were the hospital to turn over management of one of its subsidiaries to someone whose ultimate motives and control might not meet those of the inpatient corporation "parent," there may well be a question of private inurement.[22] Notwithstanding the implicit evolution of the hospital into a holding company in which, as the legal challenges suggest, phalanxes of managers, accountants, lawyers, and others are personally enriched, the federal income tax exemption for hospitals looks secure.

Property Taxation

Hospitals have always enjoyed exemption from property or *ad valorem* taxes. Generally the exemption has obtained on the theory that the hospital performs a function that the government, as ultimate bearer of responsibility for its citizens' welfare, might otherwise be required to provide and that the hospital, as a charity, qualifies for the same treatment enjoyed by other institutions operating in the community's interest.[23]

It is also argued that charitable entities enhance community values by their presence. The exemption may reflect the desire of those with a commercial interest in the prosperity of a community to save on investing their own capital by encouraging the establishment of charitable entities.

In any case, the property tax exemption enjoyed by hospitals as a privilege extended by state and local governments has been well established. And despite the universal practice of the charitable hospital

---

[21] Priv. Ltr. Rul. 8308019.

[22] G.C.M.39326 (August 31, 1984).

[23] Government's responsibility for the provision of health care, as an alternative to its provision by charitable institutions is discussed at E. Fisch, D. Freed, and E. Schachter, "Charities and Charitable Foundations," Sec. 787, at 602 (1974); Ginsberg, "The Real Property Tax Exemption of Nonprofit Organizations: A Perspective," *Temple Law Quarterly* **53**:291 (1980); Note, "Exemption of Educational Philanthropic and Religious Institutions from State Real Property Taxes," *Harvard Law Review* **64**:288, 290 (1950).

charging patients for care,[24] or its aggressive behavior in collecting delinquent accounts,[25] the community hospital has been exempt from property taxes throughout its entire history.

Only recently has a case arisen in which the exemption has been removed.[26] In *Utah County v. Intermountain Health Care, Inc.*, the Supreme Court of Utah overturned the tax exemption of two voluntary hospitals and established a six-point test for considering whether charitable hospitals would qualify in the future. They are (1) whether the stated purpose of the entity is to provide a significant service to others without immediate expectation of material reward; (2) whether the entity is supported, and to what extent, by donations and gifts; (3) whether the recipients of the charity are required to pay for the assistance they received, in whole or in part; (4) whether the income received from all sources (gifts, donations, and payment from recipients) produces a "profit" to the entity in the sense that the income exceeds operating and long-term maintenance expenses; (5) whether the beneficiaries of the charity are restricted or unrestricted and, if restricted, whether the restriction bears a reasonable relationship to the entity's charitable objectives; and (6) whether dividends or some other form of financial benefit, or assets upon dissolution, are available to private interests, and whether the entity is organized and operated so that any commercial activities are subordinate or incidental to the charitable ones. The test does not require that each of the points be equally weighted or that an institution qualify under all six points in order to qualify for the exemption.

The Utah court found that the behavior of the hospitals in question essentially supported the view of the majority of the court (greatly influenced by Paul Starr's work)[27] that a revolution in hospitals has occurred. The court was impressed that the "healing profession" has been transformed into an "enormous and complex industry employing millions of people and accounting for a substantial proportion of our gross national product." The court felt that the hospitals in question were, in fact, competing with each other in ways resembling for-profit firms. Moreover, as competing entities they could not demonstrate that they

[24] See *McDonald v. Massachusetts General Hospital*, 120 Mass. 432 (1876), which found a charitable exemption even though most of the patients paid for their care. Likewise, see *State ex rel. Alexian Brothers Hospital v. Powers*, 10 Mo. App. 263 (1881), and *Sisters of St. Francis v. Board of Review of Peoria County*, 231 Ill. 317 (1907). For modern cases, see *Harvard Community Health Plan, Inc. v. Board of Assessors*, 384 Mass. 536 (1981), and *Mayo Foundation v. Commissioner*, 306 Minn. 25 (1975).

[25] See *West Allegheny Hospital v. Board of Property Assessment*, 500 Pa. 236 (1982).

[26] The property tax exemption has been questioned, however, in recent years. See *North Star Research Institute v. County of Hennepin*, 306 Minn. 1 (1975), and *St. Joseph's Props. v. Srogi*, 51 NY2d 127 (1980).

[27] See Starr, *The Social Transformation of American Medicine*.

provided members of the community with substantial volumes of service without seeking payment in return. In other words, the test for charitable identity should be substantial and quantifiable gifts to the community, which the hospitals in this case did not demonstrate. The court dismissed the hospitals' contention that modern hospitals must be paid for their services and that the cost of care is such that endowment assets could never pay the substantive costs of any charitable hospital.[28] Finally, the court was not persuaded that government was greatly relieved of a burden because of the existence of the tax exemption, finding instead that the government already had paid substantial sums for the care of the indigent through federal, state, and county entitlement and welfare programs, and that the bill was no lower as a result of the hospitals' tax exemptions.

Tax-Exempt Debt

Some observers suggest that the hospital industry has experienced two revolutions since the advent of Medicare and Medicaid. The first resulted from the government's initial promise to fund all the costs of care for the elderly and the poor, thus insulating the hospital from the risk of financial failure caused by providing care to these two populations. In the wake of this legislation, there was a remarkable expansion of the number of hospital beds in both the nonprofit and the for-profit sectors.

A parallel provision of the Medicare Act provided for government payment to voluntary hospitals of the costs of debt financing for capital expenditures, and for-profit hospitals were provided with a return-on-equity payment. Once Medicare and other payers agreed to pay hospitals' capital costs, it was only a matter of finding the vehicle by which the second revolution, debt financing, would materialize.

Since the enactment of the first income tax law in 1913,[29] interest on state and local obligations has been generally regarded as exempt from federal income tax.[30] Hospitals expressly were found to be eligible to

[28]The fact that the case arose over allegations that the hospitals in question turned patients who could not pay over to the county, did not serve the defendant hospitals well. Notwithstanding a county budget to pay the hospitals for some indigent care, the Utah Valley Hospital had refused admission on the basis of inability to pay.

[29]I.R.C. of 1954, Sec 103(a)(1).

[30]For a discussion of this issue, see "The Taxability of State and Local Bond Debt Interest by the Federal Government," *University of Cincinnati Law Review* **38**:703, 705 (1969). The provision exists as a matter of comity between the federal, state, and local governments, and originally was also supported by a since-eroded belief that such an exemption was mandated by the Constitution. *See* id.; U.S. Department of the Treasury, Report to the President, entitled "Tax Reform for Fairness, Simplicity, and Economic Growth," (November 1984) (hereinafter "Treasury Proposal"), Vol. 1 at 135, and Vol. 2 at 290.

issue tax-exempt capital financing in a 1963 Revenue Ruling, but only on the condition that a governmental agency issue the hospital's bonds, and that the agency would obtain full legal title to the financed property until the retirement of the indebtedness.[31] As a consequence, few hospitals sought such financing.

In response to appeals from the hospital industry and investment bankers, state legislatures began to create financing agencies, generally of a quasi-governmental nature as their typical "authority" status indicates, to issue tax-exempt revenue bonds on behalf of hospitals.[32] The creation of these financing authorities allowed hospitals to use the device of "conduit financing." This technique involves the sale of bonds by a government agency and the lending of the proceeds to a specified hospital. The reference to conduit financing obtains because the government does not lend its full faith and credit to the bonds; rather, the transaction is really between the hospital and the investor, who appreciates that the ultimate payer is the hospital itself.

Since this technique developed in the late 1960s, the use of long-term debt obligations issued on behalf of hospitals by state authorities has become virtually the only way hospitals finance new capital construction. In 1968, about 34 percent of new hospital construction was supported by debt of one kind or another, and tax-exempt hospital bonds were unknown. By 1980, however, approximately 80 percent of all construction was debt-supported, with over four-fifths of this amount supported by tax-exempt bonds.[33] In 1985, over $30 billion in hospital bonds were placed, accounting for nearly 20 percent of *all* municipal bond sales that year.[34]

For hospitals, as in so many other cases, one legislative reform sows the seeds of the next. The enormous volume of tax-exempt hospital financing, coupled with the growing realization that the nation's hospitals are overcapitalized,[35] has caused Congress to consider terminating the exemption for hospital bonds. In 1985 and 1986, Congress consid-

---

[31] Rev. Ruling 63-20, 1963-1 C.B. 24.
[32] See D. Cohodes and B. Kinkead, *Hospital Capital Formation in the 1980s*, Johns Hopkins University Press, Baltimore, Maryland, 1984, p. 19.
[33] Ibid., p. 22.
[34] Much of the volume was accounted for by proposals to eliminate the tax exemption for hospital debt, discussed in the text below. In the fourth quarter of 1986, 134 issues totaling $4 billion were placed, indicating renewed activity after the tax reform law. See McGraw-Hill, *Health and Business* 2(2):4 (January 9, 1987).
[35] This observation relates to the surplus bed condition that obtains in most communities.

ered three different proposals to reduce or eliminate hospitals' access to tax-exempt financing.[36]

Although policy during the 1950s and 1960s encouraged the growth of the nation's hospital capacity,[37] there was a growing sense that hospitals were getting too large and that they were becoming financially too powerful. An analytic distinction began to emerge between tax-exempt proceeds actually used by a governmental agency in performing a governmental function and monies from bonds that were "issued [by government] on behalf" of a private user.[38] Thus, hospital bonds were often referred to as "private use" instruments by tax reformers.

In addition to resistance to continuing tax-exempt financing for what had come to be viewed as a private use, calls for reform also rested on conflicts in public policy regarding hospital expansion. The federal Administration argued that lost tax revenues represent an indirect federal subsidy, without government supervision, that encourages hospitals to build in instances where they would not spend their own revenues to support new investment.

Another line of criticism suggested that the use of tax-exempt financing for charitable hospitals created a market distortion that reduced competition between for-profit and nonprofit hospitals, causing prices to be higher than they otherwise would be.

While the tax reform initiative of 1986 left the exemption for hospital debt in place, sufficient attention has been directed to the issue to suggest that it is hardly secure for the indefinite future. Increased budgetary pressure to reduce Medicare spending will cause further examination of all components of government hospital payment — direct and indirect — and in an overcapitalized market, it is hard to see a prolonged life for the exemption in its present form. Regardless of the outcome of the question in the next few years, however, the examination paid the issue by Congress reveals the weakened rationale that undergirds the exemption and, more importantly, suggests a changed perception of the hospital's fundamental identity in the eyes of many in the federal legislature.[39]

---

[36] These were the Kasten-Kemp "Fair and Simple Tax" ("FAST") proposal, S. 325, H.R. 777, 99th Cong., 1st Sess. (1985); the Bradley-Gephardt "Fair Tax Act," S. 409, H.R. 800, 99th Cong., 1st Sess. (1985); and the "Treasury Proposal," U.S. Treas., Report to the President entitled "Tax Reform and Fairness, Simplicity, and Economic Growth" (November 1984).

[37] See E. L. Brown, "The Hill-Burton Act: Asynchrony in the Delivery of Health Care to the Poor," *University of Maryland Law Review* **39:**316 (1979).

[38] See "Treasury Proposal," Vol. 2, pp. 291–292.

[39] Several rationales have been advanced for eliminating hospital access to the tax-exempt market. For example, one suggested that this was necessary in the interest of increasing Treasury receipts. Another advanced the notion that the hospital would never become truly economical if implicit subsidies existed.

OLD RATIONALES, NEW CIRCUMSTANCES

The law of the hospital tax exemption, then, seems poised for change. Indeed the rationales that underlie the legal and administrative rules relating to the hospital as a tax exempt entity are beginning to undergo a broad-scale reexamination.[40] Without doubt, any reshaping of tax law will only tighten up the exemptions, and perhaps subject the institutions to increased tax liabilities.

This trend, as suggested at the outset of this chapter, reflects a much broader change in the way in which society views the voluntary hospital.[41] As Dr. Arnold Relman, editor of the *New England Journal of Medicine*, has observed, American medicine is now accurately viewed as a "new medical–industrial complex" that has displaced the old eleemosynary organization.[42] Likewise, Professor Robert Clark, writing in 1980 in the *Harvard Law Review* in an article entitled "Does the Nonprofit Form Fit the Hospital Industry?," concluded that "The unexorcised possibility that nonprofit hospitals actually do act in accord with the exploitation hypothesis [they seek higher than market rates of return on the sale of services], as well as the fact that they are elitist institutions engaging in cross-subsidization in the provision of public goods, should disturb policy makers."[43]

While these observations may capture the spirit of many commentators, they do not approach the more interesting underlying question of why there has been a shift in social attitudes toward the hospital. One may cite informed commentary on the way in which hospitals behave and describe the changed treatment of the hospital from the perspective of how it is taxed, which, in turn, reflects the operating values of legisla-

---

[40] The successful passage of legislation taxing Blue Cross reserves in excess of certain sums during the 99th Congress is suggestive of the scrutiny legislatures are paying to nonprofit, health-related institutions. See P.L. 99-514. More aggressive legislation that eliminates the insurance premium tax enjoyed by Blue Cross plans recently has been passed by several legislatures and is under consideration in several other states.

[41] Several other areas of the law have already undergone profound change regarding the way in which the hospital is treated. Perhaps the most enlightening in terms of an explicit policy rationale regards the change in the legal status of the hospital as a party to collective bargaining. In 1972 Congress acted to remove an express exemption of the National Labor Relations Act as it applied to hospital employees. Prior to the 1972 enactment, hospital employees were not protected in their union activity. This exclusion was premised on the assumption that hospitals were fragile institutions to be protected from the rigors (and higher wage costs) of collective bargaining. In 1972, Congress reasoned that hospitals had become such powerful economic institutions that protecting them from unionization conveyed a distinct and unnecessary disadvantage to hospital employees.

[42] A. S. Relman, "The New Medical-Industrial Complex," *New England Journal of Medicine*, **303:**963 (October 21, 1980).

[43] R. Clark, "Does the Nonprofit Form Fit the Hospital Industry?," *Harvard Law Review* **93:**1416, 1471 (1980).

TABLE 3-1
THE CHANGING VIEW OF THE VOLUNTARY HOSPITAL

Dimension	Historic perception	Current perception
Fundamental orientation	Eleemosynary	Market competence
Form	Individual, nonprofit	Polycorporate
Behavior	Charitable	Self-interested actor
Governance	Trustees	Director/trustees
Ownership	Community/ethnic/religious group	Creditors/investors
Role of government	Supportive	Regulatory
Staff relations	Physician dominated	Employer
Tax treatment	Exempt	Taxable

tors and judges. The conceptual foundation of society's attitude, however, is the more important question if one is to speculate on what the future holds for the hospital in the eyes of the law. Understanding how society forms the framework on which action is taken is the pertinent inquiry if one hopes to change the apparent course of public opinion and reassert an identity for the voluntary hospital that realigns it with its more traditional role as a charity and a social institution acting for the common weal.

The contemporary view of the voluntary hospital reflects attitudes about virtually every dimension of the hospital as an economic and social institution. Table 3.1 suggests that the changing attitude toward tax treatment of the hospital mirrors attitude shifts on several other dimensions of the hospital's identity. That these trends may be alarming to trustees and managers of voluntary hospitals, simply points out the enhanced importance of restating the case for voluntary health care institutions, and reeducating the public to their continual virtue to their communities.

Market Competence

One basis for the shifting perception of the voluntary hospital stems from what might be thought of as the economic identity of the hospital. The economic study of the hospital has disrupted society's conceptual base regarding its nature and behavior. The service provided in a hospital is now conceived of as "product," its provision is spoken of as "sales" and "delivery," and its financing is analyzed in transaction terms such as "supply," "demand," "clearing price," "shadow costs."[44] From its initial

[44]See, for example, S. Feigenbaum, in C. J. Schramm (ed.), *Risk Bearing in Health Care Finance*, W. W. Norton, New York, 1987.

use to understand the economic behavior of the health care system in the 1960s, *lingua economica* has had the appeal of a carefully crafted, albeit perhaps imperfect, framework to deal with a major, pervasive health care problem, namely, its financing.

For many observers, this concept-snatching has made the health care event between patient and practitioner look like any other purchase. Economics deals with interactions in exchange terms, forcing, for example, the care provided by a vocationally inspired nun to a destitute patient to yield to an analytic model where each individual must ultimately be posited as self-interested.

Nonetheless, economics had overwhelming odds in its favor as the captor of the conceptual field. It can be argued that a conceptual vacuum existed in health care payment analysis. The expenses of operating a hospital had risen enormously in real terms through the 1960s, causing hospitals to seek increased revenues. The preexisting rationales conceived of the hospital as a benign, charitable actor in need of protection from the community. The protections emerged for many reasons, well chronicled by Professors Clark and Hansmann,[45] but ultimately rested on the premise that hospitals did the work of the community that otherwise would have fallen to government.

While viewed as performing a government function, voluntary hospitals were never able to argue that their revenue should be increased to levels characteristic of other public services. Indeed, it could be argued that the philanthropic concept of the hospital languished because it was unable to justify increased government and private funding. Once a transaction identity descended on the health care event, the hospital was able to argue that subsidy from its own charitable resources was inadequate, that government could purchase its way out of a more fundamental responsibility for the poor by contracting with hospitals for care when they became ill, and that patients and those who insured them could not avoid the naked forces of the market as reflected in price.[46]

This market identity may also have arisen by timely coincidence. Given a crisis in the financing of health care, economics was the most likely place to look for an alternative rationale to charitable action with

[45]Clark, "Does the Nonprofit Form Fit the Hospital Industry?"; H. Hansmann, "The Role of Nonprofit Enterprise," *Yale Law Journal* **89**:835 (1980).

[46]It is interesting to note that this reasoning, to the extent that it operates, was enforced by the Medicare Prospective Payment System enacted in 1983, where government, it is argued, began to behave as a "prudent purchaser" of care for Medicare beneficiaries. In effect, this action meant that the government established a take-it-or-leave-it price and the hospitals that pursued a strategy based on the legitimacy of selling services to the government for the poor and elderly were ultimately forced to meet the handmaiden of the marketplace, namely, price regulation.

which to analyze the sector. Economics was well developed as a system of thinking, and it contemplated such social issues as welfare, human capital, and professional labor markets, all of which appeared critical to understanding health care. It can be argued that the 1960s marked the apogee of the influence and prestige of economics as a means of understanding larger social problems.

However, economic analysis, like most systems of thought, is not neutral. Indeed, classical economic thought is based on a belief that the welfare of the greatest number is advanced by permitting a price system of distribution to operate free of governmental or institutional restraints, and an assumption that all motivations in providing products or services are economically, or profit-driven.

Economics also brought a policy vision to the problems of hospital finance. The free-market and welfare-maximizing precepts of economic analysis suggest that problems of hospital finance and delivery can arise from four phenomena. First is the problem of "moral hazard," which suggests that in an insured market people demand too much of the covered good or service. Second, individual practitioners, as well as institutions, may exercise too much market power, taking profits in excess of the efficient exchange price. Third, adequate information is not always available to consumers to make choices in their own best interests. Fourth, institutions protected by price supports by way of subsidies are not efficient.

Economics produces policy prescriptions for all of these problems. To reduce moral hazard, some argue that more prudent use of health care services should be promoted by increasing the cost to the individual by reducing insurance coverage. To decrease market control by providers, it is suggested that antitrust enforcement is appropriate. Where information is inadequate, many believe that accurate price and quality information can be made readily available to consumers. To eliminate cross-subsidy, many feel that payment for the poor and elderly should be purchased by government at explicitly determined levels.

The normative vision of the hospital growing out of economics, then, is one that sees the hospital as entrepreneurial, price conscious, and stimulated to efficiency by government programs designed to reduce subsidy, increase competition, and prohibit provider dominance.[47] According to this view, necessitated by the strictures of economic analysis, the hospital can only behave best (that is, in society's best interests) when it is made to respond to the forces of supply and demand and is

---

[47]See C. Schramm and S. Renn, "Hospital Mergers, Market Concentration and the Herfindahl-Hirschman Index," *Emory Law Journal* **33**:869 (1984).

unsupported by the implicit subsidies that are embodied in current tax treatment. That there are a good many people, policymakers among them, who subscribe to this analysis, goes without saying.

Polycorporate Enterprise

The term "polycorporate" is used to great effect in the *Utah* decision to suggest the presence of multiple firms within a holding corporation.[48] This metamorphosis of the voluntary hospital from a single charitable entity into a multiple corporate presence, with several of the owned entities established as for-profit firms, is also altering perceptions about the hospital. These nonprofit holding companies, which operate research foundations, gift shops, parking companies, health clubs, management firms, home health agencies, and special food companies,[49] suggest a firm that is similar to for-profit entities. This perception of corporate form is of great importance to legal thinking, becoming more so since the concept has entered the appellate literature.

It appears that the motives of a multicomponent corporate organization operating principally as a hospital are now suspect in the minds of many. It is likely that the very term "corporate organization" suggests the demise of the smaller institution staffed by dedicated, often religious, personnel operating at submarket wages because of their dedication to the hospital's mission. In its place is now a corporation whose charitable identity often is obscured by its perceived interest in behaving like a profit-seeking firm. Indeed, inasmuch as hospitals are perceived as holding companies, they are regarded as suspect because of the traditional covert identities and activities of the components of the traditional holding company.[50] This conceptualization of the hospital is inimical to its continued subsidization through preferential tax treatment.

Self-Interested Actor

Perhaps the perception most damaging to the voluntary hospital, from the perspective of changing social attitudes, is its apparent assertion of self-interest over community interest. Of course, the hospital, like any organization, has always advanced its own self-interests. But the image in

---

[48] M. Brown, "Systems Diversify with Ventures Outside the Hospital," *Hospitals* **55**(7): 147–153 (April 1, 1981).

[49] See "For Hospitals, New Ventures and New Problems," *New York Times*, January 25, 1987, p. 1.

[50] D. Boorstin, *The Americans: The Democratic Experience*, Vintage Books, New York, 1974, p. 20.

the past was that the hospital's behavior reflected an internal management ethic that placed the interest of the community above that of the institution. Indeed, the voluntary hospital's image was so thoroughly bound together with the community's that it often mirrored the priorities of its constituencies. This vision reflected a cultural sense that hospital care should not operate at significant cost to its users — that other needs (schooling, shelter, and food, for example) should not be compromised to pay for hospitalization. This view reflected the charitable ethos of management that tied the hospital closely with the best interests of the community.

Perhaps the public now perceives its community hospitals as profligate. The naked competition for patients seen in television, radio, and printed advertising, and the frequent newspaper stories on surplus hospital beds may suggest to the public that hospitals have behaved in a financially careless manner and are now imposing on the community the costs of this ill-conceived growth.

The perception that hospitals have behaved in an economically irrational way — whether deserved or not — tends to mitigate the argument that they deserve protected status. Ironically, classical economic theory would suggest that it was in the joint interests of hospitals to restrict production by holding the number of beds constant, thus reducing costs and increasing the ability to stabilize prices. From the perspective of the price-maximizing monopolist, the hospital could not have created a more strategic blunder.

This analysis is particularly important in shaping policy because of the trust the community vests in the hospital — with its monopoly or oligopoly position — to behave as the delegated expert decision-maker regarding the optimal supply of hospital beds.

Privatization of Governance

A fourth component of the changing perception of the voluntary hospital relates to its governance. In previous times the voluntary hospital ultimately answered to a board of trustees that possessed both legal and equitable ownership of the institution. The trustees retained decision-making power over the typical charitable hospital until the Medicare era, when physicians and administrators began to dominate the institution. Medicare and Medicaid, by assuring payment for old and poor patients, were largely responsible for this transformation. The raison d'être of the traditional hospital board — the penurious husbandry of the institution's trust assets to ensure that care would be provided to all — subsided with the advent of Medicare and Medicaid.

The nearly exclusive focus of the hospital's traditional charitable endeavor — the care of the poor and the elderly — had become one of the hospital's major sources of revenue. The historic budget constraint of the charitable institution, enforced by the trustees, accordingly dissolved as a rationale without a reason.

Hospital budgetary discipline rapidly became dominated by the "reasonableness" test imposed by payers. Trustees found it painless to approve proposals to enlarge or enhance the hospital (which purported to improve the community's standard of hospital practice), because it involved no financial risk to the institution.

As the hospital has developed a polycorporate identity, trustees have begun to — indeed, have been expected to — behave more like private directors. In addition to their historic but ill-defined sense of community stewardship, voluntary trustees may be held to a strict standard of fiduciary responsibility similar to that of corporate directors.[51] Increasingly, patients sue hospital trustees, alleging personal responsibility in cases relating to the competence of the institution's physicians. In medical malpractice claims it is often argued that the trustees bear ultimate legal responsibility for the choice of physicians practicing in the hospital. By extension, then, the hospital trustee may be held to account, as in product liability cases, for damages arising from the tortious action of members of the medical staff.

Remote Financial Owners

The growth of debt financing for capital needs is of profound importance to the identity of the voluntary hospital. As a charitable institution, the hospital had to rely on the largesse of the community for its capital. The vast majority of voluntary hospitals was built with funds that had been promised or given in advance of the construction itself. Not only did this reflect the way in which charitable institutions routinely were capitalized, it was also necessary because banks have always been reluctant to provide mortgage funding for hospital buildings.

Once hospitals began to sell long-term obligations through the municipal bond market, it can be argued that the institutions' self-identity began to change. Bond holders primarily have an economic, not a health-related, interest in the hospital issuing the bonds, and they are, for the most part, geographically remote and not members of the community in which the hospital is located. Trustees now must consider the

---

[51] See *Stearn v. Lucy Webb Hayes School* (Sibley Hospital), 381 F. Supp. 1003, D.C., 1974.

economic expectations of these bond holders. In doing so, the hospital presents an image of becoming less connected with the community in which it is situated. The implicit rationale for protecting the hospital as an institution fundamentally concerned with and linked to the community is being questioned as it increasingly is perceived as a large firm operating with significant connections and interests, largely of an economic nature, beyond the community.

State as Intervening Interest

Hospitals, which in the past were protected and encouraged in their service by the state because they provided care and succor to the ill—ultimately the responsibility of the state—were sheltered from many of the legal and tax responsibilities to which other organizations are subject.

As the hospital has developed its modern identity, the state has come to view the institution as so ready to act in its own interest that an explicit government regulatory role has been made necessary. Hospitals have been limited to government-approved construction and development programs, including the initiation of new services. Some of the prices they charge are limited by federal price schedules, in the form of diagnostic related groupings (DRGs), and in several states, by agencies that regulate hospital charges. Increasingly, the medical management of hospital cases is overseen by public agencies to ensure at least minimum standards of care. In each instance where the state has intervened, the presumption seems to exist, that, absent state supervision, the hospital may not act entirely in the interests of the community at large and the patients entrusted to its care.

New Staff Relations

Historically, the hospital extended practice or admitting privileges to doctors at no cost in return for the physician's promise to provide care without charge to poor persons seen at the hospital, and historically treated as charity wards. Through time the paying patients of these physicians became the predominant users of the hospital. In treating their hospitalized patients, physicians have been largely independent of the hospital's internal economic structure, since they have been seen as neither employees nor contractors. This led Professor Mark Pauly to observe that the hospital operates as a "physicians' workshop."[52]

[52]M. Pauley and M. Redisch, "The Not-For-Profit Hospital as a Physician's Cooperative," *American Economic Review* **63:**87 (1973).

With Medicare and Medicaid, which permit even the poor and elderly to choose their attending physicians, hospital charity or "ward" practice has nearly disappeared. Because hospitals depend on physicians to fill their beds, physicians are able to exercise a good deal of leverage over the hospital to act in their interests. Accordingly, hospitals have invested in new services and equipment to compete for the loyalty — and patients — of physicians. Not surprisingly, then, hospitals and physicians often are perceived as a formidable alliance acting in each other's interests, and in the process driving up health care costs to unacceptable levels. If this view is correct, one result is that the protections once enjoyed by the hospital are at risk because of the perception that the hospitals have been taken over by physicians, and that physicians make most of their money while practicing in hospitals.

A TIME FOR SELF-ASSESSMENT

This chapter has purposely reviewed some of the widespread perceptions about voluntary hospitals — and indeed the entire voluntary health care system — that these organizations must contend with in justifying their continued tax-favored status to revenue-seeking local, state, and federal officials. Before voluntary hospitals proceed further in seeking reconciliation between their mission and their tax exemptions, their leaders would be well advised to clarify what it is that the late twentieth century charitable hospital is and does. One intent of this chapter is to spur just this sort of institutional introspection.

In the foregoing discussion, two themes emerge that can increase understanding of the voluntary hospital's past and its future. First, because hospitals traditionally have not served the economic purposes of any individuals or groups that have an ownership interest, their tax-exempt status has seemed appropriate. Americans, who, on the one hand, can be hard-nosed business people, seem disposed, on the other hand, to nurture voluntary organizations formed to advance nonmarket or noneconomic goals. We have traditionally seen hospitals in this light, and their continuing tax exemption reflects this perception.

Second, the primary purpose of hospitals has been to dispense needed care to people, and payment for this care traditionally has been a secondary consideration. This perception of hospitals is key to understanding the federal income tax treatment of hospitals and their exemption from local taxation. The comfort derived from knowing hospitals will dispense aid to the indigent infirm, as well as to paying patients, has traditionally been worth the tax tradeoff.

The quarrel that many observers and policymakers apparently have with the modern hospital is reflected in proposals to change the tax treatment of the hospital. In its essence the quarrel is one of disillusionment and the disappointment that attends the apparent failure of expectations or ideology. Commonplace perceptions of the substance, form, behavior, and governance of the modern voluntary hospital establish it as often appearing market competent and as advancing its own self-interest, frequently at the expense of community interest. This vision of the hospital, undeniable in the image that many hospitals themselves now advance in their advertising and other activities, is destined to disappoint.

Is Nothing Sacred?

Perhaps Americans embrace somewhat naive visions of how society is ordered. Private and public sectors serve separate functions, and voluntary, charitable organizations have quasi-public characteristics all their own. As hospitals are increasingly perceived as self-interested, robust economic actors, Americans feel particularly disturbed — even cynical. Are we dominated by the profit motive? Is there no place in our society for pure altruism? Will economics prevail over compassion? Is nothing sacred?

As the survival of institutions, both nonprofit and for profit, depends increasingly on the bottom line, the distinction between the two blurs. With the fall of the hospital from the mountain of the sacred, charitable, nonmarket performer, to the plain of entrepreneurial firm, many people feel that one of the last distinctive, charitable organizations has been lost.

Hospitals as social institutions seem to be caught in a broader crisis of ideology in the United States. Our community institutions, and, even more important, our sense of community itself (kinship with fellow persons in our cities, towns, and neighborhoods) are critical to our sense of communal identity, and these institutions increasingly seem dominated by forces beyond the community's control.

Voluntary hospitals traditionally have nurtured and embodied one of the most cherished values of the community in the healing of the sick and injured regardless of ability to pay. If the voluntary hospitals abandon this unconditional mission, the backlash may be significant. The loss of tax exemptions, reductions in government payments, and the forced reduction of the industry, at the hands of savvy purchasers and government regulatory agencies, are likely to result. All these possibilities testify to the special disenchantment that many Americans feel about the entity that some hospitals have let themselves become. Lost in the metamorphosis was a characteristic of hospital culture that further endeared them to their communities — their economic frailty.

It would be fatuous to suggest either that hospitals should resume the posture of the poor cousin of the community, with hand perpetually extended in search of funds, or that they should be oblivious to policies that force a constant watch over the ever-exigent bottom line. In their quest to survive in these turbulent times, however, voluntary hospital leaders should be ever mindful — indeed proud — of their origins and their community obligations. And, they should be aware that if they act increasingly like corporate players, they can expect to be treated like them, and at the expense of more important assets — the faith and sponsorship of the community, which entrusts to hospitals its most vulnerable citizens. Their care and healing is the sacred trust of hospitals, and must take precedence over other considerations.

ACKNOWLEDGMENT

The author wishes to thank Robert Liebenluft of Hogan and Hartson in Washington for expert legal research on the subject of tax-exempt capital financing.

CHAPTER 4

HETEROGENEITY AND UNIFORMITY: HISTORICAL PERSPECTIVES ON THE VOLUNTARY HOSPITAL

David Rosner, Ph.D., M.P.H.

A HISTORY OF DIVERSITY

The American system of voluntary, not-for-profit hospitals is composed of a heterogeneous set of institutions that vary widely in ethnic and religious orientation, medical school affiliation, size, financing, specialty, and patient base. Its institutions are generally governed individually by lay trustees, staffed by private practitioners and salaried personnel, and funded through an amalgam of private and public sources in widely varying geographic settings. For the past 200 years, the system of not-for-profit, community-sponsored hospitals has dominated the hospital scene, adapting to enormous changes in the social, economic, political, and medical landscape.[1]

During the late 1970s and early 1980s, however, a set of institutions

---

[1] There has been strong resistance in American history to highly centralized systems for the provision of health care. We might look back at the fate of such organizations as the dispensary or the Neighborhood Health Centers of the 1890–1920 period for examples of the destruction of more systematized attempts to organize services. Despite their exemplary intent, the harsh realities of political, economic, and medical changes undermined their support, leaving them vulnerable to decimation at the hands of their political enemies within and outside of organized medicine. Also, the harsh treatment at the hands of the American Medical Association in the Report of the *Committee on the Costs of Medical Care* during the 1930s was partly rooted in the antagonism to centralized systems for distributing health care.

arose that have substantially different organizational arrangements and characteristics. Unlike the voluntary system that has prided itself on its nonprofit, voluntaristic, and decentralized nature, for-profit hospital *chains*, run as businesses with centralized, standardized, and formal relationships to each other, have arisen in some sections of the country, particularly the West and the South. Spokespersons for the for-profit hospital chains have asserted that in light of rising health care costs and the need for more efficiency in the hospital system, their institutions, driven by the need to earn money for their stockholders, will make better use of medical resources than will the voluntary system. Despite ambiguous and often negative results of academic studies, they maintain that there is an equation between profit-making, centralization and standardization, and social and economic efficiency.

In light of these arguments, this chapter will explore the historical development of voluntary hospitals in the United States. It will focus on the tension that has existed between movements to standardize medical care, administration, and organization and the voluntary system's apparent resistance to centralization. Two parallel arguments are made. First, it is argued that the past strength of the voluntary system rests on its strong ties to communities with sometimes idiosyncratic needs. The historical heterogeneity in the organization, mission, and patient base of the voluntary hospital reflects the heterogeneity of the communities and interests served. The continually changing demographic, social, economic, political, and medical context of American society (and the apparent political and social resistance to publicly accountable, government-sponsored health care systems) will continue to make the voluntary, nonprofit form the vital element in the American health care system.

Second, it is suggested that, historically, the rhetoric of efficiency, standardization, centralization, and science has been used as an ideological wedge in the battle over the control of the health care system, but has generally been a cloak for other narrower professional and economic interests. Today, arguments that depend heavily on seemingly self-evident scientific, economic, and free-market truths should be viewed with a degree of wariness in light of the enormous financial stakes involved.[2]

---

[2] In the past, the ideological uses of standardization have revolved around the roles of the state and federal government in regulating and providing service. Throughout most of the century, the medical and hospital communities have taken aggressive stands against governmental involvement claiming that uniformity of care, payments, and organization were anathema to the needs of a diverse and heterogeneous population. Significantly, in the past, the mantle of variety and heterogeneity was used to ward off seemingly legitimate calls for compulsory or national health insurance. More recently, the ideology of business and scientific efficiency has been used by the for-profit hospital sector in their attempt to gain social legitimacy and control of a larger portion of the health care dollar. In the more

This chapter will try to peel away the various social, intellectual, and professional layers of the institution, seeking to illustrate that the cultural underpinnings of the voluntary hospital have affected their goals, structure, and organization. First is an examination of the skin of the institution, the first images and beliefs that led to the formation of community or voluntary hospitals. Some of the social forces that shaped the goals of the trustees who organized voluntary hospitals, and the needs of the patients who populated those hospitals in the late nineteenth and early twentieth centuries will be outlined. Doing so will illustrate that the hospitals' origins had relatively little to do with medical care as it is now understood and everything to do with social services and social needs.

Second, the chapter will delve deeper into the institution and look at its internal culture and workings, and the growing interest of physicians in the hospital in the decades around the turn of this century will be reviewed. Here, an emphasis on the economic aspects of their growing involvement will be provided, and specifically included will be a careful look at the jarring impact that the organizational forms of private practice had on the internal culture and organization of the facilities.[3] This analysis will illustrate that the administrative structure of the institution was rooted in the paternalist motives of a variety of trustees whose position was challenged by new commercial and seemingly "modern" business and entrepreneurial notions of the hospital. This approach will also show that even the development of private practice medicine within the walls of the hospital was influenced and shaped by the older traditions of the religious and social tenets of the institution.

Following the discussion of the developing administrative and physical organization of the voluntary health care institution, the chapter will look even further into the core of the institution by tracing the history of voluntary health care administrators through the depression. What will be illustrated is that hospital administration has always been shaped by the cultural role of the institution as a place for the care of the dependent and sick rather than its business purpose. While the rhetoric of business efficiency and standardization has dotted the pages of hospital administration texts from the 1890s on, the voluntary hospital administrators' use of ideas borrowed from business and industry have undergone profound mutations in light of the voluntary hospitals' multifaceted historical mis-

---

conservative and pro-business 1980s, administrators and trustees are far more defensive and often appear to be at a loss when asked to justify their apparent business inefficiencies.

[3]Traditional arguments regarding the growing interests of physicians in hospital care have centered on the institution's role in doctors' expanded interest in scientific medicine, surgery, and antisepsis.

sion. Finally, the chapter will conclude with some thoughts on the historical challenges to the mission of the institution during the 1950s through 1970s. The growing commercialization of medicine, the development of new incentives in the postwar years, and changing notions of community responsibility have combined to create a growing confusion on the part of trustees concerning their purpose and the reasons for their institutions. This has led to contradictory and sometimes self-defeating activities by institutional leaders who have often abrogated their responsibilities to professionals whose social legitimacy does not derive from the same ideals of stewardship.

PUBLIC NEEDS, PRIVATE MEANS

In order to understand the changing social relationships of hospitals and communities in the United States, it is important to begin with a brief review of some social and demographic factors that influenced the historical development of the hospital.[4] The American hospital developed in a unique social environment during the late nineteenth and early twentieth centuries. For most people throughout this period, life revolved around small communities and narrow personal contacts. Most Americans lived in rural villages, towns, and farms that were essentially isolated from each other. Even city dwellers, while in close proximity to each other in the nation's burgeoning cities, were far more isolated than the city dwellers of today. Before the introduction of adequate transportation and communication systems at the end of the nineteenth century, people lived in highly structured communities separated by culture, ethnicity and, in cities at least, language.[5] For most people in these so-called walking cities, life was organized around the local church, school, and other neighborhood institutions.[6] Even government, often

---

[4] Portions of the following text have appeared in slightly different forms in the following books and articles: David Rosner, *A Once Charitable Enterprise, Hospitals and Health Care in Brooklyn and New York, 1885–1915*, Cambridge University Press, New York, 1982; Princeton University Press, Princeton, New Jersey, 1986 (hereinafter cited as *Enterprise*); Rosner, "Social Control and Social Service: The Changing Use of Space in Charity Hospitals," *Radical History Review* **21**:183–197 (Fall 1979). Rosner, "Business at the Bedside," in Susan Reverby and David Rosner (eds.), *Health Care in America*, Temple University Press, Philadelphia, 1979, pp. 117–131.

[5] See Rosner, *Enterprise*; Morris J. Vogel, *The Invention of the Modern Hospital, Boston, 1880–1930*, Chicago University Press, Chicago, 1981 (hereinafter cited as *Modern Hospital*), for two local studies of the development of community hospitals in East Coast cities. There is an extensive literature on nineteenth century communities and the process of change and suburbanization. See, for example, Robert Wiebe, *The Search for Order, 1877–1920*, Hill and Wang, New York, 1967, and Sam Bass Warner, *Streetcar Suburbs*, Harvard University Press, Cambridge, Massachusetts, 1968, for two of the most influential studies.

[6] Hutchins Hapgood, in Moses Rischin (ed.), *The Spirit of the Ghetto*, Belknap Press of Harvard University Press, Cambridge, Massachusetts, 1967.

controlled in larger cities by political machines, responded on a personalized, ward-based level.

History and Heterogeneity

The origins of the American hospital are similarly linked to the heterogeneity of the country's ethnic, regional, class, and racial groups. While originally an urban, East Coast phenomenon, the hospital was born out of the changing relationship between rural and urban communities during the nineteenth century. In the early years of the nineteenth century, most manufacturing took place as part of the home or farm economy. While there were a few factories producing textiles, shoes, and other manufactured goods, most manufacturing was done by independent craftsmen who often worked part time finishing goods for sale. Sometimes, those who worked on the farm would use the slower winter season to produce handcrafts or clothing for sale. Often, independent artisans, working out of their homes in the newly emerging commercial cities, would combine homelife and gardening with manufacturing to supplement their income.[7] In this pre-factory context, few workers were solely dependent upon wages for their survival; most could supplement their income through formal and informal networks of resources based upon the predominance of the farming and nonindustrial economy.

In the second half of the nineteenth century, however, the economic revolution that overtook the entire Northeast left many without their earlier forms of support. Workers migrating to the large industrial cities found themselves dependent upon the wages that they earned in the factory. Gone were the farms or small gardens that might allow families and individuals to maintain themselves during slow periods and times of economic distress. Increasingly, families found themselves faced with periods of unemployment or forced idleness from which they had no buffer. In the closing decades of the century, dependence on the community, once a relatively rare occurrence that demanded explanation in terms of individual deviance and susceptibility, became a fact of life for millions of industrial workers.

Throughout the late nineteenth century workers in the highly industrialized states of Massachusetts and New York could expect to be unem-

---

[7] See Elizabeth Blackmar's dissertation and forthcoming book (Cornell University Press, Ithaca, New York, 1989) on antebellum artisans, land use and housing patterns. Also see Sean Wilentz, *Chants Democratic, New York City and the Rise of the American Working Class, 1788–1850*, Oxford University Press, New York, 1984, for an extended discussion of the development of republican ideology among American workers in this pre-factory period. Concerning the development of institutions for the care of the dependent, see David J. Rothman, *The Discovery of the Asylum*, Little, Brown, Boston, 1971.

ployed about three months of every year. In the New York area in 1900, 13.2 percent of all workers — male and female — were unemployed for 1 to 3 months. Another 9.3 percent were unemployed for 4 to 6 months and 2.8 percent were unemployed for 7 to 12 months. In all, 25 percent of the workforce could expect to be unemployed in any given year.

Wages were also low, with the unskilled rarely earning above $10 to $12 per week.[8] As unemployment and dependency became facts of life for millions of workers, charitable institutions such as the hospital were organized to serve a number of distinctly social services — hospitals provided housing, shelter, and care for the homeless, elderly, young, and sick. Significantly, it was the diversity of social conditions and moral beliefs and tenets in the rapidly developing cities that gave rise to the variety of institutions that are now called voluntary hospitals.

Demographic and Geographic Influences

Until the years following the Civil War, only a handful of hospitals existed throughout the country. Most of the pre-Civil War institutions were large, urban institutions that had substantial philanthropic and political support from old English or even Dutch gentry. In 1873, for example, the first hospital census was conducted, which list only 178 institutions nationwide. Of these, most were long-term care institutions, primarily state and private asylums for the insane. Others, such as Boston City

---

[8] Alexander Keyssar, *Out of Work, The First Century of Unemployment in Massachusetts,* Cambridge University Press, New York, 1986, and Rosner, *Enterprise,* pp. 25–26; also see Methodist Hospital of Brooklyn, 9th *Annual Report,* Nov. 1895–Oct. 1896, pp. 23–25 quoted in Rosner, *Enterprise,* pp. 18–19: It is significant that the period of major voluntary hospital growth, 1870 to about 1920, corresponded with the time when the industrial urban city emerged in America. With the development of this new type of community came the types of dependence that formed the core of most charity and hospital work. In some institutions, it was the out-of-luck and unemployed who formed the core of the patient population; in others it was the pregnant out-of-wedlock women unable to face unaccepting churchgoers: in others it was the unwanted or abandoned child. Still other nineteenth century institutions established themselves to care for those suffering from even more specialized forms of dependence. One Methodist institution was organized in a middle class neighborhood in order to care for housekeepers who, when taken ill, were forced to leave the brownstone townhouses of their employers. Unable to return to her home which was far away, perhaps overseas, the hospital served the social function of becoming a surrogate family. "Few, when sick, are in sorer need of a hospital than they," reported the trustees. "The [middle class] families in which they lived feel embarrassed [but] the work [of the household] must go on and another must take her place. . . . What can be done with the poor invalid," the report continued. "Her room is required. She is in the way . . . [she] is a burden and she knows it [and] the poor girl grows feverish with anxiety." The hospital provided a solution for both the wealthy family and the servant by providing her with a place to stay outside of the household.

Hospital, and Bellevue and Kings County Hospitals in New York, were municipal institutions, and sometimes adjuncts to public penitentiaries or almshouses. Only a few nonpublic, general hospitals, such as the Massachusetts General Hospital, New York Hospital, and Pennsylvania General Hospital, were organized in the antebellum period.

After the 1870s, however, hospitals began to appear in large numbers, primarily in East Coast urban communities. Generally, these institutions were diverse and served a wide variety of social and medical needs. Very often the elite of a community, generally merchants, local businessmen, and members of the clergy, would initiate and sponsor the formation of a charity hospital to serve the working class and the dependent poor. Hospitals generally differed in their religious and ethnic orientation, sources of financial support, size, medical orientation, and the type of service they provided. Most of these hospitals reflected the idiosyncratic qualities of the community they served.

Specific hospitals catered to different groups of Jews, Catholics, Italians, Germans, and blacks. Children's hospitals arose to care for orphaned children. Maternity hospitals, often located in working class neighborhoods, were as much a shelter for unwed mothers as they were a maternity medical service. In communities with a significant number of elderly and dependent persons, local merchants often organized a home or hospital for "incurables" or for the chronically ill.[9]

Atypical Is Typical Most of the institutions that developed were small, urban, locally sponsored charity facilities almost exclusively serving working class and poor patients. Because they reflected the social diversity of their ethnic and religious sponsors and working class patients, no "typical" hospital can be said to have existed. Many looked and functioned like homes or churches and, therefore, were not readily distinguishable from other structures and organizations within the community.

The hospitals that developed during the early period of growth before the 1920s were organized around different notions of purpose and function. First, there was little interest or concern with establishing a "standardized" institution. In fact, most of the hospitals were tiny in comparison to even the smallest of today's institutions and were established in a

---

[9] See, for example, Rosner, *Enterprise*, and Vogel, *Modern Hospital*, for two accounts of the development of East Coast hospital systems. Also, Charles Rosenberg, "Inward Vision and Outward Glance: The Shaping of the Modern Hospital," *Bulletin of the History of Medicine* **53:**346–391 (Fall, 1979).

seemingly haphazard manner.[10] Many institutions showed a degree of spontaneous organization, characteristic of the fluidity of nineteenth century social organization. In a historical survey of late nineteenth century Boston facilities, it was found that during the 1890s, smaller hospitals (those with 50 beds or less) showed an average life span of little more than 5 years, often being organized and disbanded with a frequency that would shock modern observers.[11]

Fragility and Fluidity Not only were these small late nineteenth century institutions likely to close at any moment, they also were in danger of immediate eviction. During the late nineteenth century, East Coast cities underwent fundamental changes in economic and social organization that placed tremendous pressure on charitable institutions, not only forcing them to adjust to new demands for services, but also forcing them to relocate and adjust to changing uses of land and space. As the older walking communities gave way to newer industrial and commercial centers, land upon which many institutions sat often became more valuable. Streets were widened, electric trolleys lines were installed in many cities, elevated train lines were introduced, and new means of personal transportation, such as the bicycle and later the automobile, forced city governments to widen, pave, and clean streets. Sleepy commercial shopping districts that aimed to serve local neighborhood clientele suddenly emerged as busy, bustling downtowns with large department stores, massive traffic jams, and crowded streets. New pressure for space arose from newly established stores, warehouses, and government establishments in growing downtown commercial areas. Older commu-

---

[10] *First Annual Report of the Chinese Hospital of Brooklyn, 1892,* quoted in Rosner, *Enterprise,* p. 17: An extreme example of the spontaneity characteristic in the era before the JCAH, state planning and review boards, licensing and public financing was the organization of the Chinese Hospital of Brooklyn, established in 1890. This organization was begun by the King's Daughters of China, a Protestant missionary society. In little over one month in late 1890, this group of laywomen conceived of the need for the facility, rented space, and opened its doors to patients, admitting five Chinese patients. "The project for a Chinese Hospital . . . owes its fruition and consummation to the 'King's Daughters of China,'" began its Annual Report in 1892. "The rent being guaranteed by these ladies and acting upon their advice, I leased for the term of one year, the premises at No. 45 Hicks Street for Hospital uses, commencing our term as tenants upon November 1, 1890, at the rate of $50 per month. . . . Preparations were made at once to receive patients, and by the last week of the month we were ready for them, beginning with only 5 beds."

[11] This study of smaller Boston facilities was done by the author as part of a research exercise using existing newspaper listings, Boston guides and handbooks, city directories, and physician directories for the period 1890 to 1900. In the absence of any central public or professional agency that kept track of the variety of hospitals, homes, and dispensaries that continually appeared and disappeared during this period of time, it was necessary to cull these sources to identify when institutions were founded and when they ceased to exist.

nities were destroyed as people moved out to the newly arising "streetcar suburbs" that began to develop on the periphery of the central city neighborhoods.[12]

The relative fluidity of the nineteenth century hospital might be understood as a sign of its weakness or instability. Yet, this would be only partially accurate. While individual institutions were subject to tremendous social, demographic, and economic pressures that often forced them to move or to go out of existence, the system as a whole flourished. Charity hospitals increased in number continually throughout the period, and the system continued to experiment with form and function, selecting out certain institutions while killing off others. The tremendous variety of institutions that served the dependent poor in nineteenth century America gave the system as a whole a dynamism and stability that is remarkable from today's rather static vantage point. Voluntary hospital organizations, while apparently disorganized, unstandardized, and unstable produced a variety of forms that proved to give the system its future strength and vitality.

Multipurpose Institution

Unlike the modern-day hospital, the nineteenth century urban East Coast institution was not solely a medical facility. It was a facility that provided shelter, food, and care to those in need. Community leaders and the middle class were generally cared for in their homes; hospitals treated those working class residents who were forced to become dependent on the larger society during times of hardship. The forms that this hardship took varied significantly for different segments of the working class communities. Some dependence was created by illness, but often social circumstances caused the growing dependence of a class of the population. In fact, the urban hospital can be understood to have its

[12] See Warner, *Streetcar Suburbs*; Vogel, *Modern Hospital*; Rosner, *Enterprise*, p. 29. The same pressures that forced older communities to disband and move forced older institutions to move as well. One hospital administrator in downtown Brooklyn complained that the "widening of Livingston Street" had deprived the hospital of "thirty feet of frontage," forcing the trustees to consider moving their facility. The Memorial Hospital in the same city moved no fewer than six times in eight years, and a dispensary also found land costs too expensive and decided to relocate to a place "where they were more needed." The obituary of one of the founders of Brooklyn's Jewish Hospital pointed out one of the ironies of the man's life. Abraham Abraham, the founder, was also "a pioneer in the development of the big shopping district of Brooklyn" and his department stores and warehouse facilities covered more than seven acres of formerly residential land in downtown Brooklyn. The unavailability of land in the early 1900s forced the Jewish Hospital to choose to build in the newly emerging streetcar suburb in the Bedford section of Brooklyn. By the 1950s, with the migration of the Jewish population to Long Island and Queens, this hospital would find itself serving a primarily black population.

origins in the variety of forms that dependence, not illness, took in the later nineteenth century. Within this context, the nineteenth century institution played a varied and ambiguous role. It functioned simultaneously as a health care facility, a social service, and an agent of social control. Admission to the hospital depended less on a patient's medical state than on the determination by wealthy patrons that the patient's physical and social circumstances made him or her an appropriate candidate for admission.[13]

The importance of community notions of moral and social suasion was not limited to the small, charity institutions. Larger, more established, hospitals also began with a concern for the moral lessons that their facilities could impart to their patients. For example, the Children's Hospital of Boston, today a leading teaching institution for Harvard University, was established with a dual role of moral and medical treatment. But, in the case of Children's, the community to which it responded was the elite Protestants of Boston's Back Bay.

As Morris Vogel has illustrated in his work, this facility's concern for the welfare of poorer children was often confused with its concern regarding social and political dissolution within the poverty-struck Irish Catholic community of Boston: "Think how hard it is to say 'no room' when a sick child is brought to the hospital; to see the hope die out of the mother's face as she turns to carry her boy back to the noisy street," reported a public relations piece appearing in the Boston *Evening Transcript* in 1879. "Then a bitter thought comes, and she is ready to curse the rich people who . . . cannot spare one bed for her sick child; and she goes fiercely on her way, ripe for any evil deed. . . ." The article, seeking to appeal to the general public for funds, appeals directly to their fear of the potential for political unrest in the poor neighborhoods. "There is a practical side to this charity, which may commend it to thoughtful men. In it I think I see one clew to the future settlement of several of the questions of the hours, such as communism, socialism, and

---

[13] Methodist Hospital of Brooklyn, 9th *Annual Report*, Nov. 1895–Oct. 1896, pp. 23–25, quoted in Rosner, *Enterprise*, pp. 18–19: "Some [patients] were at the point of death and others were apparently in robust health, their diseases . . . obscure or simply annoying," casually reported one hospital superintendent. See also, *First Annual Report of the Chinese Hospital of Brooklyn, 1890–91*, 1892: While many nineteenth century hospitals served as a refuge or social service facility for the poor, others served a religious function. The Chinese Hospital, for instance, a small, five bed facility located in the fashionable Heights section of Brooklyn, was organized by the King's Daughters of China, an evangelical Protestant missionary society, to convert as well as to cure. In its annual reports, its superintendent generally listed both the number of medical procedures performed as well as the number of converts produced "while on their beds of suffering." The superintendent noted that his patients "would go forth from the hospital better fitted morally, as well as physically, to fight the great outside battles."

the reconciliation of labor to capital . . . while [in the hospital], in addition to their medical treatment . . . they are carefully taught cleanliness of habit, purity of thought and word, and as much regard is paid to their moral training as can be found in any cultivated family."

Morris Vogel points out that such an integration of moral functions within the walls of the hospital were central to notions of social and moral control during this period of hospital formation. "Think what a widespreading influence this becomes when the children return to their homes." The report continues by pointing out that all members of the family "unconsciously rise a little in the social scale" under the influence of this newly reformed child.[14]

A Moral Enterprise For many of the older Brahmin class, hospital work was often motivated by an amalgam of social, moral, and political beliefs regarding the moral origins of illness, the role of the individual in creating his or her own susceptibility to disease, and the need to maintain social order. The immoral, deviant, outcast, and outsider were viewed as individually susceptible to the ravages of illness because of their own personal failings. In this pre-Keynesian world, societal explanations for the spread of disease barely existed in any other than highly moral terms. The poor, as a group, were clearly more susceptible to illness than were the wealthy; but the poor, as a group, were understood to be of a more suspicious moral fiber than were the wealthy, at least from the perspective of the organizers of many of these institutions.[15]

In other communities, the social beliefs and origins of the trustees had much less of an impact on the organization and function of the institution. For example, Alan Derickson, in a fascinating forthcoming volume on miners' hospitals, indicates that in the closing years of the nineteenth century, a number of institutions were organized in the Far West with substantially different motivations and organizing principles.[16] These institutions, organized in the 1890s by the Western Federation of Miners, were begun in the context of severe labor disputes that arose between mine owners and workers. It appears that in the ongoing struggles between the miners and management over mine safety, health issues and

[14]See Vogel, *Modern Hospital*, pp. 23-25, for a fascinating analysis of this institution and of this document: " 'The Children's Hospital,' What 'Fireside' Thinks About It," *Boston Evening Transcript*, January 29, 1879; see also Janet Golden and Diane Long (eds.), *Hospitals and Community*, Cornell University Press, Ithaca, New York (forthcoming).

[15]See Charles Rosenberg, "Inward Vision and Outward Glance," op.cit. and *The Cholera Years*, University of Chicago Press, Chicago, 1964, for interesting discussions of the persistence of moralism as an explanation for individual susceptibility to disease.

[16]See Alan Derickson's description of the development of these facilities in a forthcoming volume from Cornell University Press, Ithaca, New York.

health services were central. Given the extremely dangerous working conditions, safety was a major reason for labor unrest, and owners soon developed a corps of "company doctors" to care for injured and diseased miners. However, miners deeply suspected the loyalties and motivations of this company-sponsored system of health services, especially in the aftermath of a series of incidents in which the physicians sought to cover up the tremendously high rates of lung disease among the workers.

Also, it appears that accidents within the mines were often the reason for labor walkouts and wildcat strikes. The company-controlled hospital and ambulance services were used to spirit injured or killed workers away from the worksite because of the fear that public disclosure of accidental death and injury would lead to disruptions in production if workers walked off the job to protest unsafe conditions. In reaction to the fear that both the political and medical apparatus of the community were under the control of the mine owners, the union decided to invest their own resources in establishing a set of hospitals under their control, staffed by physicians whose loyalties, while suspect, could be monitored by the union itself.

In the South as well, institutions also catered to special needs and interests of target populations. A number of facilities that arose in the early years of the twentieth century were organized by a variety of philanthropies that sought to accommodate the realities of a highly segregated system of health services by funding and building institutions that catered primarily to blacks. Elsewhere, philanthropists sought to establish institutions that functioned much like an urban, modern, teaching hospital only to find that the realities of local medical politics mitigated against their success.[17]

A Diversity of Values   In many ways, the hospital reflected the diversity of the communities that sponsored, organized, and populated them. Often the values of trustees, patients, and workers were incorporated into the very order of the institution. Assumptions regarding the meaning of dependence and disease, its moral context, and its relationship to poverty or occupation were active ingredients in shaping the diverse institutions that addressed the special needs of particular neighborhoods, religious groups, occupations, and races. Institutions differed

[17]See Peter Buck and Barbara Rosenkrantz's forthcoming volume on rural hospital development and the role of the Commonwealth Fund, The Milbank Fund, and a number of other foundations in establishing southern institutions; Vanessa Gamble, "The Negro Hospital Renaissance," Ph.D. dissertation, University of Pennsylvania, Philadelphia, 1987.

from each other much in the way that the diverse communities that founded them differed.

The moral and political objectives of these diverse nineteenth century institutions had a profound impact on their internal order and organization. In general, the use of large, undifferentiated wards with many beds, the usual form of housing in the nineteenth century hospital, met the needs of an institution trying to supervise and control patients confined there for long periods of time. First, the ward, with beds lined along its walls, allowed nurses or attendants to watch many patients simultaneously and guaranteed strict supervision of potentially disruptive or untrustworthy poorer "inmates."

Second, the ward arrangement allowed patients to socialize in an institution that in practice substituted for the home. Third, patients who were ambulatory could learn good work habits by serving as orderlies and nurses and by helping those other patients near at hand who were incapable of helping themselves. By performing assigned and necessary tasks, patients made the administration of the hospital less complex and also "paid" for their stay. At the same time they learned the value of work by performing vital tasks for their fellow patients — a lesson considered an important part of their cure.

The only social characteristics that were used to separate patients in wards were sex, age, and medical condition. Although the institutions were often administered by specific religious or sectarian orders, most trustees believed in a moral obligation to admit poorer patients regardless of race or religion. In fact, given their strong missionary zeal, many trustees understood the inclusion of a wide range of religious, racial, and ethnic groups to be an important indication of the usefulness of the institution. Furthermore, the missionary function of some of the facilities dictated that the hospital not only accept poor patients who presented themselves, but also seek out and welcome such people. Every year the annual reports of the various hospitals remarked on the wide variety of races, religions, and nationalities who appeared in their beds. Even the architectural detail of many institutions reflected the overriding concern with its social and moral objectives, with many institutions built to resemble churches, mansions, and homes rather than prisons, schools, or factories.

INFLUENCE OF MEDICAL PRACTICE

The relationship of doctors to the voluntary hospital is also rooted in the nineteenth century social context, for during much of the nineteenth century the responsibility for health care also rested within the community. It was widely recognized that medical knowledge was inexact at best, and professionals often exhibited bitter and highly publicized disagreements about the cause of disease and its proper management.[18] Consequently, the choice of treatment was often a reflection of the customs and medical beliefs of a particular community or group of practitioners rather than of standardized professional or scientific consensus. The medicine practiced in one area of the country or by one group of practitioners was often quite different in form and theory from the medicine of another area or group.[19] In much of rural America, lay people combined local folk custom with information gleaned from medical dictionaries and popular medical texts to form an idiosyncratic body of therapeutic practices. Similarly, doctors, not yet an elite professional group, were generally locally trained through a combination of formal medical school preparation and apprenticeship. The large number of medical schools were generally "proprietary" institutions organized for the profit of local practitioners in which students, often from lower middle class or lower class backgrounds, paid a price to attend lectures of dubious worth.[20] Formal medical education, largely unregulated and nonstandardized, could vary in length, content, and structure and was, from 1848 when the American Medical Association was formed, criticized for its lack of standardization of practice.

Few, during the nineteenth century, could agree on what might constitute appropriate practice among myriad individuals who ascribed to the wide variety of schools of medicine. Furthermore, most practitioners and educated laymen of the period were skeptical of those who sought to unify practitioners under any one therapeutic umbrella. Generally, calls for uniformity in practice were perceived by both professionals and laymen alike as little more than political ploys to gain a measure of social legitimacy for a particular sect of medical practitioners.

Throughout much of the nineteenth century, the disparate demands of different groups in different areas of the country created a diverse body of therapeutic knowledge and practice. Accordingly, training dif-

---

[18] For a discussion of the political ramifications within medicine of these deep splits, see Gerald Markowitz and David Rosner, "Doctors in Crisis: Medical Education and Medical Reform During the Progressive Era," in Susan Reverby and David Rosner (eds.), *Health Care in America, Essays in Social History*, Temple University Press, Philadelphia, 1979, pp. 185–205; John Duffy, *The Healers, The Rise of the Medical Establishment*, McGraw-Hill, New York, 1976, pp. 228–236.

[19] See, for example, Guenter B. Risse, R. S. Numbers, and J. W. Leavitt (eds.), *Medicine Without Doctors, Home Health Care in American History*, Science Publications, New York, 1977.

[20] Kenneth M. Ludmerer, *Learning to Heal, The Development of American Medical Education*, Basic Books, New York, 1985 (hereinafter cited as *Learning to Heal*).

fered for rural practitioners, urban practitioners, homeopaths, ailopaths, eclectics, Thomsonians, and the host of other practitioners of the "art" of medicine. Even those treating different classes and ethnic groups within the population were forced by the realities of the medical marketplace to adjust their practice.

This disparity between educational requirements of various schools was reflected as well in the differences between medical nosologies, views, and theoretical positions. Different groups of practitioners generally identified with differing "schools" or "sects" of medicine. Rural areas produced a wide variety of practitioners who depended mostly on herbal treatments. Thomsonians and later eclectics were among the various botanical schools that developed throughout rural New England, the South, and Midwest.[21] Generally, these groups incorporated local folk custom into their therapeutics. In urban areas, regular practitioners, homeopaths, and a host of others with differing medical viewpoints and practices competed strongly with each other for the patronage of patients.[22]

Multiple Choice

Unlike today, when patients have little meaningful control or choice over the types of therapies used, patients in nineteenth century America could choose from among a host of practitioners and a fairly wide variety of therapies. Doctors, by and large, were private "family" or "community" practitioners, who were engaged in general medicine. While a small number of doctors specialized in surgery, ophthalmology, or other areas, specialism and hospital practice were largely tangential to most physicians.[23]

Family practitioners, the bulk of the profession, generally lived within the communities where they practiced, providing health services in the patients' homes or in their offices, which were generally located in the doctor's house. They served a patient population that lived within a few block area and they were often members of the same church or other

---

[21] See William Rothstein, *American Physicians in the Nineteenth Century*, Johns Hopkins University Press, Baltimore, 1971, for a fuller account of the variety and types of American medical practitioners.

[22] See Rothstein, ibid., and Paul Starr, *The Social Transformation of American Medicine*, Basic Books, New York, 1982, for extended discussions of the development of the medical marketplace in urban communities.

[23] See George Rosen, *The Specialization of Medicine*, Froeben Press, New York, 1944; Markowitz and Rosner, "Doctors in Crisis, Medical Education and Progressive Reform," op.cit.; Rosen, *The Structure of American Medical Practice, 1875–1941*, University of Pennsylvania Press, Philadelphia, 1983, for discussions of the role of specialization in the development of the modern medical profession.

local community clubs and organizations. The family doctor would preside at the significant events in peoples' lives; he would be fetched for births as well as deaths. He saw it as his role to comfort the family and it was not unusual for him to move into the patients' house for the duration of an illness.

The relationship between doctors and patients was not necessarily a product of a deep-seated intellectual or professional belief in democracy nor of the importance of trust and understanding in the therapeutic process. Rather, it was in large measure an outgrowth of the professional environment where practitioners, working in an era of significant medical uncertainty with regard to procedures and outcomes, were in severe competition with each other for clients. A large number of loosely organized and nonregulated medical schools combined with loose licensure requirements uncontrolled by the state or the profession resulted in a surfeit of practitioners. Without the now-available options of research positions in universities, hospitals, or institutes, and without highly specialized forms of practice, doctors depended on the good will of their patients for their economic survival. Competition among practitioners for patients was fierce by the end of the nineteenth century and familiarity, dress, demeanor, courteousness, cultivation, and common understanding were essential qualities for the successful practitioner.[24]

Because medical knowledge was not standardized and because practitioners depended on their patients for a living, they tended to practice in ways that were familiar and accepted by their patients. This does not mean that doctors were providing treatments in which they did not believe; but in many ways their knowledge was just more sophisticated than that of their patients. Regular practitioners — the largest number of practitioners — employed bleeding, cupping, purging, and other seem-

[24] Arpad G. Gerster, *Recollections of a New York Surgeon*, Paul B. Hoeber, New York, 1917, pp. 23 – 24: One European physician who had recently arrived in New York observed the effect of this uniquely American physician's relationship with his clients. He noted that the "science and technique of practice" were less important to American doctors than were "the personal relations between physician and patient." He remarked that "physicians in America were concerned more with establishing a feeling of confidence and trust, hence comfort in patients, then were" Europeans. He ascribed this to their highly competitive environment of practice and to the relatively low social and educational status of American practitioners. The "medical men had to be more modest; he had to be more circumspect, even deferential" when treating patients, even when the patients were ignorant or ill mannered. It was the unique quality of highly isolated communities which created a marketplace where personal relationships and involvement were at a premium. See also D. W. Cathell, *The Physician Himself*, 1882 (reprinted by Arno Press, New York, 1972): Cathell, a physician who authored a widely distributed and oft-repeated late nineteenth century practical guidebook for practitioners, began his volume by pointing out that "there is nothing more pitiful than to see a worthy physician deficient in these qualities, waiting year after year for a practice . . . that never comes."

ingly Draconian measures to treat their patients. Because illness was often equated with moral failing, what today may be seen as cruelty of treatment was, in a sense, viewed in the nineteenth century context as an appropriate punishment for transgressions.

Those who rejected regular therapeutics might turn to other, milder forms of practice. Appealing to merchants and other urban groups, homeopathy provided milder therapies and perhaps more elegant rationales. What might have been lacking in scientific rigor and specificity was made up for by the intimacy of practice itself. The authority of the practitioner rested as much on his social relationship to his patient as it did upon the consistency or scientific basis of his therapeutics.

A Move to Standardize

In the decades surrounding the turn of the century a significant reform movement arose within medicine itself that held as its guiding principles the need to standardize medical education. Underlying this reform effort lay the notion that by standardizing the training of physicians and by controlling entry into the profession through licensure, medical practice itself would become more uniform. The movement culminated in the now-classic Carnegie Bulletin Number Four, or the "Flexner Report," that called for the reorganization of medical school curriculum.[25]

The Flexner Report illustrates some of the diverse strands that divided the medical community during the early years of the twentieth century and the centrality of arguments regarding standardization to those who sought to gain leverage over the health care system. First, it called for the establishment of a common medical education built around laboratory science, a hospital experience as well as didactic lecture. Second, it posited that the guiding principles of professional behavior would be determined by the "science" of medical practice rather than the "art" of individual attention. Like the busy machine shop and industrial factory that was proving so successful in turning the country into an industrial power, so too would medicine transform into a technically exact scientific enterprise. Finally, it called for the standardization of the social background of practitioners.[26]

[25]See "Medical Education in the United States and Canada," Report No. 4, The Carnegie Foundation, New York, 1910.

[26]See E. Richard Brown, *Rockefeller Medicine Men*, University of California Press, Berkeley, 1976; Howard Berliner, "A New Perspective on the Flexner Report," *International Journal of Health Services* **5:**573–592 (1975); Berliner, *A System of Scientific Medicine, Philanthropic Foundations in the Flexner Era*, Tavistock, New York and London, 1985, for the radical interpretations of this effort to control the direction of medical education during the Progressive Era.

The Flexner Report was an end-product of a long and tortured movement among medical educators, predominantly within the American Medical Association's Council on Medical Education, to standardize American medicine.[27] But it was only successful in certain narrow respects. While medical practice would remain a field filled with medical uncertainty and nonstandardized procedures performed by individual practitioners, the standardization of the social background of medical practitioners would be achieved. By the end of the nineteenth century, the eclectic nature of medical practice and the largely unregulated environment in which medicine developed had created a large and diverse set of educational institutions that catered to women, black, and poor students. In fact, there were 16 women's medical schools by 1900, and 10 black medical colleges, primarily in the southern states, by the same year. Also, the majority of medical students attending the various proprietary medical colleges were lower or lower middle class in social class background. But, by 1916, only one women's college and two black schools remained in existence, and many of the proprietary institutions that once catered to part-time and working students went out of existence.[28]

The Coming of Medical Science

Reformers saw little need for protecting these poorly endowed medical schools, in part because of their belief that the future era of scientific medicine would make social diversity within the ranks of medicine unimportant. If the physician of the future was to become a scientist treating patients irrespective of social class, then there was little practical justification for protecting certain social groups in medicine. Doctors were to treat organs rather than people, and they were to cure diseases irrespective of the social, racial, and class characteristics of the bodies these diseases attacked. In Flexner's model of the new science of medicine, it mattered little who the practitioner was as long as he was trained in modern scientific institutions. If the "best" turned up to be the white, upper middle class male, so much the better, for then the general social position of medical practitioners would be enhanced as well. Abraham Flexner's discussion of the future of the "Poor Boy," "Women," and "Negros" in medicine showed a simple and, from today's perspective,

---

[27] See Gerald Markowitz and David Rosner, "Doctors in Crisis, The Uses of Medical Education Reform to Establish Elitism in Medicine," *American Quarterly* **25**(March, 1973); Ludmerer, *Learning to Heal*; Daniel M. Fox, *Health Policies, Health Politics, The British and American Experience, 1911–1965*, Princeton University Press, Princeton, New Jersey, 1986.

[28] See Markowitz and Rosner, ibid.

naive belief in the ability of medical science to solve the issues of equity and equality that became the central concerns of health planners and professionals in the 1960s and 1970s.[29]

While the effect of the movement around science and standardization had profound implications for the social characteristics of American physicians, it had less of an impact on their practices. By and large, practitioners were still tied to their private offices and were very defensive about any possibility of interference from those who might seek to standardize or evaluate their treatment of patients. With no central organization capable of oversight, practitioners adopted the mantle of science and the aura of scientists while maintaining their autonomy over treatment and procedure. Unlike Britain, where there was a long tradition of central government regulation, the American situation functioned to undermine centralized authority or standardization.

Daniel M. Fox, in his new book *Health Policies, Health Politics*, develops this theme in a telling analysis of the development of health policy in the United States. Looking at the role of foundations, he illustrates that they "had power and influence but they lacked control" and were especially unsuccessful in trying to get specialists to become "full-time" hospital practitioners. Rather than become employees of the medical school hospitals, the practitioners brought their private model of practice into the hospital setting, thereby undermining the centralizing and regulatory function that the university medical center might have otherwise played in standardizing physicians' practices. "The coalition supporting the reform of medical education soon disintegrated . . . when the Rockefeller philanthropies decided to make grants to schools on the condition that they establish full-time chairs in clinical departments," Fox points out. While the rhetoric and ideological power of science and standardization was effectively used to undermine different social

---

[29]The current arguments over the reform period revolve around whether or not these changes were intentional or unintentional. Some see the social transformation of the medical community into one dominated by elite white male practitioners as an unintended or secondary by-product of a more admirable effort to reform medicine, while others see it as an essential ingredient in the development of the new male-dominated or capitalist model of health care then evolving. See the books and articles by Fox, Ludmerer, Brown, Berliner, Markowitz and Rosner for extended discussions; see also Mary Roth Walsh, *"Doctors Wanted, No Women Need Apply": Sexual Barriers in the Medical Profession, 1835–1975*, Yale University Press, New Haven, 1977; Virginia Drachman, *Hospital with a Heart, Women Doctors and the Paradox of Separatism at the New England Hospital, 1862–1969*, Cornell University Press, Ithaca, New York, 1984, for extended discussions of the position of women in medicine. See also the work of Vanessa Gamble on black hospitals and physicians that will be published in a book edited by Janet Golden and Diana Long, tentatively entitled *Hospitals and Community*: "The Negro Hospital Renaissance: The Black Hospital Movement, 1920–1945," Cornell University Press, Ithaca, New York, forthcoming, 1989.

groups within medicine, even the elite specialists balked when confronted by an institutional affiliation that might imply greater standardization, for standardization implied oversight and regulation.[30]

Susan Reverby has also published a fascinating study of the reaction of the medical community of Boston to the efforts of Ernest Codman, a prominent surgeon at the Massachusetts General Hospital, to institute his "End Result" system. The End Result system was an outcome measure he devised for determining the effectiveness of various surgical interventions by his colleagues at the hospital. Here, the surgeons of the Massachusetts General Hospital banded together to force Codman to resign from the staff rather than accept oversight of their surgical success or failure rates.[31]

Despite the ideological power that the ideals of standardization carried, the reality of a heterogeneous health care system built upon the assumptions of individualized practice, independent hospitals, heterogeneous communities, and isolated populations, mitigated against any long-standing ability to install a system of standardized care. In fact, the very strength of the system was its variation. Its ability to adapt to rapidly changing environmental, political, and social issues rested on the very antithesis of standardization.

Proliferation and Promise

Between the late 1890s and the beginning of the depression, the voluntary hospital changed its mission, reorganized its services, and altered its financial base. First, the number of hospitals increased sharply — in 1923 it stood at some 6,500, a 40-fold jump in 50 years. Second, trustees began to envision an entirely new kind of institution — vast, hotel- or factory-like in appearance, and operating as a voluntary rather than as a charitable facility. In the process of seeking to change from a charity to a voluntary institution, hospitals underwent fundamental shifts in function, organization, administration, and purpose, which altered relationships, particularly among trustees, their medical staffs, and their administrations.

---

[30] Daniel M. Fox, *Health Policies, Health Politics, The British and American Experience, 1911–1965*, Princeton University Press, Princeton, New Jersey, 1986, pp. 39–40; see also E. Richard Brown, "He Who Pays the Piper: Foundations, the Medical Profession and Medical Education," in Susan Reverby and David Rosner (eds.), *Health Care in America*, pp. 132–153.

[31] Susan Reverby, "Stealing the Golden Eggs: Ernest Amory Codman and the Science and Management of Medicine," *Bulletin of the History of Medicine* **55:**156–171 (Summer 1981).

Most of the rhetoric for change came in the form of appeals for efficient management or scientific necessity, but, in the process of change, the older role of the hospital as a charity was undermined by new rationales based upon medical ideologies. Hospitals increasingly sought to attract patients from the middle or upper classes of society and built services with more amenities and greater comforts than previously had been necessary in the purely charitable institution. Private and semiprivate wards began to replace the charity ward; private wings and private nursing were introduced into facilities that previously made few, if any, class distinctions regarding patients. Similarly, visiting medical personnel became ubiquitous in institutions where, only a few decades before, few physicians could be found in the wards on any regular basis. A series of organizational and economic changes were instituted, often using the rhetoric efficiency, science, and business as a legitimating cover.

The organizational changes that overtook American voluntary hospitals during the early years of this century affected profoundly the relationship between trustees and their medical staffs. In part, the new relationship was forced on the trustees and their physician staffs by the changing social conditions under which both medical and hospital care now functioned. In part, the changing internal economy of the institution altered the traditional paternalistic control that many trustees had exerted in their institutions. While it is sometimes said that the voluntary hospital has become a workshop for the physician, a closer inspection of the history of trustee–physician relationship shows that the modern professional–administrative structure of the hospital was a product of a series of profound compromises and adjustments in the running of the facility.

Cost as a Catalyst

To understand the changing relationships between trustees and their medical and administrative staffs it is necessary to review briefly some of the central elements of the crisis in hospital financing that overtook American hospitals in the late nineteenth century. For most of that period, the charity hospitals of the country were inexpensive institutions that could run on relatively small sums of money each year. In New York in the 1890s, for example, the average voluntary institution in the city spent less than $30,000 to provide care. In other parts of the country the cost for running a facility was similarly low. In Worcester, Massachusetts, in 1890, for example, the City Hospital was operated for $33,000; in Portsmouth, New Hampshire, the General Hospital cost $38,000 to run, and the Rhode Island Hospital operated for less than $45,000. Partly because they were small institutions, rarely with more than 150 beds, partly because patients provided much of the labor power, and partly because of the fact that medical care was a decidedly low-tech enterprise, these institutions generally cost less than $1.50 per patient-day. Funded by the institutions' benefactors, a variety of state and local government sources, and a minimal amount of patient payments, these institutions ran at modest deficits every year, deficits that were generally covered by trustee contributions.

By the end of the century, however, the cost for patient care began to increase substantially as advances in medical technology and changing standards of cleanliness began to affect the care provided. Also, as philanthropists faced competing demands from other agencies and as the number of poor increased substantially, hospitals found themselves strapped for funds. Increasingly, hospital trustees were forced to make hard choices about the future of their charitable enterprises and began to turn to new and untested sources of income: private middle class patients.

In order to attract paying patients into the charity hospitals, however, trustees needed to change both the types of services and administrative structures of their facilities. First, they needed to bring into the facility private community practitioners who had previously been excluded; for it was the private practitioners who largely controlled the loyalties of paying patients. Without the private practitioner, there was no mechanism for attracting the patient who could afford to pay for care. Second, the hospital had to underplay its traditional image as a facility for the poor. Finally, it had to introduce new services and amenities that would be expected by a wealthier clientele. During the decades before the depression, many hospital trustees would face wrenching decisions about whether or not to fundamentally restructure their facilities.

The Advent of Private Practice

In many institutions, the introduction of private practitioners into the voluntary institution was the most troubling aspect of restructuring. Previous to this period, the trustees had governed very closely controlled institutions in which most workers, patients, administrators, and even "house staff" physicians, co-existed in a closed environment. In fact, within the older closed "house" in which the limited number of physicians were younger house staff, who depended upon the paternalistic authority of the trustees, the institutions' leaders generally did not hesitate to reprimand, limit, and even dismiss rebellious doctors. In Brooklyn, New York, for example, as late as the 1890s, protests by physicians over living and working conditions in one hospital resulted in the dismissal of the entire staff. In another facility, doctors who protested their treatment at the hands of the head nurse and who demanded her dismissal, were themselves dismissed by indignant trustees. As late as 1900, many voluntary trustees believed that the efficient functioning of the institution depended more on the nursing staff than on the medical staff.[32]

From the beginning, trustees recognized the threat to their authority of an "open" institution. By opening up their institutions to private doctors, the trustees faced a danger of losing moral, medical, and cultural control of the institution. From the perspective of many upper class trustees, local private practitioners understood nothing about the underlying moral and social rationale of the facility. Unlike the younger house staff who depended upon trustees for closely guarded learning experiences, private practitioners had little understanding of the larger goals of the institution and exhibited loyalty only to their private patients. From the perspective of the trustees they brought with them a strange, petty, bourgeois entrepreneurial focus and undermined the paternalism, communality, oversight, and structure of the hospital.

Reluctantly, trustees slowly opened up their facilities to private community practitioners. For example, at the Brooklyn Hospital, every trustee meeting in the beginning of 1901 was the scene of a debate over staff enlargement. "Though the Committee has given the subject the most careful consideration, no satisfactory method of decreasing the expenses or of increasing the income [of the hospital] has been discovered. . . . The recommendation . . . that the private accommodations of the Hospital be increased and thrown open to the regular profession of the City is reluctantly though unanimously endorsed by the Committee, who recognize . . . the numerous objections to such a course."[33] At other New York institutions, similar crises resulted in the gradual opening of hospital privileges to the profession. At New York Hospital, Roosevelt Hospital, and St. Lukes Hospital, trustees, faced by growing deficits and shrinking incomes, threw open their institutions to new and largely untested physicians.[34]

Twin Loyalties and Dual Obligations

For many trustees faced by the challenge of allowing private practice in their previously closed houses, while at the same time hewing to the

---

[32] See Rosner, *Enterprise*, pp. 105–107; also Susan Reverby, *Ordered to Care, The Dilemma of American Nursing, 1850–1945*, Cambridge University Press, New York and Cambridge, 1987.

[33] Brooklyn Hospital, *Minutes*, 5(Jan. 23, 1901), pp. 103–104.

[34] Rosner, *Enterprise*, pp. 97–100.

institutions' time-honored social goals, the answer lay in organizing two parallel structures of health service within the hospital. In part, the parallel structures were meant to protect the charity institution while providing the amenities demanded by a new, wealthier class of patient. In the process, however, the trustees institutionalized certain elements of two-class care by providing the charity patient with what they assumed was a more appropriate service and allowing the paying patient to be placed in the hands of practitioners who the trustees generally saw as undereducated, crass, and ill-prepared to care for most of their charity patients. First, the trustees sought to protect the traditional charitable institution from the entrepreneurial private practitioners by giving local doctors visiting privileges rather than staff appointments in their institutions. By keeping the local practitioner outside of the formal structure of the facility, trustees believed that they could effectively shield the charitable hospital for the deserving poor from the commercial aspect of private care.

Second, trustees organized private wings, wards, and rooms within the institution as much to shelter the charity patient from the commercialization of medical care that paying patients, private practitioners, and private services represented. While private practice was to become an intrinsic part of the voluntary hospital, it was not introduced by trustees solely to reward private practitioners and private patients. Rather, it was introduced in its particular way to protect charity patients — the true objective of the hospitals' mission — from an unaccountable and commercial private practice. Far from attempting to turn the institution into a "physician's workshop," many trustees sought to isolate private practice in private wings, wards, and rooms.

The worst fears of these trustees were soon realized as private attending physicians and their private patients began to alter the work relationships, attitudes, and culture of hospital wards. "In our effort . . . to please our Attendings," complained the Superintendent of Methodist Hospital in Brooklyn, "we have built up an intricate piece of machinery which is becoming more and more difficult to handle every day." The machinery of which he spoke was the complexity of organizing the service in which numerous private attendings ran in and out of the hospital, paying attention only to their own patients, and showing little concern for the overall efficiency of the wards. "Certain of our doctors try to force us to receive patients for which we have no accommodations," he noted. "They are indifferent as to where we place them so long as they can get them in. Then the friends of the patients complain and, as a rule, the doctor does not try to shield us by explaining our difficulties." The Superintendent ended by stating that he believed "that some of our doctors rejoice more in criticism made concerning the Hospital than in its praise."[35]

Introduction of Fees

In other instances, the very paternalistic underpinnings of the institution were challenged as private practitioners sought to collect fees from patients in the charity hospitals. Traditionally, charity hospital patients paid little or nothing for their care in the institution; but, with the entrance of the private doctor into the hospital ward, this apparent "right" was severely tested. Attending physicians complained that hospitals were "supported by charity, donations, grants, etc., and therefore the presumption is . . . that all treatment is to be free." This assumption was seen to work to the detriment of the attendings and they sometimes sought to remedy this apparent defect. Some doctors called for "nothing less than . . . a readjustment of [the hospitals'] foundation." All the "sentimental nonsense about the inhumanity of it to the contrary," observed one physician, charity only served as a "cloak [that] covers too many unpaid doctor's bills."[36]

When doctors seeking to charge their clients in the hospital encountered opposition from trustees, they sometimes sought legal help. In 1902, one physician who had visiting privileges at three major Brooklyn institutions sued eight patients who had refused to pay for his professional services. "This is a fight for the sake of principle," he declared to the newspapers of the city. "Surgeons have suffered . . . a long time and I propose to see whether or not the law will allow us to be cheated out of what is due us." He "determined to try out in the courts the question of whether or not a man with plenty of money could go into a [voluntary] public hospital and get the benefits of a skillful and high-priced operation for nothing." "These suits are test cases," he concluded, "and by them I hope to vindicate a principle that is being abused in every hospital."[37]

The conflicts within the new hospital were not easily resolved. Trustees, increasingly dependent upon private attending physicians for their paying patients, also found their authority challenged by the grow-

[35] Report of Superintendent Kavanagh to Trustees, p. 3, attached to Methodist Hospital, *Executive Committee Minutes*, June 3, 1914, p. 221.

[36] Heber Hoople, "Economics of the Practice of Medicine," *Brooklyn Medical Journal* **17:**270 (June, 1903).

[37] See "Surgeon Sues Patients to Uphold a Principle," *Brooklyn Daily Eagle*, May 21, 1902, p. 1; "Dr. Fowler Wins One Case," *Brooklyn Daily Eagle*, May 22, 1902, p. 1; "Physicians and Hospitals Suffer Much from Deadbeats," *Brooklyn Daily Eagle*, June 1, 1902, p. 2.

ing expertise and aura of medical science that came with many of these practitioners. Increasingly, trustees sought means by which to maintain their authority within their own institutions. One compromise solution was to cede control over private patients to the attending physicians and the medical boards. Another tactic, already mentioned, was to protect the charity end of things by isolating the ward patients from the paying patients. In the process of this reorganization, a tentative and temporary balance was often reached between trustees and their attending physicians. As the hospital became increasingly dependent upon paying patients referred through the attending staff, and as the institution began to downplay its charitable tradition, power slowly shifted to the physicians.

Professional Autonomy and Institutional Goals

The struggle for control of patients reflected the very different communities to which the newly arising physicians and the traditional institutional stewards were responding. On the one hand, the physicians were clearly adapting their practices to the needs of a socio-economic class of patients—the prosperous or middle class. On the other hand, the trustees, while seeking to reorient their institutions to the new financial realities that plagued them, still grounded their attempts at reorganization in older notions of community, based upon ethnicity, religious belief, and obligation.

   Those institutions that were wealthy enough to withstand the devastating effects of rising health care costs or that resisted the temptation to become more modern acute care institutions could avoid many of the problems that the development of private practice medicine brought with it. But even for those that succumbed to a variety of pressures, the long-term growth in the power and authority of the physician was an unintended by-product of trustees' attempts to control and maintain an institution organized around the variety of social forces that originally gave the trustees their authority.

MINISTERING TO THE ADMINISTRATORS

The bureaucratic changes that were about to be instituted depended in large measure on the development of administrators who would be capable of coordinating the increasingly complex institution with its complex set of professional, social, medical, and economic goals. This section will describe some of the changes that occurred within the field of hospital administration, illustrating the uses of the notions of efficiency and standardization and their political implications. It will be made clear that before the 1940s, administrators often saw their role, first, as a provider of moral and medical service, and second, as financial agents. In more recent decades, the field of voluntary health care administration has sought to align itself more closely with the generic fields of business management. However, the alliance of hospitals with the business community was always suspect at best, and strong strands of nineteenth century paternalistic and maternalistic attitudes profoundly influenced the definitions of professional responsibility that were taught both formally through training in public health schools, and informally through experience with the realities of the hospital experience. The highly heterogeneous set of institutions gave rise to principles of hospital administration that clearly distinguished the hospital administrator from managers in other fields.

The history of training in hospital administration is closely related to the history of charity hospital growth in the United States. In the half century between 1875 and 1925, the enormous growth in the number and complexity of hospitals in this country created a real demand for hospital administrators. In the time that the number of hospitals grew from 150 to about 6,500, the number of hospital beds increased from 35,000 to 860,000.[38] Because of the close alliance with the various community leaders who organized the institutions, most early hospital superintendents often were drawn to the institution because of their own desire to be part of a larger charitable effort.

In the late nineteenth and early twentieth centuries, urban society, where dependence, poverty, and illness were often interpreted as interlocking indications of a general morality — or immorality — of patients, medical cure was seen as intimately linked to the success of moral reform within the institution. Hence, the administrator, as the person responsible for the total life of the institution, largely controlled the program that would teach patients acceptable standards of moral behavior. Internally, facilities reflected the underlying moral goals of the founders and the head administrator. The superintendent was responsible for the daily running of the institution and he or she functioned as a patriarch or matriarch of the extended family that the hospital was supposed to resemble. The entire structure of the administration of the facility was modeled on the ideals of the middle class family of late nineteenth and early twentieth century America: The superintendent and/or matron served as father or mother; nurses, Sisters, long-term

---

[38]See Rosner, *Enterprise;* also see Michael M. Davis, *Hospital Administration: A Career, The Need of Trained Executives for a Billion Dollar Business, and How They May Be Trained,* New York, 1929 (hereinafter cited as *Hospital Administration*) for a brief description of the importance of this rapid growth on the functions of the administrator.

patients, and young house staff physicians played the role of older children with varying degrees of responsibility for the care and house-keeping chores that were required in the institution; newly admitted patients, not yet socialized into the life of the institution were effectively the "infants" in need of constant guidance and supervision by parents and siblings alike. Only the trustees, the institution's spiritual leaders, escaped the confining environment of the "house," as it was called.[39]

Changing of the Guard

Given the integration of the hospital into the larger system of charity and benevolence, it should not be surprising that until the 1920s a majority of hospital administrators, then called superintendents, were women. In fact, as recently as 1929, women comprised nearly 40 percent of all head administrators in the country. In a 1929 survey of superintendents of the 7,610 institutions in the United States and Canada, Michael M. Davis reported that 20 percent were nurses, 8 percent were Sisters, and 11 percent were laywomen. Of the 61 percent remaining, 37 percent were male physicians, and 10 percent were laymen; the remaining 14 percent unspecified.[40]

The significant roles that women have played in shaping modern health care administration have hardly been recognized. In the years when the health care system grew dramatically, the administration of the hospital and the clinic was seen as the natural preserve of largely single, middle class women whose vision of their social function was to maintain the harmony, stability, and cohesiveness of their communities. Just as the married women ran the household, single women, often Sisters in Catholic institutions or nurses and laywomen in smaller ethnic facilities,

---

[39]See Charles Rosenberg, "Inward Vision and Outward Glance, op.cit.; Rosenberg, "And Heal the Sick: The Hospital and the Patient in 19th Century America," *Journal of Social History* **10**:428–447 (1977); Vogel, *Modern Hospital*: and Rosner, *Enterprise*, for extended discussions of the structure of the nineteenth and early twentieth century voluntary health care facilities.

[40]Davis, *Hospital Administration*, pp. 8–9. This data was collected by the American Medical Association and reported by Davis in a section of his book entitled "How Are Hospital Administrators Trained?" It is also significant that before the 1930s, hospital administration texts often assumed that women would play a leading role in the institution. See, for example, John Hornsby and Richard Schmidt, *The Modern Hospital, Its Inspiration, Its Architecture, Its Equipment, Its Operation*, W. B. Saunders, Philadelphia, 1913, p. 253 (hereinafter cited as *The Modern Hospital*): "the man or woman who was a competent hospital director a few years ago may be today so far behind the times that the whole institution is out of date."

were appropriate candidates to run the community's voluntary institutions. In these generally smaller institutions, they were responsible both for the caring and business functions of the facility.[41] For a significant portion of the first third of the twentieth century, the caring and financial abilities were co-equal elements in the qualities considered necessary for the hospital administrator. Women, therefore, with their claim on the household and emotional lives of the community, made excellent candidates for administrative health care positions, and shaped the goals of the administrator, emphasizing the caring and social service aspects of that training.

In light of the unique administrative structure of the hospital, for much of the first decades of the century there was an indistinct separation of traditional nursing and administrative functions in many smaller charity facilities. In the Brooklyn Nursery and Infants' Hospital, for example, the head administrator was responsible for the "entire supervision of the House, and control of the servants and nurses," as stated in the facility's constitution in 1892. But, in addition to these traditional administrative roles, she was required to make certain that the children's "deportment is proper at the table" and that "on Sunday the inmates of the house [were] called together, and [were] present at [Sabbath] services."[42] Separating out the qualities necessary for clinical and administrative roles in many smaller hospitals was difficult or impossible until very late in hospital history. "The former superintendent was also a director of nurses," complained one female superintendent. "I am not, and the task of separating the two positions in the public (and private) mind is requiring great persistence as well as care."[43]

Generally, the early generation of female administrator was drawn from the ranks of the hospital nurse or that class of genteel society that was deeply involved in charity work. Their salaries were relatively low, with over 50 percent receiving less than $2,000 a year, plus room and board, in 1929. The lay male administrators generally were drawn from the fields of social work and engineering.[44]

---

[41] May Ayres Burgess, *Nurses, Patients and Pocketbooks*, Committee on the Grading of Nursing Schools, New York, 1928, pp. 404–409, quoted in Davis, *Hospital Administration*, p. 29: As late as 1928, one woman administrator noted that "A hospital superintendent should have a working knowledge of business methods. I am confident that many hospitals need and want as superintendent women who have health, business ability and some understanding of medical and nursing problems."

[42] Brooklyn Nursery and Infants' Hospital, "Constitution and By-Laws," Annual Report, 1892–1893, p. 11.

[43] Quoted in Davis, *Hospital Administration*, p. 29.

[44] Davis, p. 16.

New Notions of Hospital Management

The last tumultuous decade of the nineteenth century and the first decades of this century inflicted tremendous damage to the older maternalistic relationships within the charity hospitals and set in motion a struggle for control of the institution among those interested in integrating modern notions of efficiency, bureaucracy, and order into the older, informal facility. Not surprisingly, the events of these decades began to undermine the traditional role of the head administrator as the moral steward for the patients.

In the early decades of this century, as financial problems increasingly plagued hospitals, trustees sought new types of personnel to administer their institutions — primarily *men* with a background in both medicine and business. While the goals of the institution still revolved around providing human services, the new mission of the institution began to abandon the older charity ideals in favor the new rising credibility of medicine and business. Medicine, unlike the earlier charitable rationale for institutions, lacked the clear class identification of charity care and helped trustees in their efforts to begin the process of cleansing their institutions of the class-bound identification of a charity facility. As medicine became a more accepted justification of a hospital's function and physicians became more integral to the financial and service structure of these institutions, trustees sought persons whose identity was more intimately associated with medicine and business rather than charity. Also, trustees sought individuals who could identify for them potential problems associated with the medicalization of the institution. When able, trustees turned to physicians to administer the institution.

Although 50 percent of all administrators were women in 1920, by 1929, fully 37 percent of all administrators were male physicians. In teaching hospitals, the percentage was even higher, hovering around 53 percent.[45] "Standards of hospital administration have been practically revolutionized within the past five or ten years, and the standards of hospital managers have changed within the same time," announced one important hospital administration text in 1913.

The new need to standardize the hospital resulted in the ouster of large numbers of women administrators. In addition to fulfilling the traditional housekeeping chores, the new administrator must "keep abreast of medical and surgical progress, to know what new apparatus of a medical or surgical kind should be bought and used. He must know the laws of asepsis, and at least enough about the character of the communicable diseases to guard not only against their appearance . . . but to

[45] See Davis, p. 12.

prevent their spread.''[46] Such tasks were considered beyond the scope of the older, caring traditions of the female administrator. The dual role of service and efficiency of the administrator was taking on a particular sex as medical expertise became a new criteria for the efficient manager, replacing social service as the primary administrative function. "If the modern superintendent is not a surgeon or internist . . . he must at least be sufficiently well informed on all of these subjects to engage in intelligent conference with members of his medical staff," remarked the authors of The Modern Hospital in 1913.[47]

By the 1920s, the institution was reorganizing itself to respond to the new needs of new potential customers, and, with this reorganization, the basis for the maternalistic, female administrator began to disappear. While the public image of the institution was that of a social service, women began to complain of the preference that trustees now showed for males interested in becoming head administrators.

> There has . . . been great injustice shown toward the woman executive," complained one hospital administrator from Pennsylvania. "A woman builds up on a substantial foundation but [w]hen the institution has expanded in its capacity for increased service, in its popularity with the public, in its whole-some influence upon the community, the question seems to be raised in the minds of [these trustees], should we not pass on to a man's control, and this often when a woman has mortgaged her health in her impassioned service to the institution."[48]

The Rise of Academia

The new social and medical functions of the voluntary hospitals upset some hospital administrators, and many turned to the university and formal education process for answers. It was hoped that academia could give the field of administration a new standard focus and agenda, one that could stand in place of the amalgam of idiosyncratic charitable ideals that marked the older style of administration. S. S. Goldwater, the head administrator of Mt. Sinai Hospital in New York, reflected the frustration that many physicians and laymen experienced in the rapidly changing hospital environment of the early twentieth century. "The country has drifted into its present chaotic condition because there was nobody whose business it was to furnish guidance in matters of medical adminis-

---

[46] Hornsby and Schmidt, The Modern Hospital.
[47] Ibid., pp. 253–254. It is remarkable how quickly the hospital literature began to refer to all head administrators as "he" while only a few years before the most popular texts always used both male and female pronouns.
[48] Quoted in Davis, p. 30.

tration," he complained in 1919. "Incomparably the best way to treat the matter is to have the study of medical administration organized and directed under university auspices," he suggested.[49] Repeated often throughout the 1920s, the demand of hospital administrators for formal training reflected their increasing sense of drift during a period of tremendous disruption in the relationship of the administrator to his or her institution.[50]

As hospital administration exited from the relative stability of a culture of paternalism and charity, there was a strong sense that the traditional values and roles of administration were of little relevance in the new environment of modern medicine. But there were few alternatives to this older notion of the administrator as the moral, social, and organizational voice of the institution.

In 1922, the Josiah Macy Jr. Foundation responded by forming a committee to evaluate the need for more formal training. In their concluding report, the committee developed a mission statement for future education courses, one that merged traditional service ideals to a broad mandate of educational reform along the lines of modern business administration. "An interpretation of the principles involved in hospital functions, organization, and tendencies and a presentation of their relationships to the broad problems and activities of community life . . . should be the basis of training for hospital executives," the report remarked. "A philosophy of community responsibility in matters of health is rapidly growing," it continued.[51] For those involved in developing formal educational goals for hospital administrators during the 1920s, the first order of business was to merge the community and medical service function of the hospital with a new set of business skills.

The Chicago Experiment

Perhaps the most promising development of the 1930s was the organization of an MBA program in health care administration at the University of

[49] S. S. Goldwater, "Civilian Medical Administration and the Need for Trained Leaders," *Journal of the American Medical Association*, May 24, 1919, reprinted in S. S. Goldwater, *On Hospitals*, Macmillan, New York, 1947, p. 26.

[50] See Report of the Committee on the Training of Hospital Executives, *Principles of Hospital Administration and Training of Hospital Executives*, Josiah Macy Jr. Foundation, New York, April 1922.

[51] Ibid., p. 8; See also, S. S. Goldwater, "Ideal Aims of Hospital Organization," *On Hospitals*, Macmillan, New York, 1947, pp. 4–5, reprinted from "The Search for the Ideal Hospital Organization," *Modern Hospital* (Feb. 1922): "To define the relation of the hospital to the community is today the essential theoretical problem of hospital administration. . . ."

Chicago. The only formal business program for administrators, it was begun with the goal of providing the foundations upon which the dual responsibilities of caring and managing could be addressed through formal education. Its goals were to provide a place where administrators "absorbed in institutional detail"[52] could stand back and reflect on the broader social currents that affected their jobs as managers of social services.[53]

What is interesting about the early efforts at formal education in a field where most administrators previously drifted, was the degree to which it acknowledged the traditional missions of the institution, seeking to ground the role of manager in the earlier service mandate of the charity hospital. This new manager was to maintain the service orientation of the facility while augmenting his management skills with ideas and concepts borrowed from the business community. Organized during the depression and coincidental with the publication of the report of the Committee on the Costs of Medical Care, the Chicago experiment was part of a broader attempt to substitute voluntarist language of the nineteenth century with twentieth century notions of business, efficiency, and standardization. However, the overall effect was to institutionalize the traditional caring responsibility while changing gender and ideological commitments of the administrator.

In following years, in many educational programs, the tensions that the abandonment of traditional charitable ideals might have had, remained relatively muted among administrators, as formal education in administration moved primarily into schools of public health rather than into schools of business. Within these educational environments, the object of all courses was to design delivery systems little concerned with business notions of efficiency or costs of providing service. Furthermore, even when administrators came from the few MBA programs in health administration (like the one at the University of Chicago), they quickly adopted the paternalistic (or more appropriately, maternalistic) ideals of caring for a community's sick, dependent, and helpless.

---

[52] M. M. Davis, "Development of the First Graduate Program in Hospital Administration," reprinted in The Journal of Health Administration Education **2**:121–134 (Spring, 1984).

[53] There were other shorter courses provided for a variety of administrators throughout the 1920s. New York University, Temple University, Teachers College of Columbia University, the Illinois Training School for Women, McGill University, Iowa University, Marquette University, Yale University, Cincinnati, and Harvard University School of Public Health all provided either special short courses or attenuated curricula throughout the teens and 1920s. None, with the possible exception of Marquette University, provided more than a short sequence of courses and most were not offered regularly.

Sympathy and Compassion

In community institutions managers could only institute business measures to improve efficiency and effectiveness and to balance the budget if the measures were in compliance with the goals of the caring professions. The trained administrator could not afford to maintain true allegiance to his academic training in management, standardization, and economic efficiency. The very skills that this new administrator brought from his student days would undergo a fundamental change when faced with the culture of caring and the realities of hospital practice. When hospital administrators—whether female or male—"borrowed a volume from industry," they did more than crudely adopt business principles as if there were no distinctions between money-making corporations and charitable enterprises. Rather, they essentially transformed business concepts to suit their needs as administrators of a special community trust.

S. S. Goldwater, the Head Administrator of New York's Mt. Sinai Hospital from 1902 to 1929 and a major participant in shaping the New York public hospital system (and Blue Cross as well), stated the evolving rationale for the field of hospital administration—a rationale that guaranteed that the field would remain separated from many other fields of business: "The hospital is a social institution whose true origins are deeply embedded in the human character," he wrote. "It is the response of prudence and sympathy to man's hatred of suffering and his fear of death."[54] Here, he adopted service as the primary motive for hospital organization. Elsewhere, he differentiated the hospital administrator from other business executives, adopting the rhetoric of the charity administrator of a generation before:

> If you were asked what you considered the most important single quality in a hospital administrator, what would you say? . . . I would answer, "sympathy and compassion." Not the emotional type of compassion which gives way to tears and ends in helpless despair, but the kind which arouses action, which intuitively grasps the meaning of a critical situation, which senses the need of appeasement, and eventually does something. The future will see a widening of the beneficent influence of this type of compassion to the extent that men of good will can be enrolled in the ranks of administrators.

Goldwater sought to make a distinction between a manager of a business enterprise and the health administrator. He differed from his female counterparts of 30 years before, only in rhetorical style, not content. He wanted "sympathy and compassion"—traditional adminis-

[54] S. S. Goldwater, *On Hospitals*, p. 20.

trators' ideals — but "sympathy and compassion" fortified with a strong dose of hard business sense.

The distinctions between health care and other forms of business administration were not merely the product of older administrators bringing forward old notions of *caritas*. Both business and health administrators through the first half of this century used the rhetoric and language of science, management, and the assembly line. But the hospital administrators' definitions of efficiency and accountability were generally intertwined with ideals that had given life and purpose to the voluntary hospital: providing care for the community's dependent and vulnerable. In that context, it is not surprising that the ideas borrowed from industry underwent a mutation that often made them unidentifiable by the business communities in which they first appeared. By the depression years, hospital administration defined its mission as applying the tools of industrial organization to the unique and complex setting of a human service where the "bottom line" could not be measured by merely looking at profits and losses, but by assessing human happiness and comfort.

But clearly, there was growing tension in the administrators' role. Increasingly, the patient care aspects of their professional mission was absorbed by the doctors, nurses, and various professionals who increasingly dominated daily ward life. Administrators tended to avoid conflict over professional matters for which they were not trained. Increasingly, they saw their position in the institution as tied to the financial survival of the institution, and often saw themselves as in opposition, rather than in league, with the very professionals that they paid. Hospital administration would, in the 1970s, become an adverserial profession, as sources of funds began to dry up and as administrators were increasingly divorced from direct patient care functions.

Blurring Vision

The tensions that have plagued the hospital administrator reflected larger pressures that were affecting the very leadership of the institution. In the years following World War II, many trustees lost sight of the earlier commitment to charity care and the community, as they traditionally had been defined. The growing involvement of the federal government in financing research, construction, and medical education altered the relationship between institutions and their local communities. Furthermore, the long, historical movement of private practice medicine out of the private office and into the hospital significantly changed the internal culture of the institution as trustees lost their role and legitimacy as guardians of the poor, the dependent, and the sick.

Slowly, along with the changing social class makeup of the institution, went the commitment to traditional religious, ethnic, and economic constituencies. In their place, a newer commitment to the communities of professionals — most notably doctors — developed. With this new community, came the abandonment of the older, traditional rationales of social service and the development of new, if vaguer, definitions of success. Medical definitions of disease replaced the older social definitions of dependence as the reason for the institution, and less specific community needs took a back seat to medically defined priorities. The institution relied less and less on the decisions of trustees who understood little about the technology and medical decision making in the hospitals. The trustee became solely concerned with the finances of the institution.

The very idea of community was significantly altered in the aftermath of World War II. While earlier generations of trustees and patients would often share certain religious or moral assumptions, the development of highly stratified communities divided along class or race lines made the whole concept of community a lot more vague. As the highway system spurred the growth of wealthy suburbs and hastened the economic decline of the "inner cities," trustees found themselves even more removed socially and physically from the communities of the poor they ostensibly served. The social origins of the patient in the hospital became a mere abstraction in the larger efforts of trustees and administrators to maintain the economic integrity of an institution dedicated to medical care rather than social service.

By the mid-1960s, as hospitals responded to calls for unionization, the notion of an institution closely connected to its community seemed like a romantic remnant of a "pre-scientific" era. Health planners and activists alike began to trumpet calls for community-based services as the very institutions that once appeared to be central to community life appeared more remote. Federal programs through the Office of Economic Opportunity were organized under the rubric that health was "a community affair" that demanded the creation of Neighborhood Health Centers that would respond to locally defined needs. At the very time that there was a rebirth of interest in locally based health services, hospital leaders seemed increasingly distant, and even antagonistic at times, to such efforts. In some communities such as the South Bronx, Chicago, and elsewhere, hospitals, once the cornerstone of community social service, were perceived as the enemy by many people, and even stormed and occupied by some. The growing distance between the community leaders and the hospital trustees spoke to the tremendous historical journey our community hospitals set out upon during the twentieth century. Along with hospitals' abandonment of community came the pressure for national standards to measure progress and success.

THE STRENGTH OF HETEROGENEITY AND DIVERSITY

This chapter has outlined certain historical traditions that have been characteristic of the development of the modern voluntary hospital. Though necessarily brief, it has attempted to point out that the seemingly heterogeneous character of the modern hospital is not the product of chance or happenstance. Rather, it is the product of a set of important choices and realizations about the nature of the health care enterprise in a socially diverse society. Central to understanding the history of the institution, and particularly the relationship between its governing body, professional staff, patients, and administration, is the fact that the social functions and the scientific and demographic base of these diverse institutions are ever-changing and will continue to shift.

In light of this continually changing social, medical, and political environment, it is important to recognize that the variety of institutional forms and arrangements that make up the voluntary hospital system is a source of strength, both for the system itself, and for the larger society that depends upon it. The danger lies not in the heterogeneity of the institutional form, or in the variety of assumptions that underlie its social base; rather, the danger to the system lies in the subtle erosion of the values, assumptions, and ideals that formed the system in the first place.

As the hospital abandons the various social constituencies that form the core of its population base, the institution is in danger of losing its most precious form of political, social, and economic support. As new constituencies develop, the willingness of the institution to serve their varied needs will determine the support provided by the society at large. To a large degree, the recent antagonism shown toward the voluntary form is an index of the degree to which the institution has deviated from its mission. While it may not be the for-profit hospitals that pose the greatest threat, they certainly do play on the current weakness of the voluntary institution's moral and social argument.[55]

A New Clarity of Purpose

There are clearly major improvements that should be made in the voluntary hospital system, and our history might give us an indication of their

[55] These observations are not lost on some hospital administrators. See Edward J. Connors, "The Mission and Social Responsibility of Health Care in a Changed Environment," presented at Iowa Hospital Association, Annual Meeting, April 23, 1986; Kevin O'Rourke, "An Ethical Perspective on Investor-Owned Medical Care Corporations," *Frontiers of Health Services Management* **1:**10–26 (September, 1984).

direction. This chapter has tried to examine the motives of the original founders of our community institutions to see how their very well-defined moral mission infused the structure, purpose, and organization of the voluntary health care institution. The clarity of that vision was challenged over the course of the twentieth century by the growing power of the ideals of scientific medicine, but neither the moral nor medical models were ever universally successful in gaining their objectives. Finally, it is good to question how far we have come from the clarity of the original founders of the voluntary health care system, and pose the question whether we should pause now and seek methods for regaining a community focus. It is clearly time to rethink and to reassert the traditional goals of the institution while adjusting to the changing communities who must now be served. The poor are still there, as are the homeless, although they may now look and act in ways that seem alien to trustees far removed from the reality and immediacy of their existence.

If anything, this history may indicate the direction of necessary change: guaranteeing the diversity of the voluntary hospital system, and encouraging community accountability. Responsiveness to community needs will entail even more diversity in types and kinds of care than exist today, and will require even more complex and idiosyncratic arrangements between local communities, hospital trustees, and providers. Simple assumptions that a profit-making, publicly unaccountable, uniform, standardized, and businesslike hospital system is necessarily "more efficient" should be regarded with suspicion, especially in a country as diverse as the United States.

Doing Well and Doing Good

For all of this century, the voluntary hospital has dominated the American health system. But today provides a "critical moment" for health care because, for the first time in many decades, the field has become increasingly responsive to ideological and economic forces outside of the institutions themselves. Today, administrators, physicians, and planners are spending their professional careers in corporations or consulting firms organizing health benefits packages. Others are organizing Preferred Provider Organizations (PPO) or Health Maintenance Organizations (HMO) for corporations. In these new settings, it is unclear whether the culture of the hospital, with its focus on care rather than profit, will continue to be a central factor in determining a health professional's identity. Fifty years from now, other historians may look back at this time and note that it was a period of change, when the basic contours of health care were altered by a business community that defined success in terms of dollars rather than in terms of human comfort and well-being.

S. S. Goldwater wrote a letter to C.-E. A. Winslow in 1928 that sought to explain his reasons for entering the field of health care administration. In that letter, he revealed some of the basic ideals that informed the early generation of hospital administrators:

> I originally dedicated myself not to medical or public health work, but to economics. With an ethical background and with the love of and belief in justice that characterizes the youthful enthusiast, I speedily arrived at the conclusion that a mere analysis of economic conditions without a social objective was hardly worthwhile. . . . This line of thought led me straight away back to . . . health and suggested that any system of applied economics designed to satisfy human needs would eventually have to be directed by . . . health officers. I at once decided to abandon economics [to begin] a [public] health career.

In this letter, Goldwater reveals the mixed historical baggage of hospitals: They were institutions that defined their mission at one time as doing well financially but also as doing good for their clients. Their administrators and planners, despite their attempts to adopt the language of science, business, and efficiency, found their views of their own particular mission shaped by the institutions in which they worked.

CHAPTER 5

THE VIRTUOUS HOSPITAL: DO NONPROFIT INSTITUTIONS HAVE A DISTINCTIVE MORAL MISSION?

Daniel Wikler, Ph.D.

THE MORAL IMPORT OF EMPIRICAL DATA

America's health care system is composed of public, nonprofit, and for-profit institutions. Among hospitals, the nonprofit — or voluntary hospitals — have been predominant, both in numbers and influence. Hospitals of the other types filled niches: public hospitals mainly served populations for whom the government had special responsibilities, such as veterans and the poor, whereas for-profit hospitals, mostly small and undistinguished, served the needs of physicians and their patients where nonprofit hospitals had not been established.

Voluntary hospitals, as a result, served as exemplars. Though not all of them were exemplary, it was to this group that one looked to gain an idea of what a hospital should be. Their conduct defined the virtues of the hospital, setting expectations on the part of the public, and establishing the social contract under which they won the public's support.

After years of unquestioned hegemony among America's institutional providers of health care, however, these hospitals are being challenged. Large chains of for-profit hospitals scout opportunities for skimming the cream of the patient population, leaving the voluntary institutions with a less lucrative clientele. Governments and insurers are encouraging competition among providers, pitting voluntary hospitals against each other.

Nonprofit hospitals perceive the need to stand and fight, eat or be eaten, however uncongenial this behavior might feel to a charitable institution.

Economic pressure from competitors and predators, however, has not been the only force acting to change the character of nonprofit hospitals. An important accompaniment has been a marked change in the nation's prevailing political ideology. The "pro-business" tilt of the 1980s emphasizes the putative efficiencies of the market and ignores its moral and social failings. It lionizes those successful at profitmaking, while giving little attention or admiration to those dedicated to public service. The allocation of resources brought about by competition — including market segmentation, overemphasis of price, and cessation of cross-subsidization of clients and services — are deemed optimal almost by definition, thereby tainting the fruits of cooperative planning and regulation.

In short, both the current (economics) and the wind (justifying ideology) act to steer voluntary hospitals in the direction of ordinary commercial enterprise. Operating a nonprofit institution as though it were but a special kind of profit-oriented company comes to seem not only self-protective, but morally acceptable, as realistic rather than opportunistic.

Nonprofit hospitals, however, may not have complete freedom to redefine themselves. Communities that support nonprofit hospitals have formed expectations over many years that demand behavior not keyed so directly to profit-seeking. Public support for tax exemptions may rest on the fulfillment of these expectations. Health care workers, including managers and professionals, may have been attracted to these institutions precisely because they wished to be part of a team motivated by nonmonetary goals and ideals. Their professional identity demands that the hospitals with which they are associated strive to be something distinctive, and even noble.

Despite the pressures and opportunities this new business climate is creating, the public's need for a commitment by voluntary health care institutions to nonprofitable services is even greater than in previous years. The rapid, albeit apparently brief, rise of the for-profit companies converged, not coincidentally, with a series of trends that exacerbated existing problems of access to health care, now affecting even the middle class. The trends include raging inflation of health care costs, a retreat from governmental support for the welfare state, and a reduction in workplace-based health care insurance. Far from condoning an abandonment of its social mission, the public may look to voluntary institutions to expand their role and shoulder some of the burden jettisoned by government in these trying times.

In the face of these countervailing pressures, it is understandable that many nonprofit health care institutions are uncertain of their mission. Should they remain distinctive, answering to higher ideals and a more demanding notion of virtue than other hospitals? Should they claim a special covenant with the public, in return for which they could claim tax breaks and other forms of support? On what terms would this relationship be based? And, why would they, because of their nonprofit status, be exclusively qualified to pursue this kind of mission?

Some observers counsel the voluntary hospitals to accept the continuing convergence of the nonprofit and for-profit hospital types as inevitable, however regrettable. Perhaps the nonprofit hospitals were not so different, after all. Or perhaps a hospital's behavior is largely determined by the environment in which it operates, in which case contemporary pressures acting similarly on hospitals of all types will bring about similar institutional behavior, and in turn, similar tax and other public policy treatment. In this view, there is no special role for nonprofit institutions to play, nor do they have any special character or nature that peculiarly suits them to such a task. This suggests that hospitals are a dependent variable in health policy: the basic decisions are made elsewhere, in government, industry, or in the market; hospitals of all types are then left with the job of adapting and surviving in a similar environment.

The debate over the role of voluntary hospitals in America's health care system is partly "philosophical," a reflection of differing beliefs and assumptions about the proper place of public, private, and voluntary institutions in health care and in society generally. For the most part, however, these relatively abstract considerations remain buried in the discussion of the role of the voluntary hospital: assumed rather than argued for, they are often unrecognized sources of continuing disagreement over the importance of available data.

Some of the reluctance to deal directly with the philosophical issues stems from the perceived futility of that kind of debate. Neither side is likely to convert the other, and the propositions in dispute are often so general and abstract that even when both sides seem to agree on a given principle, its implications for policy and management remain obscure.

Attempting to avoid the philosophical issues, however, may be equally futile. At a minimum, the parties to the debate must attempt to formulate their assumptions with some precision — for how else can they know what agenda to defend? And some effort to understand the sources of the other side's values and outlook is necessary both for effective presentation of one's own case and as a way of finding common ground. Finally, some of these assumptions look much less self-evident once unearthed and made explicit. Taking time out for review of the basic assumptions can free the debate of the influence of weak ideas.

This chapter examines three of these abstract considerations. The next section of this chapter addresses the issue of whether nongovernmental institutions, such as voluntary health care facilities, ought to take on the job of performing what are, in essence, public or governmental functions. This goes to the heart of the definition of a voluntary hospital, for what is in question is whether institutions should define and pursue any substantive moral goals of their own. Even assuming that they should, conceptual uncertainties remain: it is not clear what kind of institutional behavior is required, beyond the formulation of a mission statement, nor is it apparent how to decide how much effort on behalf of the mission suffices. These questions are posed in the chapter's third section. The chapter closes with a discussion of arguments supporting and disputing the key assumption that voluntary hospitals are uniquely suited to their distinctive mission — that they are inherently virtuous — because of their nonprofit form of organization.

This chapter aims more to amplify the range of opinions on these issues than to establish one view as immune to rebuttal. Nevertheless the discussion has an outcome: no convincing theoretical ground is found that suggests the abandonment of the quest for a distinctive moral mission for voluntary facilities. Though the nonprofit status alone may not guarantee praiseworthy institutional behavior, this chapter suggests that the concept of the virtuous hospital, understood as commitment to substantive moral goals, is especially congenial to the voluntary role as developed both historically and functionally in the American health care system. Thus, even if many nonprofit hospitals act like for-profit hospitals today, there remains a significant difference between the two types: if not in how they are, then certainly in how they *should be*. This promise, if buttressed by renewed commitment to its fulfillment, supports their claim to continued support in public policy.

SHOULD HOSPITALS ASPIRE TO VIRTUE?

Are hospitals moral agents? Should they set moral goals: aspire to good character; engage, at their own initiative, in good works? Posed in these words, few would respond negatively to these questions. Every competent individual, and every human institution, is a "moral agent" in the sense of having to make choices and accept responsibility for the consequences, of being appropriate objects of praise or blame.

Nevertheless, there remains a nontrivial and undecided question regarding the moral agency of hospitals. Though every hospital aspires to act honorably, the "virtuous hospital" goes further: it pursues *independent substantive* moral goals. In its independence it seeks to define its own mission, to be not only responsive to its environment but to play a leading role in creating it. Its moral goals are broader than providing good medical care and "keeping its nose clean"; it identifies and targets unmet needs and accepts broad responsibilities in health care that it is not required to shoulder.

Principles or Pragmatics?

Thus defined, it is far from axiomatic that America's hospitals ought to be virtuous hospitals. Indeed, current health policy suggests the opposite. Pressure on the part of payers of health care, led by the government, to encourage competition among providers, rather than cooperative community planning, and to resist paying prices that reflect cross-subsidization of services and patients, discourage precisely those activities by which hospitals define a distinctive, independent moral mission for themselves.

The case for these policies, however, is not ordinarily made at the level of moral principle. Payers merely want to pay as little as possible. If competition and unbundling of services reduce expenditures, this is justification enough. This pressure from payers need not be understood as an expression of any particular opinion on the moral issues involved, but simply as a statement of their priorities.

All the same, the questions of principle are — or certainly should be — a part of the health policy debate. The current transformation of the health care system could not take place without the relaxation of certain taboos, such as those that discouraged advertising. The pro-market ideological cheerleading of recent years undoubtedly helps to soothe the concern of administrators, physicians, and other health care professionals who had been socialized in an earlier ethic. Let us proceed, then, to assess the case for an independent moral mission for hospitals at the level of principle.

"Public" and "Private": Exhaustive Categories?

Health care institutions, be they hospitals, nursing homes, or other entities, that were established and operated by religious orders had no uncertainties about the appropriateness of pursuing independent, substantive moral goals. The hospital's operations were part of the order's work, and dedication to moral ideals was an important part of the group's *raison d'être*. Much the same was true of other charitable institutions.

However, some of these voluntary institutions, hospitals in particular, have changed in character. Revenues started to flow from charges to patients rather than from donations, and hospitals became the site of trading rather than of giving. Thus it becomes an open question whether, and why, the hospital should try to be anything more than the institutional setting in which this exchange of services for dollars occurs.

Indeed, the argument in opposition to the view that hospitals should attempt to define a moral mission is worthy of consideration. It proceeds by sorting responsibilities and activities in health care into one of only two categories, the social and the private. In this view, most of what transpires in health care is a matter of interest primarily to individuals: patients and those to whom they turn for services. But there are other matters that are irreducibly social in character, the most important of which are questions of social justice having to do with the allocation of resources and access to health care. These are the responsibility of the society as a whole, which usually acts through government. This purely two-category view, which briefly will be elaborated here, deals no hand to voluntary private hospitals in the nation's health care system. Though they may be the sites of health care, according to this argument they are not among the principals in the system's workings.

The location of the boundary between social and private will be determined differently depending on one's political ideology. One polar view expands the social realm widely. It regards much of health policy as pursuant to ideals of social justice: who gets what care, and how it is delivered, are irreducibly social concerns, just as when similar issues are raised with voting rights or political speech. From this perspective, morality demands, and the nation's interests are best served by, an integrated (though not necessarily centralized) health care system of practitioners, clinics, and hospitals, either run or closely regulated by government. The system as a whole would decide investment priorities, eligibility for care, standards of quality, and other factors affecting the fairness of the allocation of resources. Individual institutions would be expected to carry out the system's mandate. They would not be morally autonomous, in the sense of acting as moral agents with their own goals and self-determined mission, any more than would a particular ward in one of today's independent hospitals.

This view does not require that health care be exclusively public; there is no incompatibility between this vision and private philanthropy. Individuals who held this view could consistently create charitable institutions that served as adjuncts to the government's efforts. The important point, however, is that questions of social justice are concerned with the sharing of resources among the population as a whole. Individual philanthropy may alleviate some need and suffering, but it cannot in this view, determine the overall pattern of sharing of resources. If people have a right to a given set of health care services, their claim ultimately can be made good only by government. Philanthropy is episodic, and hit-or-miss: an individual has no assurance that any particular charity will take him on as its particular responsibility. Since social justice should not be hit-or-miss, this view concludes that this responsibility in the health care field must be carried out by government or at its direction.

Some of the same conclusions about the hospital's moral mission are supported by a view closer to the opposite pole, one that would reject a broad role for the state in overseeing health care in favor of individualistic solutions. In this perspective, health care is a marketable service, its terms to be negotiated in markets by buyers and sellers and their representatives. Buyers will want the best service available for the dollars they wish to spend, but ordinarily will have no particular interest in supporting any special moral goals and ambitions of individual sellers. Though nothing in this view of health care transactions requires that the hospital's retailing services be operated for profit, neither is this mode of operation proscribed. From the buyers point of view, the seller's status relative to profit-making is immaterial; what counts is its ability to offer attractive products at low prices. This is not to say that this perspective ignores the moral qualities of hospitals. Honesty in dealing, fair competition, full comportment with the law, and similar kinds of behavior are required. But the notion of virtue made up by these standards is narrow and largely procedural. They do not demand any particular set of substantive goals.

Though this individualist perspective views health care delivery as primarily a private matter, it too may include a role for the state and for philanthropy. Yet in neither case is it congenial to the view that health care institutions *should* actively pursue substantive moral goals.

The state's role, in this view, is restricted to policing fair dealing and, perhaps, to taking some responsibility for the deserving poor. The indigent would thus be provided with insurance at public expense and would use these dollars to buy health care in the market. Individual hospitals, however, would be given no special responsibility for these patients and would treat them like any other customers with the same ability to pay.

Similarly, the individualist perspective does not rule out, and typically encourages, a broad role for private charity. But the decision to allocate resources to and through charities is to be made by those having original title to the wealth, rather than to the hospitals from which they purchase their health care. Thus, individual health care institutions may act as moral agents to the extent that they function as charities, supported by donations, but not ordinarily in their role as sellers of health care services in the marketplace. An individual buyer may, of course, choose to patronize a hospital that, say, adds to charges to support charitable ends. The buyer is in effect making a charitable contribution when he purchases medical care. Most informed buyers will not choose to make payment of health care bills the occasion for their philanthropy, and the individualist perspective champions their right to make health care buying decisions on purely self-regarding economic grounds.

Thus, in the individualist perspective, there is nothing in the nature of health care, or of hospitals, that requires the buying and selling of care to be tied to charitable activity. In this view, individuals pursue their private interests, perhaps including charity, while government may have responsibility for some collective obligations; there is no *separate* responsibility of institutions, such as hospitals, to pursue either the private or the public ends.

Private Institutions, Public Ends

A mandate for pursuing an independent, distinctive moral mission for nonprofit, voluntary institutions, requires a third, opposing view, according to which some social problems are best assigned to moral agents that are neither governmental nor individual. In this view, not all social problems are to be resolved through governmental action, and not all concerns of individual purchasers are best addressed by providers whose character is defined solely by their activity in trading for services. The health care system, at least as presently constituted in this country, thus requires institutions that dedicate themselves to substantive moral goals they themselves define and that are pursued independently of actions of either government or individual purchasers of health care.

Why Should Private Hospitals Address
Moral and Social Problems?

Those who seek to define a moral mission for voluntary hospitals may pursue two lines of argument in response to the claim that it is government, not individual hospitals, that should take on the job of addressing problems of access and other issues of social justice in health care.

First, there are some moral functions that voluntary hospitals are uniquely capable of serving. By their nature, they are expressions of voluntarism, which is valuable in its contribution to the community in addition to the benefits it provides to those directly helped. Voluntary hospitals can also cater, as public institutions often cannot, to the needs, tastes, and mores of particular religious, ethnic, and cultural groups within the larger community. Indeed, many nonprofit hospitals had their beginnings in their sponsors' interest in this function, and some institutions continue in this tradition. Catholic hospitals, for example, are one of the most visible means of expressions of that faith's distinctive moral tenets regarding life, death, and reproduction.

Moreover, the admittedly social character of the problem of just allocation of resources does not negate the desirability of individual contributions. Even where government does a fully adequate job of ensuring social justice in access to and allocation of health care services, other institutions can play an important supplementary moral role. Though there is no consensus on the extent of society's obligation to provide health care to all those in need, many advocates of the right to health care call for provision of some kind of basic package of benefits rather than a commitment to provide any and all services that might be of any benefit.[1] This is merely to say that the requirements of justice have some limits. Indeed, there are arguably some services that, given the scarcity of resources, government should not provide. These are services that have a low expectation of benefit in relation to cost, such as a screening program for a low-risk population or a burn unit that accepts relatively hopeless cases. If the money would do much good elsewhere, the government should not channel limited dollars in this direction; and if the benefit-to-cost ratio is very unfavorable, it should not attempt to divert funds from non-health-related purposes. Yet these services are valuable for those who would in fact be helped. The hospital or clinic that provided the service would be fulfilling a moral role in the allocation of health care services that would go beyond that of the government. Since the government has an obligation to assign health care dollars equitably, which often means where they will do the most good, it is not as well positioned as private, voluntary institutions for this kind of service.

A second important function of voluntary institutions in the allocation of health care resources is providing services the government should sponsor but does not. Though the doctrine of a right to health care now appears to have somewhat fewer defenders than in recent years, there is still a consensus in the literature of health care policy that favors ensuring each citizen access to at least a decent minimum of care. By any definition of "decent minimum," this social obligation is not met in current

---

[1] "President's Commission for the Study of Ethical Problems in Medicine and Biomedical and Behavioral Research," *Securing Access to Health Care*, Vol. 1, U.S. Government Printing Office, Washington, D.C., 1983; Ibid., Vol. 2, foundational essays by Gibbard, Buchanan, Gauthier, and Daniels; A general survey of the foundational arguments appears in Daniel Wikler, "Philosophical Perspectives on Access to Health Care," loc. cit.

programs. Millions face barriers even to routine care. Individual hospitals can, and do, help to fulfill these unmet, deserving needs. In the debate over the mission of voluntary hospitals, these facts are more important than the point of principle that assigns primary responsibility to government. What matters, from the point of view of social justice, is that the job gets done, not which agency does it. Thus, even if allocation of resources would be no part of a hospital's moral mission in a perfectly just health care system, it can be an important part of that mission in the system we actually have.

The Insufficiency of the Market

Just as a case for a moral mission for individual hospitals can be made despite the claims of those who would assign these functions to government, so too can hospitals legitimately seek a role transcending the workings of the market.

Much of the argument against a system of health care delivery relying solely on the market is familiar, referring to the difficulties consumers have in assessing the need for and quality of the health care services they may wish to buy. It also stresses the lack of information and freedom of choice from which the marketplace in health care inevitably suffers. Equally important for the purpose of this chapter, is a line of argument that points out distinctive features of health care that seem to require distinctive providers. This suggests that from the moral point of view, and perhaps also to best fulfill the individual interests of health care consumers, the health care delivery system should be composed of institutions that pursue a substantive rather than a procedural kind of virtue.

What features of health care require "virtuous" providers? Health care is, to begin with, of the highest personal importance. We are more concerned with the quality and dedication of our doctors and hospitals than we are with the character of those who sell other services because our health — and even lives — are at stake. And health care is concerned with even more than survival. The medical world intrudes on our coming into being and our passing away, our sharing of life-cycle milestones and sexuality, our emotional problems and relationships. Physicians and hospitals are privy to events and information normally confined to intimates and to the home. Not just anyone or any institution is worthy of this trust.

The nature of health care requires its provision to be governed by virtues we associate with the professions. At this stage of its development, at least, practitioners of the art of medicine must rely on clinical judgment, providing services as they (and their patients) see fit, and eschewing formulas and schedules that would more naturally be governed by contracts. Practitioners and institutions are granted a great deal of autonomy in return for the expectation of dedication to the patient's interests. The professional must be equal to this task.

Professional status implies several important conditions for the would-be provider. One stems from the inevitable difference in power between provider and patient. The provider knows more than the patient about the patient's need for treatment and the kind of therapy required, and the patient must often rely on the provider's judgment. The patient's plight is made more difficult by the fact that the injured and ill are often weakened, vulnerable, and less capable of monitoring and directing the course of treatment. For therapy to occur, the patient must feel able to place himself or herself in the provider's hands without trepidation.

A second implication of professional status is that the health care provider must answer to a professional ethic — a sense of right conduct —enforced largely by peers and which may at times conflict with the demands of patients. Physicians should not offer Laetrile for cancer, for example, even when patients insist on it. They should not offer treatment of dubious effectiveness for substance abuse, arthritis, or other conditions, just because they would be able to find a large clientele. The virtuous provider will not seek to "stimulate demand" unless this precisely coincides with "meeting need," as defined by professionals as well as by consumers. Indeed, the appropriate motive for launching any new service, and for marketing it to the public, is that this represents the most effective and equitable use of health care resources in preventing and relieving illness. If this stance is "elitist," requiring the provider to use professional judgment rather than the client's, it is the kind of behavior the professional's contract with the public calls for.

Finally, as noted earlier, health care is a service that no one should have to do without. That the United States has never fully complied with this requirement is no evidence against its continuing appropriateness as a moral goal.

These characteristics of health care suggest that from the moral point of view the buying and selling of those services should be different from that of ordinary commerce. The "buyer" must feel completely free to trust the "seller." The provider who lets demand be the only determining factor in deciding whether to offer a service will not be satisfactory. And providers who, acting on their own, do something to address existing problems of access to care will, everything else being equal, be more worthy of approbation and support.

None of these considerations decisively points to the need for the nonprofit norm in health care facilities. For-profit hospitals, for example, may find that for-profit hospitals fail when they violate these norms, for customers' allegiance may be at stake; and the powerful influence of physicians may not let managers stray from these paths even if their orientation to the bottom line tempts them to do so.

The fact remains, however, that good health care, more than most other revenue-producing activity, requires behavior, which, at least in the short-to-medium run, is directly contrary to profit maximization. Some of these norms are, moreover, inherently institutional: hospitals must adopt these norms themselves, for if their commitment is lacking, no government vouchers or programs can take up the slack. Optimal health care, then, requires substantive virtue. Historically, as well as in theory, voluntary hospitals have defined themselves in reference to this kind of ideal. For-profit institutions have not.

Thus, governmental and individual initiatives and decisions do not obviate the need for health care institutions that act as moral agents pursuing substantive moral goals. The government's responsibilities are limited, and in any case remain unfulfilled. And in view of the special nature of health care, individual choices in the marketplace are inadequate as a guide for institutional behavior.

THE VIRTUOUS HOSPITAL: CONCEPTUAL PROBLEMS

The health care system will, then, be best served by institutions that are virtuous. This requires these institutions, including hospitals, to allocate resources according to what Stanley B. Jones and Dr. Merlin K. Du Val call the institution's "community services mission."[2] Thus, the measure of an institution's virtue is the extent of its devotion of resources to these largely uneconomic services. This criterion, then, would seem to offer a way of ranking hospitals in moral terms and to provide a broad goal for hospital management. But there are a host of conceptual difficulties attendant to this criterion; though none of them deprives the notion of virtue of its usefulness in the debate over hospital conduct, a full treatment of the moral issues requires that they be examined and understood. This section of the chapter will look more closely at those difficulties.

Antidemocratic Reallocation

The first difficulty stems from the fact that the voluntary hospital is not a state. This being the case, it has no direct authority or legitimacy in

---

[2] Stanley B. Jones and Merlin K. Du Val, "What Distinguishes the Voluntary Hospital in an Increasingly Commercial Health Care Environment?" (this volume).

playing a Robin Hood role. Cost-shifting in an effort to fulfill its community services mission involves making its own, private determinations of who should pay and who should benefit. That these are not necessarily optimal is demonstrated by the unavoidable fact that the necessary funds are, in effect, raised by a tax on the (insured) sick, who are already burdened. And covert cross-subsidization undercuts the claim that nonprofit status provides reliable assurance to patients that their inability to judge quality and value will not be exploited. That the cross-subsidizing hospital exploits its insured or self-paying patients on behalf of the indigent does not alter this conclusion.

These problems, raised by Robert Clark and others opposed to a special status for voluntary hospitals, can be at least partly answered. First, the allocations made by the institution may be steps in the direction of overall social justice, and the undemocratic way in which the decisions are made may not be a large enough wrong to offset these gains. Second, the hospital can gain legitimacy by obtaining delegated authority. Payers may consent to a certain amount of cost-shifting, with the precise allocations left to the hospital's good judgment. The government's legitimacy can be passed along in this way to the hospital. Third, the putative tax on the sick is usually not really that. With third-party payment, the "tax" is on the insured, or more precisely, on the insured's employer or insuring mechanism. Since most non-poor are insured, this kind of "taxation" not only falls upon the well, but is also progressive with regard to income. Finally, the same critics that protest the rake-off from better heeled patients on behalf of the medically indigent do not protest when, in a for-profit hospital, income from paying patients is used in part to enrich stockholders. Is this not "exploitation" in the same (not especially interesting) sense?[3]

Virtue No Substitute for Justice

Virtue is defined independently from justice. A virtuous person or institution is charitable to an appreciable degree. A just society distributes goods and services to the deserving poor. But there is no a priori assurance that the amount of charity produced by a society of adequately charitable individuals and institutions will be sufficient to effect a just distribution of burdens and benefits in the society as a whole.

Thus, whatever level of charity care and other community service the

---

[3] Estelle James, "How Nonprofits Grow: A Model," in Susan Rose-Ackerman (ed.), *The Economics of Nonprofit Institutions: Studies in Structure and Policy*, Oxford University Press, New York, 1986, pp. 185–195.

virtuous nonprofit hospital engages in, it is still possible that unmet and deserving need will remain (though, of course, the demands of charity are greater when the need is greater).

Further, the virtuous institution acting alone in a competitive market lacks the means to coordinate its good works with other hospitals. In a recent issue of the *New England Journal of Medicine*,[4] Norman Daniels observed that American physicians are reluctant to ration care to patients because there is no overall scheme of allocation and hence no assurance that the resources denied their patient would be put to more effective use elsewhere. The problem of institutional virtue and social justice stands this observation on its head: the individual hospital has less reason to be virtuous if it lacks the assurance that other hospitals will also be virtuous and will do so in ways that harmonize and extend the virtuous institutional behavior.

Indeed, some authors[5] have questioned whether "fair share" is even a coherent notion in this context. In their view, a fair share of the burden of social justice cannot be defined without reference to an overall scheme of (forcible) taxation and a national system of benefits. This, however, requires the state. Institutions thus cannot be judged according to the adequacy of their efforts to meet some imagined quota of good works.

Virtue Is Easier for Some Than for Others

Some people are morally lucky: life rarely poses tragic choices; it makes charity easy to bear; and it poses few temptations. Others must continually grapple with the hard questions and face up to morality's demands with few resources at hand.

The same is true of voluntary health care institutions. The suburban nonteaching hospital, for example, may have no problem handling the uncompensated care it provides to the occasional uninsured patient. The hospital left behind in the ghetto, however, must struggle to balance the books each day. The latter may turn away patients, and thus be deemed "unvirtuous," though in reality it makes fewer resources go further toward community service than the suburban hospital does.

Furthermore, this "moral luck" is manipulable. Siting and marketing decisions can determine the degree to which a hospital's virtue is chal-

[4] Norman Daniels, "Why Saying No to Patients in the U.S. Is So Hard," *New England Journal of Medicine* **314**:1381–1383 (May 22, 1986).
[5] Dan W. Brock and Allen Buchanan, "Ethical Issues in For-Profit Health Care," in Bradford Gray (ed.), *For-Profit Enterprise in Health Care*, Institute of Medicine, National Academy Press, Washington, D.C., 1986.

lenged. Fulfillment of mission, in the sense of day-to-day virtue, can be made much easier if the problems can be deterred before they approach the door. Hospitals can, figuratively, walk away from their moral problems.

Institutional Virtue and Social Deterioration

An institution can behave "virtuously" — never dumping patients, and sponsoring uncompensated care, teaching, and research — while actually reducing the level of justice in the community. This can occur, for example, if the hospital obtains its revenues at the expense of other, even more virtuous institutions; or if its refusal to close its doors in an overbedded community drives inner-city hospitals to bankruptcy.

This suggests that care be taken in explicating the notion of the virtuous hospital to ensure that it is not merely an exercise in *etiquette*. Since justice is one of the virtues, a fully virtuous institution will be concerned not only that it do good but also that good, in sufficient amounts, be done; not only that it do no evil but that evil not be done. A narrower notion of virtue, more akin to politeness or gentility, is concerned simply with keeping the individual institution's record free of blemishes. If the institution's concern is only to keep its moral appearance spotless, it will act differently than if it is bent on solving the community's real moral problems. That takes dedication of a different sort: active, outward-looking, and occasionally trouble-making. In many circumstances, a hospital can stay polite — narrowly virtuous — while the community's health deteriorates alarmingly.

Problems in Calibration

Jones and Du Val[6] observe the difficulty inherent in a commitment to fulfill a "community service mission" as well as a "business mission": the standards for success are much fuzzier. This is not a trivial problem.

It is, first, difficult to state precisely what it is that needs calibrating. An institution might argue, for example, that providing medical care — even if for high fees — is itself a community service. In some cases, this seems to have been sufficient to win the right to continued exemption from taxes. But this sort of service is beside the point, unless the service is rare, or of unusually high quality.

The community service in question seems to require activity that is *not* "good business." If this were the case, then virtue in hospitals would

---

[6] Jones and Du Val, this volume.

be defined by the degree to which it engaged in uneconomic behavior of the appropriate kind. This would have a strong advantage if it were an adequate answer, because it is, in theory, quantifiable. The hospital's accountants would need merely to determine how much revenue was foregone, or how much extra cost was incurred. The dollar figure thus computed could be compared to a benchmark amount, expressed either in absolute terms or as a percentage of revenues.

Unfortunately, conceptual problems lie in the path of this resolution. Foremost is the fact, also noted by Jones and Du Val, that what appears to be uneconomic behavior is often good business. It may draw patients to the hospital who will bring money in on other occasions. It may be an unavoidable cost of a profitable venture (as with an outpatient clinic that results in many admissions of insureds but also brings in a few indigent patients). Or, most generally, it may bolster the hospital's reputation as a "caring" institution. This good publicity may serve the hospital's balance sheet in the event that public opinion influences the awarding of contracts, Certificates of Need, or other privileges. It may also protect its autonomy, as the community will trust it to run its own affairs in the public interest.

Finally, some institutions may seek to fulfill a community service mission in ways that are impossible to quantify and compare. One institution may voluntarily submit to community control in order to enhance the democratic character of the hospital and community; another may become, or remain, consumer-owned- and -controlled, thus providing a similar good to its members. These qualify as contributions to the public good, but their worth cannot be figured in dollar terms.

What conclusion should be drawn from this recital of difficulties in the concept of the virtuous hospital? Not that the concept is too unclear, weak, or confused for use in the formulation of health policy. The argument in its favor, reviewed in the second section of this chapter, provides some justification for its use. The conceptual problems noted here do show, however, that institutional virtue is a limited source of justice in the system as a whole and that it is inherently imprecise as either a guide for management or as a criterion of institutional evaluation.

VIRTUE AND NONPROFIT STATUS

Nonprofit hospitals are often regarded as better for society than for-profit hospitals precisely because they aspire to, and often do, achieve virtue. This section examines the case for this claim, beginning with its theoretical basis and proceeding to the empirical evidence.

Theoretical Considerations Favoring Nonprofits

The Nondistribution Constraint The obvious reason derives from the definition of the voluntary form itself, that is, that it is prohibited from distributing profits to owners. This "nondistribution constraint" suggests, according to Harry Hansmann,[7] that nonprofit institutions will not attempt to take advantage of the consumer's informational deficits and provide inferior services. The reason is that the staff, or those who direct them, will lack the financial incentive to do so. The assumption, apparently, is that the staff would, everything else being equal, be inclined to act in the patient's interest. For-profit firms, on the other hand, are beholden to stockholders who expect to see maximum returns on every dollar. Consumers who cannot protect themselves by independent assessments of quality may have reason to be concerned.

Thus, actual and prospective patients would, if this account were correct, have reason to prefer that their care be delivered in voluntary hospitals. Government, too, can benefit from an inclination toward quality, if it exists, for by favoring nonprofits it can, in theory, reduce the need to police and regulate those institutions.[8]

Though something like this view seems to underlie much of the animus that is expressed toward for-profit hospitals, Hansmann denies that his analysis — part of a general theory of nonprofit hospitals of all kinds — applies directly to hospitals. Patients, he points out, are represented by their physicians, who are expert "purchasing agents," and though the patients may lack information about the physicians, they stand to be on equal terms with the hospital.

Hansmann's point, however, holds only as long as patients have reason to trust their physicians to use their knowledge in the patient's interest. As long as patients are at an informational disadvantage vis-à-vis their physicians, they equally will be unable to determine whether their physicians have effectively and honestly represented them. And the increasingly common conflicts of interest traceable to physician investment in health care facilities and other forms of physician entrepreneurship threaten to undermine patients' general inclination simply to trust their doctors.[9]

It remains true, however, that this surmise — i.e., that in nonprofit hospitals the staff has no reason to compromise quality — is purely theo-

---

[7] Henry B. Hansmann, "The Role of Nonprofit Enterprise," *Yale Law Journal* **89**:835–898 (April 1980).

[8] James, "Comments" (On Contract Failure and Information Asymmetry), in Rose-Ackerman, op. cit., pp. 154–157.

[9] See, generally, "Physicians and Enterpreneurism in Health Care," in Gray, op.cit., Chapter 8.

retical. No important differences in quality have been demonstrated in acute-care hospitals between nonprofit and for-profit institutions. And a considered judgment on even the theoretical incentives would have to take into account certain untoward incentives for nonprofit staff. As David Easley and Maureen O'Hara point out,[10] those who cannot appropriate surplus as profit may still, theoretically, take advantage of the patient's lack of knowledge by refusing to work hard. That the public associates nonprofit status with quality and dedication is no iron-clad proof that the favorable attitude is deserved. Indeed, Clark[11] argues that nonprofit hospitals trade on this reputation and therefore — if the reputation is in fact undeserved — they are guilty of something like fraud.

Thus, no easy judgment can be made on whether nonprofit hospitals are constitutionally inclined toward maintaining quality on behalf of informationally disadvantaged patients. That they *should* do so is, as this chapter has noted, easier to affirm.

Consumer Control   A second source of assurance for patients in nonprofit institutions may be the control exerted by the patients (and other patrons) themselves. If, for example, a nonprofit women's health clinic is set up by a group of women dissatisfied with local services, and if these women stay involved in the operation of the clinic, then the clinic will be responsive to their interests. Some health maintenance organizations (HMOs) fit this model; on paper, at least, they are owned by their members and authority is officially vested in a consumer-elected council.

This sort of assurance, however, is limited. Most nonprofit hospitals are not set up, monitored, or governed by actual or prospective patients. And for-profit firms can be monitored by their more knowledgeable customers. All the same, certain groups who want to ensure the provision of some collective-consumption goods (such as institutions engaged in research or care in a particular field at a higher standard than the government is willing to support) may be able to assure satisfaction of these preferences only by supporting a nonprofit institution.[12]

Selective Recruiting   Since nonprofits of all sorts are generally dedicated to "higher" goals than financial gain, perhaps they attract staff who provide better or more considerate service. Hansmann states, for exam-

---

[10] David Easley and Maureen O'Hara, "Optimal Nonprofit Forms," in Rose-Ackerman, op.cit.

[11] Robert C. Clark, "Does the Nonprofit Form Fit the Hospital Industry?" *Harvard Law Review* 93(7):1417–1489 (May 1980).

[12] See, generally, Burton Weisbrod, *The Voluntary Nonprofit Sector*, Lexington Books, Lexington, Massachusetts, 1977.

ple, that "The nonprofit form . . . may select as managers precisely that class of individuals whose preferences are most in consonance with the fiduciary role that the organization is designed to serve . . . employees who are more interested in providing high-quality service and less interested in financial rewards than most individuals."[13]

Though this claim may seem intuitively correct, it is necessary to be specific about which individuals are involved. Physicians typically have privileges at several hospitals, some of which may be nonprofit and others for-profit or public. Who, then, are the staff who are selected for altruism by the nonprofit hospital's mission? Hospital executives are increasingly trained in graduate programs based in business schools, with no separate "corporate" and "nonprofit" tracks. Do nurses, orderlies, and other staff sort themselves out along these lines? Research showing that they do could be a powerful marketing tool for nonprofit hospitals; without such data, however, the people-sorting hypothesis remains interesting but speculative.

Historical Trajectory   The weight of history and tradition may serve to guide nonprofit hospitals toward morally appropriate goals. Voluntary hospitals were once charitable institutions dependent on philanthropy. The proprietary hospitals never had a tradition of charity, and this may continue to influence the institution's behavior even though, today, neither most nonprofit nor for-profit institutions derive significant revenues from donations. Nonprofit hospitals can exhibit the same tendency by making greater efforts to cross-subsidize, drawing on the surplus gained from treating insured patients to provide for the uninsured and for those whose treatment is not a source of profit. Similarly, the nonprofit hospital may exhibit more interest in contracts and other arrangements with governments to provide care for the poor. Of course, these are not perfect substitutes; the tax exemption for nonprofit hospitals, for example, was granted in part to encourage philanthropy and serves no similar purpose in cross-subsidization. Still, the sense of purpose remains when the redistribution is carried out in the new forms.

Why would a nonprofit hospital be inclined to continue tradition in these ways, when the wishes of donors are no longer such a factor? In some cases, the hospital may be tied to — though not necessarily financially dependent upon — a community or a religious or ethnic group that expects charitable activity to continue. And, as noted above, public

[13] Hansmann, op.cit. See also Susan Rose-Ackerman, "Introduction," for similar remarks, and an elaborate treatment of the people-sorting phenomenon by Dennis R. Young, "Entrepreneurship and the Behavior of Nonprofit Organizations: Elements of a Theory," both in Rose-Ackerman, op.cit.

expectations, developed over a long period, may constitute an operating environment the hospital must take care to respect in its policy choices. Although a process of "demythologizing" regarding nonprofits and the service ethic may be under way, as Theodore Marmor et al. claim,[14] it may not yet be complete—nor yet irreversible.

Apart from this line of reasoning, however, this "charitable" function presents a formal problem to other claims of moral superiority for nonprofit hospitals. The need to generate surplus for Robin Hood-style redistribution, to the extent that this actually occurs, provides an incentive to charge more, or to provide less, than the patient's care actually warrants. When this is done without the knowledge and consent of the patient, it undercuts the general claim that nonprofit institutions can be trusted to deliver high quality at lower cost. Though the rake-off is done for altruistic reasons, the altruism does not directly aid the paying patient who may have chosen the nonprofit hospital for its purported lack of incentives to undertreat and overcharge.

Indeed, there is no particular assurance that the surplus so achieved by altruistic managers will be used within the institution. The chief executive officer of one Catholic acute-care hospital chain, for example, disclosed that his mission was to wring every possible dollar from operations. The difference between his system and an investor-owned, for-profit chain lay only in the use (charitable, but not necessarily in health care) made by the religious order of the profits generated.[15]

Attributes Inherent in the Voluntary Hospital Form   Finally, the category of nonprofit hospitals defines certain traits, which can be counted toward a hospital's virtue. These include providing a channel for voluntarism and charity, serving as a locus and a forum for shared communal activity—particularly when community representatives sit on hospital boards—and furnishing a continuing means of affirming the community's solidarity with fellow citizens in gravest need, thus enhancing social solidarity and providing a measure of psychological security to its citizens.

The importance of these functions for a community's well-being is undoubtedly underappreciated in contemporary America. The extent to which existing voluntary facilities serve these functions, however, must

[14] Theodore Marmor, Mark Schlesinger, and Richard W. Smithy, "Nonprofit Organizations and Health Care," in Walter W. Powell (ed.), *The Nonprofit Sector: A Research Handbook*, Yale University Press, New Haven, Connecticut, 1987, pp. 221–239.

[15] This hospital system, and its public and for-profit competitors, are profiled in Jessica Townsend, "Hospitals and Their Communities: A Report on Three Case Studies, in Gray, op.cit., pp. 458–473.

not be overestimated. Though the contributions of volunteers are impressive, it remains true that many citizens never become volunteers. Similarly, most people are unaware of the governance structure of the voluntary hospitals in their communities, even when community representation is present. But these forms of participation could be encouraged, thereby enhancing this contribution of voluntary hospitals.

CONCLUSION

The voluntary hospital form presents certain intrinsic advantages. The incentive structure, the potential offerings to specific groups of patients, the potential for attracting altruistic staff, and the tradition of charity and volunteering all present certain theoretical grounds for looking to nonprofits as mainstays of a health care system.

It must be kept in mind, however, that each of these advantages is theoretical and speculative. Some of these observations are useful primarily for generating research hypotheses. The debate over the special moral character of voluntary health care institutions cannot be settled on the basis of theory alone, for observers skeptical of the nonprofits' pretensions provide theoretical arguments of their own. Several of them are noted here, along with the rejoinders available to the defenders of voluntary institutions.

Theoretical Considerations Against the Voluntaries' Claims

The skeptics' first and principal observation is that any differences that may have existed in past years are eroding as the economic environment changes. In this view, differences between the hospital types are not, and have never been, explainable purely in terms of abstract features of the hospital form. Differences between the types, when they were significant, were traceable to other features. Not-for-profit hospitals attracted philanthropy, for example, while proprietaries did not. Voluntary hospitals generally arose because of a set of public good-oriented reasons, and demand by cohesive ethnic and religious communities; while proprietaries came into being largely for other private interest-oriented reasons.

These earlier differences no longer have much effect on hospitals. Few hospitals enjoy significantly large sums from philanthropy. All rely on payments made on behalf of patients, mostly by governmental programs and private insurance. Many of the founding ethnic and religious communities are largely assimilated and no longer so cohesive. This is also true of most of the other factors that once accounted for differences in the character and conduct of health care institutions.

Today, in this view, the chief difference between nonprofit and for-profit hospitals lies in the way they raise capital. The for-profit hospitals obtain money in exchange for stock, the nonprofit hospitals exchange bonds. True, bondholders do not vote, but since institutional behavior must be geared toward meeting the expectations of future bondholders, the interests and wishes of the investor community influence hospital behavior without a direct vote. For most intents and purposes, then, voluntary and for-profit hospitals have become more or less the same kind of entity, and the role for the one must be about the same as the role given to the other.

The problem with this argument, which is historical in character, is that it is insufficiently historical. The fact that the two kinds of hospitals have become more alike does not show that they are alike in character. They may be very different kinds of entities, which happen to act alike in certain ways or in certain kinds of environments. If they are in fact different, their behavior could diverge again when and if the health care environment changes. It is entirely possible that, under the new system of prospective reimbursement and payer resistance to high prices, or in a regime of national health insurance with vouchers, or in a new system as yet unenvisioned, for-profit institutions would respond differently than voluntary hospitals to incentives and opportunities. It has happened before. Speculation on precisely how these hospital types would respond to these diverse operating environments must proceed from the observer's particular theory of these institutions' respective characters. No consensus exists on which to base a confident prediction, but that very diversity of opinion suggests that the hospital types may have distinctive capacities and interests. This in turn suggests a divergence in behavior if present trends in the health system change direction.

Thus, that same history that causes today's convergence may also be a factor that distinguishes the two types in the future. As suggested above, their historical origins and historical record condition expectations on the part of the staff, patients, and the general public, and these create an operating environment that constrains and shapes the institutions. This social definition helps to determine what sort of entity each type of hospital is, and this, in turn, generates a set of expectations of what constitutes the hospital's paradigmatic conduct or ideal. These may differ according to type. This is the point underlying the earlier claim that the biggest difference between for-profit and nonprofit hospitals is not how they *are* but how they *ought to be.*

Image and Reality Skeptics further insist that the discussion must take account not of how the hospitals present themselves, but as they really are. The popular image of the purely benevolent voluntary hospital is largely a myth, say the skeptics, and health policy must not rely on it. Thus, Clark[16] notes the hypothesis that the nonprofit hospital functions mostly for the convenience and profit of the physicians who practice in it, and that the significance of the nonprofit form lies largely in the image of selflessness it conveys to consumers.

But even if this argument were largely correct, it does not show, in itself, that no differences exist between nonprofit hospitals and their rivals. Again, different public expectations may serve as limits to what doctors can do with and in their workshops: they may be constrained by the image they have benefited from. And though physicians may have much of the effective authority over the institution in their hands, that power is shared, and may be decreasing. The aspirations and aims of the other parties may be more in keeping with the hospital's image. Finally, Clark's argument fails to take account of those differences that persist in institutional conduct. Though these may not be as impressive as earlier differences were, their significance may be considerable.

The Larger Picture   Critics of voluntary hospitals may complain that the nonprofits' advocates ignore the larger issues of health policy. According to this argument, the most important thing that must be taken into account is that inflation and overspending have necessitated a corrective approach, i.e., the competition strategy, which must be permitted to accomplish its ends. As Jones and Du Val note,[17] promoting competition and instituting other cost-containment measures may impinge on features of the health care system that have distinctive moral importance: community planning and cooperation among health care institutions; prices set not to permit price-comparison but to give institutions the freedom to pursue various public-spirited ends; and first-dollar insurance coverage. All these losses will be worthwhile, however, if cost-containment can be achieved.

Thus, according to this view, the pursuit of voluntary hospitals' public service mission was good in the previous environment, but may either be irrelevant or antithetical to today's environment. The turn to the competitive strategy is an attempt to use the strength of the invisible hand, which imparts its benefits through the self-serving acts of the players. Adam Smith urged that in dealing with others, we "address ourselves not to their humanity but to their self-love, and never talk to them of our necessities but of their advantages."[18]

[16] Clark, op.cit.

[17] Jones and Du Val, this volume.

[18] Adam Smith, The Wealth of Nations, Vol. 1, Oxford University Press, New York, 1976, p. 27; see, generally, Sheldon Wolin, "The New Public Philosophy," Democracy **1**(4):23 – 36 (October 1981).

The problem with this argument lies both in its unquestioning acceptance of the merits of the competition strategy and in the assumption that the success of that strategy not only accommodates but demands self-aggrandizing behavior on the part of health care institutions. Evidence for the latter is lacking; the weakest part of the argument for the competitive strategy is precisely in the moral aspect, particularly in regard to the fairness of the burdens imposed. The argument assumes that the cost savings achievable by competition make up for the loss of the morally important features of the system, but these are not necessarily commensurate.

Suboptimal Solutions   Finally, in attempting to undermine the claims of nonprofit hospitals to virtue skeptics remind us that responsibility for ensuring access to care, and for many other morally important elements of the health care system as well, is inherently social and is thus in the province of government rather than private institutions. In this view, any existing or even potential differences between voluntary and for-profit hospitals regarding care for the indigent, and other non-profit-maximizing practices, are beside the point. The government should address the access question directly, and if ensuring access is deemed important it should target the funds appropriately. Thus, even if nonprofit institutions are more likely to cross-subsidize and to accept indigent patients, we would do better to press for governmental action and permit the contest between voluntary and for-profit hospitals to be settled on other grounds.

This argument, however, does not address the most important question. Let us grant the point: all would be best if government, particularly the federal government, took responsibility for the problem. This does not bear on the evaluation of the extrinsic value of the nonprofit hospital unless the government actually *does* assume that responsibility. If it does not—and there is no sign of its intending to do so in the immediate future—then we must look to other solutions. If voluntary hospitals provide such an alternative, they can be valued for that. As Admiral Rickover might have advised President Carter, Why not second best—when first best is not available?

Looking at the Record

The theoretical argument for the claim that nonprofit hospitals are inherently more virtuous than their nonprofit rivals is best paired with a review of the record to date. The empirical data may be a better indicator of the character of nonprofit hospitals. Theory on this subject is still rather primitive, and no general account of the genesis and function of nonprofit institutions has gained wide acceptance.

Do voluntary hospitals deserve their largely favorable reputation? As with any institution that generates a lot of cash, there may be opportunities for nest-feathering and exploitation of patients. But according to Hansmann, even despite the lack of enforcement of the rule barring distribution of profits

> . . . abuses appear to be the exception rather than the rule . . . presumably due to adherence to social norms. . . . Indeed, such ethical constraints may be far more important than legal sanctions in causing the managers of nonprofits to adhere to their fiduciary responsibilities . . . such norms may have achieved more substantial development in some industries than others . . . in hospital care . . . predominately nonprofit for centuries in Anglo-American society, it appears that norms prohibiting profiteering have taken deep root. . . . The importance of such ethical constraints may also explain why so many nonprofit institutes . . . are affiliated with religious groups. For such an association may help to keep the norms intact and at the same time assure potential patrons that in fact they are intact.[19]

Even if we accept Hansmann's finding that the voluntary hospital records are admirable in these respects, we are not driven to the conclusion that for-profit institutions lack the moral character of their rivals. The ethical norms Hansmann posits are hypothesized, not observed directly, and are invoked to explain why those who manage voluntary hospitals have not responded to incentives to cheat and underserve. Unless we find measurable differences in behavior in these respects between voluntary and for-profit hospitals, the same kind of argument would imply that for-profit companies have an even higher dedication to ethics, for the incentives for misbehavior brought by the profit motive are, at least in theory, much greater.

This points to the need for less theoretical, and more close-to-the-data accounts of the behavior of voluntary and proprietary health care institutions. Unfortunately, these data are hard to come by. No agency has the obligation to undertake the expense involved. Few institutions like to collect and retain information that makes them look bad. The result has been that the heated debate over the ethics of nonprofit and for-profit hospitals has proceeded largely on the basis of theory and anecdote.

In hopes of reviewing all existing empirical studies, and of sponsoring new research to fill in some of the gaps, the Institute of Medicine (IOM) recently conducted a 3-year, multimillion dollar study. The advantages of the voluntary hospitals, as compared with their for-profit rivals, were

[19] Hansmann, op.cit.

partially elucidated in its report, *For Profit Enterprise in Health Care.* This report has been widely proclaimed to be neutral between the two types of hospitals, and, indeed, it recommended that federal policy neither encourage nor discourage the for-profit sector in health care. But the same report supports a much less even-handed conclusion. As seven members of the study committee (including this author) stated in an appended statement.

> In our opinion, the major finding of this report is that the investor-owned hospital chains have so far demonstrated no advantages for the public interest over their not-for-profit competitors. The report shows that on average the for-profit hospitals have been slightly less efficient, have charged payers more, and have rendered less uncompensated care to uninsured patients than not-for-profit hospitals. Their most notable capability has been their greater access to capital, which in some places may have allowed them to build or renovate needed facilities. However, the current underutilization of hospital beds, most evident among the investor-owned hospitals, suggests that easy access to capital has also encouraged overexpansion of inpatient facilities and may not always be a virtue.[20]

The IOM committee found significant, if not very impressive, national differences in levels of charity care. In states in which the concentration of for-profit hospitals was highest, and hence where there were relatively fewer nonprofit facilities to share the burden of uncompensated care, the difference between the two hospital forms in this dimension was striking. Finally, the voluntary hospitals accounted for the lion's share of teaching and research support.

The IOM report, moreover, may have missed the most important phenomena. Limitations of available data did not permit the study committee to examine the widely alleged skimming and dumping behavior imputed mostly to for-profit institutions. These practices have an immediate impact on the distribution of health care and, because they weaken the very facilities that presently do the most to alleviate inequities, threaten significant deterioration in the future.

Nor could the committee assess the long-term significance of the growing concentration of lobbying power and economic clout now being concentrated in the hands of the few largest investor-owned chains. The interests of these corporations will, in the ordinary course of things, be enhanced through the exercise of this power. It is conceivable that the chains could lobby for governmental intervention on behalf of the poor, thus alleviating the uncompensated care problem faced even

---

[20]Gray, ed., op.cit., supplementary statement, Alexander Capron et al., p. 205.

by them. But other policies they would be likely to favor might exacerbate the access problems. For example, the funding of rival hospitals might be a target, as would proposals to pool the risk posed to hospitals by service to the uninsured.

From these data it seems reasonable to conclude that, given the present avoidance of responsibility on the part of the federal government for ensuring access to health care and for ameliorating other moral failings of the current health care system, the system will be more just if the nonprofit hospitals persist; indeed, the more care provided by them and the less by the for-profit facilities, the better off the system. What matters is not the precise function of the voluntary hospital in the economic system, nor the intentions of the individuals in those institutions, but the documented fact that as a group the institutions are more likely to be part of the solution and less a part of the problem than their chief rivals, the for-profit hospitals.

VIRTUE AND THE VOLUNTARY HEALTH CARE INSTITUTION

The claim of special virtue, honored by special tax status and by public esteem, is problematical at best. Skeptics begin by challenging the very idea that health care institutions should aspire to virtue independently of the market and of government. Hospitals and related facilities aspiring to virtue face further problems in defining and calibrating virtuous character. It is an elusive concept.

Caution must be taken, too, in evaluating the claim that voluntary health care institutions are inherently superior in the relevant moral dimensions. Other nations' hospital systems, made up not of voluntary but of public hospitals, may provide most of the advantages of our voluntary-dominated system. And the most familiar grounds for asserting the inherent virtue in voluntary institutions can tend toward the a priori and speculative.

While these doubts and uncertainties must be faced in the effort to define the special mission of voluntary health care institutions, however, they do not doom that effort. In the health care system we actually have, the voluntary institutions play a vital role, serving both private charitable goals and public functions, which the government has not shouldered. Their history, ideology, habits, and reputation incline them toward virtue, even if their nature does not require it. It is thus both appropriate and necessary for the public to look to voluntary health care institutions to fulfill an independent moral role, and for the voluntary institutions to respond to these expectations.

CHAPTER 6

PROFIT AND NONPROFIT ORGANIZATIONS IN HEALTH CARE: A SOCIOLOGICAL PERSPECTIVE

Merwyn R. Greenlick, Ph.D.

You can't expect private firms to do less in pursuit of profit than the law allows.

(Richard Pratt, the former chairman of the Federal Home Loan Bank Board—
Newsweek, Nov. 10, 1986)

As recently as ten years ago, the focus of the public policy debate within the health care community was on the relative roles of government and nonprofit organizations. With the expansion of profit-making corporations into the provision of health care services, however, the debate has shifted to the relative roles of nonprofit institutions and profit-making corporations. This debate has been made most relevant by the Reagan Administration's support of "pro-competitive" proposals, an approach one commentator has attributed to a desire to deregulate the health care field and reduce federal spending for federally funded programs.[1]

Just a few years ago Dr. Arnold Relman raised this issue for the medical care community when he catalogued a set of concerns made salient by the growing influence of the "medical-industrial complex" on

[1] Philip Caper, "Competition and Health Care: A New Trojan Horse?," *New England Journal of Medicine* **306**(15):928–929(1982).

the provision of health care services in this country and abroad.[2] Relman recommended, among other things, that more attention be paid to the new health care industry, particularly to the respective roles of the profit-making and the nonprofit sectors. This chapter reviews the issue from a structural – functional perspective, with some focus on the special case of managed health care systems such as health maintenance organizations (HMOs).

The thesis presented here is that the most appropriate form of organization within the health care system is that which most effectively addresses certain specific functional needs of the system. After briefly reviewing the relationship between function and structure in specialized institutions generally, the chapter examines the functional requirements of the American health care system. These include the need to protect the patient, historically provided by the unique nature of the physician role; the need to mediate the clash between business and professional subcultures within the system; and the need to resolve the special problems involved in bureaucratizing physicians. Noting the salient characteristics of profit versus nonprofit organizations, the chapter concludes that as more health care services are delivered in complex organizations, the corporate culture that emerges within nonprofit institutions is more likely to provide these functional needs of the health care system.

SPECIALIZED INSTITUTIONS: FUNCTION AND STRUCTURE

The discussion of the respective roles of for-profit and nonprofit organizations in health care should differentiate the functional requirements of different social institutions in our society.[3] Western industrial society, is both complex and differentiated. Even in those countries that are capitalistic, the business of society is divided up among government, profit-making companies, and nonprofit organizations. Countries that are viewed as relatively socialistic also divide up their enterprise among these three organizational forms. The difference among these classes of countries is the degree, not the fact, of differentiation.

[2] Arnold S. Relman, "The New Medical-Industrial Complex," *New England Journal of Medicine* **303**(17):963 – 970(1980).

[3] Merwyn R. Greenlick, "On the Consequences of Profit-Making Organizations in Medical Care," presented at the Esselstyn Foundation conference, "New Era in Medicine," Claverack, New York, 1982; Greenlick, "The Sociological Viewpoint: On the Consequences of Profit-Making Organizations in Medical Care," in *The Investor-Related Academic Health Center and Medical Education: An Uncertain Courtship*, proceedings of the conference of American Hospital Association/American Medical Association/Association of American Medical Colleges, American Medical Association, Chicago, 1986, pp. 142 – 153.

All social systems must deal with a set of difficult problems. The more complex the social system, the more difficult the problems. New members of the society must be introduced to the culture, goods and services must be produced and distributed, and the unknown must be brought under control. Other disruptive forces—such as illness, death, and physical disruption—must be controlled or the society will fall apart. In complex social systems, such as societies, a set of specialized social institutions have evolved to deal with these societal problems. These institutions, which often compete with one another, must be intermeshed and must integrate their activities. Their form and structure evolve as the society evolves and their survival in the society depends on the consistency between their structure and their function.

The assignment of roles among the government, the profit-seeking, and the nonprofit organizations is not random within the various social institutions. The nature of the different institutional bundles and the functions these bundles perform dictate which organizational form will be most common in that specific sector of a society. Some examples will clarify this point.

Predominantly Governmental

The social system that is responsible for criminal justice is generally organized so that the most common organizational form is governmental. This area is not necessarily nor exclusively the province of government, since some aspects of the criminal justice system in the United States have been given to nonprofit organizations, and even a few to for-profit companies. Examples that come to mind are the various organizations for running halfway houses. Profit-making organizations also affect the criminal justice system in the United States, but in relatively minor ways. For example, the suppliers of police equipment have an impact on the system, but their effect is relatively insignificant compared to that of the various official governmental agencies. There is currently some move to privatize prisons, both in the United States and abroad. The most notable example in the United States is in Tennessee and there is a proposal, now being hotly debated in France, to privatize the French prison system. These activities certainly must be viewed as departures from the norm.

Governmental and Nonprofit

The social institution for the formal socialization process in our society —the education system—is characterized by both governmental and nonprofit forms. This is particularly true for secondary education, but even in primary education the nonprofit sector is a strong influence through the presence of religious and other private grade, high, and prep schools throughout the country. Private nonprofit schools are a very important element in college and graduate education. The American education system includes some proprietary schools, but for the most part they operate at the margin, usually offering trade school training. Other for-profit activity in the education field has been limited to certain experiments, such as a large demonstration project by the Westinghouse Corporation in a school district in Ohio several years ago. As in the criminal justice system, the effect of the profit-making sector has been felt more in the area of supplies and equipment.

Predominantly Nonprofit

The institutional bundle of our society that is responsible for our spiritual needs — the religious system — is almost totally dominated by the nonprofit form of organization. In the United States, unlike some other countries, the option of formal government involvement in religion has been restricted by the constitutional separation of church and state. While not constitutionally excluded from the religious system, the profit-making form of organization has not been significant in the religious system for a number of other reasons.

Predominantly Profit-making

In contrast to the above sectors of American society, the institution responsible for the production of most of the goods consumed and many of the services provided in the United States — the economic system — has been almost totally dominated by the profit-seeking form of organization. With the exception of certain producer cooperatives, almost none of the consumer goods in the United States is produced by either governmental or nonprofit organizations. This obviously is not true in other countries, and in the socialist countries almost all of the goods produced, certainly the nonfarm goods, are produced by governmentally organized enterprises.

The patterns that emerge are not random. The relative influence of the three forms of organization in each of the segments of society is a function of both the requirements of that segment and of the nature of the three forms of organization. All this is moderated, of course, by the political and ideological constraints of the culture within which the activities take place. To determine the appropriate role of the various organizational forms in the health care system, therefore, we need to examine (1) the functional requirements of the health care system, and (2) the nature of nonprofit and profit-making organizations, as well as to explore the political and ideological constraints in the culture.

FUNCTIONAL REQUIREMENTS OF THE AMERICAN HEALTH CARE SYSTEM

Background and Development

Health care systems take different forms in different societies, depending on the nature of each culture and particularly on the prevalent view of illness and its consequences in that culture. While the health care system has been of consequence in American society throughout its history, its importance has increased during this century as the system has become more successful in affecting the course of disease — probably beginning with the development of aseptic surgical techniques at the beginning of the twentieth century.

The new centrality of this system has gained recognition since World War II, as has the notion that access to health care is the right of every American citizen. Before the system actually had the ability to do positive good, little significance was attached to the organizational form that dominated the system. For example, that medical education was dominated by proprietary medical schools before the turn of the century was of little moment. Abraham Flexner's strong statement (*The Flexner Report,* 1910) against proprietary medical schools would likely have fallen on deaf ears (except among physicians hoping to limit competition) if the services of the physicians so trained were not worth worrying about. The same could be said of the fact that many of the hospitals of that day were also proprietary, or that all the worthless drugs available could be purchased without a prescription.

The health care system has become more and more central to human life, and access to it has become more important within the society. With increased acceptance of health care as a right, comes added responsibilities for providers of the service. When the notion of health care as a right swept western Europe, the response was to increase the role of government in the health care system. In the United States the response was to increase the role of the voluntary, nonprofit form of organization.

Even more critical to this discussion is a second and more basic characteristic of the health care system, namely, that the most vital interaction in this social system is the one between physicians and patients. This interaction is structured in a unique way within our culture, because of the functional requisites of the modern healing process.

Some of the characteristics of the process are so pervasive that they have become a part of the larger American culture that determines the organization of the health care subculture. Talcott Parsons, in his classic work in the early 1950s, provided the conceptual framework for this assessment.[4] He pointed out that the patient's role is characterized by relative helplessness, a lack of technical competence, and emotional disturbance. The patient is in a situation where a high level of rational judgment is difficult and is therefore particularly vulnerable to exploitation.

The physician, on the other hand, works in a situation that requires the acquisition and use of a high degree of technical competence and a basic responsibility to do everything possible to forward the complete, early, and painless recovery of the patient. The physician is required to have and use a "rational orientation." Because of the nature of disease and the state of the medical sciences, the physician is faced with a difficult situation of considerable uncertainty and ambivalence. Given this, the evolving characteristics of the physician's role have included an achievement orientation, universalistic perspective (rather than the particularistic view of the patient), functional specificity, and affective neutrality.

This institutional pattern of medical practice serves to protect the interest of individual patients and society generally in a potentially exploitive situation. The physician is unique in having access to the patient's body and to the integrity of the individual and is given access to key confidential information about the patient to hold as a privileged communication. The patient is exposed to potential physical, sexual, financial, and personal exploitation. All this is required by the nature of the healing process and is more or less freely given by the patient.

Up to now, the interest of the patient has been protected in our society by the professionalization of the medical practitioner. The socialization of the physician is totally geared to instilling the social control mechanism as an internalized component of the practicing professional. All the social control mechanisms of the profession work to create group norms to protect patients' interests, and the social pressure mechanisms work to enforce these norms. The system works relatively well in western society, considering the significant pressures medical practice puts on the situation, as long as physicians practice alone or in small social groupings and make critical decisions in an environment where the pressures are for conformity to professional norms that protect the patients.

That is not to say that the current system is without difficulties, partic-

---

[4]Talcott Parsons, *The Social System*, Free Press, New York, 1951.

ularly when the dominant form of reimbursement in the system is dependent on the fee-for-service mechanism. Since a physician's income is intertwined with the decision-making process, the conflict of interest built into this payment approach adds to the potential for the medical practitioner to exploit the patient. But the situation, while not necessarily desirable, seemed manageable when the risk was limited to an individual physician's own professional income. The situation, however, is rapidly changing.

The health care system increasingly is becoming characterized by concentrations of resources. Critical decisions are being made in situations where economic power is highly concentrated such as in the highly complex and technologically intensive academic medical centers and where the social control influence of the individual physician's professional norms is greatly weakened. More of these decisions are taking place in the context of large organizations, which also include other large hospitals, HMOs, and other organized practice settings. When this occurs—and the trend is definitely accelerating—the nature of the organization becomes a controlling factor. This consideration will be critical when we examine the relevant characteristics of profit-making and nonprofit organizations.

Conflicting Cultures

As more of the interaction of our nation's health care system takes place within organizations, the relationship between two diverse and often conflicting cultures becomes central. These are the culture of professionalism, represented particularly by physicians but also by other health care professionals, and the culture of management (or administration or "business"). Such conflict of cultures is common in other aspects of society. Consider, for example, academics in relation to administrators in colleges and universities, teachers versus administrators in our public schools, and scientists interacting with managers in many high technology enterprises.

Although the field of personal medical care is not unique in this respect, the divergence, and frequently the conflict, between the cultures of the professionals and management may well be more pervasive and influential in medical care than in any other major activity in the United States. It is informative to focus on this conflict because it is central to the way services ultimately are provided in an organization and because the manner of its resolution is ultimately defined by the corporate culture of the organization within which the conflict takes place. This analysis begins with a review of the nature of culture.

The Nature of Culture   The term "culture" is used here to designate the composite characteristics of a society, or a distinct unit within a society, that include knowledge, beliefs, morals, customs, laws, language, material facilities, attitudes, and symbols that people acquire through environmental and social influences present in the society or unit.[5]

In addition to a national culture in the United States, there are numerous smaller unit cultures, or subcultures, based on profession, occupation, and other characteristics, that tend to represent a common and often distinctive bond between members of that group, but that include significant components of the larger, national culture. In the sense in which the term is used here, different professions have their own cultures (or subcultures), as do businesses and other economic organizations, profit-oriented or nonprofit. Culture is a powerful influence on behavior, and divergences among cultures can be important sources of friction and misunderstanding.

Culture embodies not only what humans have created (material culture) but also the ways in which they have thought and behaved (nonmaterial culture), including language, knowledge, beliefs, values, rituals, and the whole array of ideas that characterize a society or distinct unit within a society. People who belong to the same cultural group are generally inclined to think of their ways as "normal" and "best." By contrast, other people's ways appear different, to some extent strange, and therefore less valid or correct. This phenomenon, referred to as ethnocentrism, appears most clearly in the case of national or ethnic groups, but in more subtle and elusive forms it is apt to be a factor in relations between persons from any two distinct subcultures.

Nonmaterial culture is divided into cognitive features, which include knowledge and beliefs, and normative features, which include values and expectations. The cognitive component of culture includes those elements that are testable, including elements that have not been properly tested and are therefore of questionable validity, and beliefs, including conceptions and ideas that are untestable, but which, nonetheless, may be important determinants of behavior.

The normative aspect of culture includes values and abstract standards that tend to persist over time and identify right and proper behavior in that culture. Significant values in the culture of medicine include commitment to the best interests of the patient, confidentiality of patient communications, and professional autonomy and responsibility on the

[5] Robert Perrucci et al. *Sociology: Basic Structures and Processes,* William C. Brown Company, Dubuque, Iowa, 1977.

part of the physician. Related values in the management or administration culture include orientation toward organizational goals, acceptance of less autonomy, and a place within an organizational structure.

The normative structure includes the rules guiding the behavior of the individuals involved. These rules, called norms, define what is proscribed and what is prescribed in society. Norms carry with them appropriate "sanctions" or rewards for following the norms, and penalties for violating them. The definition of the professional role is carried within the normative structure of our larger culture.

One significant characteristic of culture is the persistence of values, norms, and ideas over time, although often with more or less gradual changes. The process of socialization transmits culture from one generation to the next in the larger culture, or through successive classes in a business school or medical school, or successive management generations in a complex organization such as a hospital or an HMO. Thus, the process of medical education is the major vehicle transmitting and maintaining the culture of the medical profession. But, within an organization, the creation and management of the culture is the responsibility of the board of directors or trustees and top management.

Points of Conflict   Conflict between physicians and managers in an organization can be expected because of the very different cultures from which they come. Understanding the underlying strain is required before the consequences of the struggle and its mediation can be assessed. The important aspects of the medical culture are imbued in the physician as a part of the socialization process that takes place during medical education. While greater attention is given to the cognitive elements of medicine in medical school, the transmission of the remainder of the subculture has been well documented. The rigor of the medical education leads physicians to remember the acquisition of medical "knowledge." For example, long after they have become committed to medical management, physician managers tend to prize their continued ability to use their medical skills. Because of the centrality of healing in all societies, the ability to heal is significantly rewarded, and physicians tend to value the cognitive elements of their culture over the cognitive elements of the administrative culture.

It can be argued that the management culture does not include an analogous set of cognitive elements. The knowledge of managers consists of a set of tools that can be applied to management problems (such as management by objective, strategic planning, zero-based budgeting), specific information about the particular organizations which they have managed, and a wealth of practical experience with the management process.

The normative structure of the two cultures is significantly different as well, and this difference accentuates the potential conflict between physicians and managers. The normative pattern of the medical culture (which derives essentially from the fee-for-service world) includes both the role definition for the physician and a set of values to which physicians are socialized to subscribe. We have already touched upon the relevant specifications of the physician's role in this situation — namely, those developed by Talcott Parsons and validated by a body of systematic research. The physician works in a situation that requires the acquisition and use of a high degree of technical competence and a basic responsibility to do everything possible to forward the complete, early, and painless recovery of each individual patient.

The management role, on the other hand, derives from the specific requirements of the organization within which the manager works. The responsibilities and rewards of the management role derive from the specific formal procedures of the organization and are defined for each management job by the particular organization. The objectives of the organization define the role of the manager, and the values of business tend to reinforce the appropriateness of this relationship.

The values of managers tend to include a positive attitude toward authority figures, competitive motivation, power motivation, and a positive attitude toward a differentiated role and administrative responsibility. Studies confirm this tendency and point out that business students and managers have positive attitudes toward leadership: being in charge of other people, having authority over others, or being in a position of leadership or power.[6]

Finally, the two subcultures feature a completely different set of symbols. These symbols tend to create greater distance between the members of the diverse cultures. The use of medical culture symbols on the part of physician managers within an organized medical care program are readily observable. For example, physicians tend to wear white coats, even while serving in medical management roles. It is common to see a stethoscope hanging out of the pockets of physicians in meetings. The walls of medical managers tend to be covered with certificates and diplomas, a practice much less common among business managers. This practice derives from the requirement that individual physicians display their certification, because no one organization certifies the credentials

[6]Geert Hofstede, "Businessmen and Business School Faculty: A Comparison of Value Systems," *The Journal of Management Studies* **15**(1):77–87(1978).

of all individuals in the fee-for-service, private practice world. Managers, on the other hand, are certified by their very appointment to office by their organizations.

The symbols of managers tend to be those defined as valuable by the particular organization, and usually related to external symbols of office, rather than intrinsic symbols such as white coats and stethoscopes. The differential symbols of different organizational management roles have to do with the size, nature, and furnishings of the physical office where the manager spends the day and within which organizational business is transacted. This varies according to the culture of the particular organization, but participants of each organization can generally gauge the level of different managers by the size, location, or furnishings of each office or by the symbols displayed in the office.

These differences in subculture between physicians and managers must be mediated—or at least better understood—if the health care system is to function successfully. It can be argued that nonprofit organizations can better develop a corporate culture for mediating this difference, and that nonprofit organizations do so in a manner that provides not only an effective system, but also the safeguards that patients need when they receive their health services in large, complex health care institutions.

Bureaucratizing Professionals

Several assumptions underlie the general proposition that health care services can be rationalized, but the central assumption is that the work of professionals can be successfully bureaucratized. In introducing a paper published in 1961, Mary Goss reviewed the sociological opinion on this proposition.[7] She discussed whether the hierarchical principle formulated by Max Weber can be applied, without significant modification, to the formal organization of professionals. She pointed out that this concept had been considered problematic by many sociologists and reviewed the literature concerning the potential of the bureaucratic organization of professionals.

Goss reported an empirical study of a medical bureaucracy that described how the physicians were formally organized, and she analyzed the types of supervisory control that were institutionalized among the physicians. Physicians working in the medical bureaucracy (or complex organization) under study recognized and distinguished between two

[7]Mary E. W. Goss, "Influence and Authority Among Physicians in an Outpatient Clinic," *American Sociological Review* **26**(1):39–50(1961).

major types of supervisory prerogatives, the right to make decisions and the right to give advice. Goss reported, in other words, that physicians appeared to come to grips with the conflict between their need for freedom to make professional decisions according to their own trained judgments, and the administrative needs of a complex organization.

In the organizations Goss studied, the culture left a great deal of room for differentiating between the professional culture and the management culture. In the 1960s the large health care organizations were either medically dominated or had an organizational culture that provided for a split in the decision-making process, with professionals making the medical decisions and nonprofessional managers making other decisions. Apparent strain between the need for individual authority required for professional work and the administrative needs of an organization were thus mediated. The physicians did not perceive the need to be autonomous in every sphere of activity, only in areas of professional decision making. Goss concluded that when both supervisor and supervised are physicians, the control-oriented behavior of each is largely predetermined by established professional norms and values that each knows and accepts in advance.

Goss further pointed out that professional obligations take precedent over administrative decisions in the minds of physicians. But in areas perceived as administrative, physicians grant those in charge the right to make decisions affecting their action, a right they do not concede in the realm of patient care. While physicians appear to be able to separate these spheres in their own minds, almost every administrative decision affects successful functioning of a medical bureaucracy in one way or another. In fact, Goss asserted that the physicians draw the line in their own minds on a decision-by-decision basis, essentially by process of elimination.

Certain types of decisions seem to fall more clearly in the administrative realm, while others seem more clearly to fit in the professional realm. Many decisions, however, have very complex manifest or latent ramifications for both spheres. For example, the issue of hospital utilization is one with obvious consequences for both the professional and the administrative spheres, but serious consequences also follow from the resolution of such issues as the hours of work expected per professional, the time of operation of facilities, and the method of allocation of various professional resources within the organization. Yet another example is the development of quality assurance programs. Potentially conflicting decisions spread across the full range of operation of medical organizations, and the question of how a decision-making line is drawn within an organization is central to determining that organization's ability to be successful in meeting the functional requirements of the health care system. But the major point is that, presumbably, the line is drawn in significantly different places by professionals in different organizations, and even by different professionals in the same organization. And it is the organizational culture that defines where that line is drawn and how the conflict that underlies this decision is mediated.

The prepaid group practice illustrates this point. A critical aspect of patient care and of administrative involvement in an HMO, particularly a group practice HMO, is the question of control over the utilization of scarce and expensive economic resources, such as hospital beds. Physicians believe that the individual decision to discharge a specific patient from the hospital at a specific time falls almost entirely within the realm of the professional decision-making authority of the physician. The process by which professional norms for hospital discharge are established has been jealously guarded by physicians. On the other hand, the use of hospital beds is extremely expensive and the success of prepaid group practice HMOs depends on the establishment of professional norms for hospital utilization that result in lower hospital utilization patterns relative to other forms of medical care. To have a successful group practice, therefore, the established norms must result in a utilization pattern that may be somewhat deviant from the pattern in the remainder of the community. The process through which this deviant pattern is developed depends to a large extent on the leadership qualities of the physicians directing the group practice system.

Amitai Etzioni has reviewed the question of dual leadership in complex organizations.[8] Etzioni focused on the concept of leadership in complex organizations and synthesized the work of those investigating organizational effectiveness in complex organizations. Since power in complex organizations is generally institutionalized, Etzioni considered the question of positional power versus personal power and pointed out that a critical question for effectiveness in organization is the relationship between leadership power and organizational power.

Etzioni also suggested that while the two kinds of leadership might be provided by a single actor — the so-called "great man" — they generally tend not to be found in the same person because the psychological characteristics that modern leadership requires are rare. Further, such leadership requires the same person to engage in opposing patterns of social behavior: to be assertive and supportive simultaneously. And yet the great man style of leadership still may be required in complex profes-

---

[8] Amitai Etzioni, "Dual Leadership in Complex Organizations," *American Sociological Review* **30**(5):688–698(1965).

sional organizations as a matter of organizational genetics, particularly in the early stages of organizations. Because administrative and professional decisions in medical organizations are integrally related, organizational effectiveness in the medical side of many HMOs might indeed depend on the ability of a single leader to supply both influence and authority in blending social and task leadership. This, of course, must be stated as a hypothesis, since data on both leadership style and on the effectiveness of professional organizations are rather sparse.

One can, however, speculate on the functional requisites of effective professional bureaucratization. The operation of a successful group practice involves constant mediation establishing normative patterns consistent with the organizational objectives of a complex organization. An equilibrium must be established between the effectiveness of the system, which requires meeting sets of medical goals (guarded by the professional interests), and the efficiency of the system, which requires meeting sets of economic goals (guarded by the administrative interests).

The question of how to establish this equilibrium and how to integrate physicians into the modern health care institution, while at the same time representing the interests of patients and society, can be addressed by looking at the nature of the different organizational forms and by examining how these forms affect the probability that certain character- istics will be developed within the organizational culture. Specifically, we need to inquire what characteristics for-profit and nonprofit organiza- tions have in common, and where they diverge.

ORGANIZATIONAL FORMS: PROFIT/NONPROFIT

Misconceptions

Before examining which type of organization is more likely to meet the functional requirements of the health care system, we would do well to acknowledge the dominant political biases influencing the current de- bate and to dispel some misconceptions.

The functional requirements framing this discussion can be viewed from numerous perspectives, including economic and sociological. The dominant political perspective in the 1980s seems to suggest that the country would be better off if most functions in society were returned to their rightful place, the free market. This representation is only slightly facetious. The free marketeers appear to be running the show, and the ghost of Adam Smith sits smugly (perhaps uneasily, if I read The Wealth of Nations correctly) at the discursive banquet. Their argument is the simple notion that the world is best served by strengthening the marketplace for all goods and services, and by allowing the collective wisdom of consumers and producers to plan, organize, and operate most segments of society.

While some elegant arguments have been advanced on behalf of the free-market approach, others point out the inadequacies of the market-place for distributing the highly personal health care services. Relman touched on this point in discussing the medical-industrial complex, and Milton and John Roemer provided an excellent overview in a 1982 article in the *International Journal of Health Services*.[9] The Roemers point out, as have other authors before them,[10] that several characteristics make the medical care field particularly inappropriate for traditional market approaches. These observers have shown that the five necessary conditions for the achievement of a balanced market structure are inoperable in the health care market. These conditions are (1) many buyers and sellers freely interacting, (2) no substantial economies of scale, (3) low transaction costs, (4) adequate information on the part of buyers, and (5) the absence of significant externalities. Without recapitulating these arguments here, suffice it to say that there is no basis to assume that the personal health services market is anything like the classic efficient market.

The Roemers use this platform to argue for replacing free trade in the health care field with systematic social planning in order to achieve a health care system that allocates resources and distributes services both efficiently and equitably—an argument aimed at moving the public policy debate back somewhat to the left. Accepting this argument, however, is not necessary for the question at hand: what are the appropriate relative roles of nonprofit and profit-making organizations? Other grounds suggest that increased involvement in health care by profit-making organizations can be quite dysfunctional.

Before examining those grounds, however, we need to dispose of a couple of red herrings. One is that profit-making organizations are inherently more efficient than nonprofit organizations. If efficiency is defined as the ability to produce a unit of a given output for a measured unit of input, not a shred of evidence suggests that the simple nature of profit-making influences efficiency.

Certainly, profit-making organizations in the health care field produce

[9]Milton I. Roemer and John E. Roemer, "The Social Consequences of Free Trade in Health Care: A Public Health Response to Orthodox Economics," *International Journal of Health Services* **12**(1):111–129(1982).

[10]Eli Ginzberg, in H. E. Klarman (ed.), *Empirical Studies in Health Economics: Proceedings of the Second Conference on the Economics of Health Care*, Johns Hopkins University Press, Baltimore (1970), pp. 161–164; Merwyn R. Greenlick, "The Scope and Bound of Health Economics and Medical Economics," *Israel Journal of Medical Sciences* **10**(1–2):81–85(1974).

different units of output than do nonprofit organizations in similar situations. These different units may be less costly than the units of production of the nonprofit organization. But that situation does not represent greater efficiency.

In this era, all forms of productive enterprise in the health care segment of society are characterized by professional management. This management is hired by boards of directors that in turn represent the owners, in profit-making organizations, and society (or a large societal group), in nonprofit institutions. The professional managers manage as well as they know how in each situation and report to their boards about the results. The recently completed study of the Institute of Medicine, *For-Profit Enterprise in Health Care*, validated this point. This study found no evidence that for-profit institutions were in any way more efficient that nonprofit ones.[11] The study specifically reported that

> The rise in investor ownership of hospitals has increased health care costs to payers under both the original cost-based reimbursement approaches used by Medicare and some other third-party payers and the charge-based reimbursement methods still used by a large number of third-party payers.[12]

A second red herring is that since nonprofit organizations can (or must) produce a surplus of revenues over expenses in given years, they are the same as profit-making organizations. This is patent nonsense. Any organization in the health care system, or for that matter in any other field, must balance revenues and expenses over time in order to survive. Furthermore, if the organization is a capital-intensive one, such as a hospital or facility-based HMO, then it must produce earned surpluses at various times in its life in order to produce and replace the capital stock it needs to serve its clients. The profit-making organization must do this and must, in addition, produce a profit for distribution to its shareholders. This balancing of revenues and expenses does not make a profit-making organization out of a nonprofit one.

In fact, a critical problem with the current profit-making institutions in the health care field is that they appear not to be focused on producing a reasonable amount of revenue greater than their expenses. Rather, their focus seems to be on manipulating their equity position. Consider for example, the following statement by Fred Wasserman, chairman and CEO of Maxicare Health Plans, Inc., from an interview in *Hospitals:*

> ...the stockholders of Maxicare are mostly very large institutions. There's less

---

[11] Institute of Medicine, Bradford Gray, ed., *For-Profit Enterprises in Health Care*, National Academy Press, Washington, D.C., 1986.
[12] Ibid., p. 185.

than 80 institutions that own about 80 percent of all Maxicare stock. They're not enthusiastic about seeing a Maxicare stock price at 14.[13]

In order to understand what really does make a difference in the nature of the organization, we need to examine what qualities go into creating a successful organizational culture.

Successful Organizations

The solution to the above problems — the diversity of the two subcultures and the special difficulties of bureaucratizing physicians in a complex organization — is greatly assisted by the creation of a corporate culture that provides the structure and process required for the successful operation of the program. At the same time this culture must produce a normative structure that can protect the interests of the patients as the power of the professional normative structure is diminished. There has begun to be a particular interest in investigating the cultures that have developed in successful business organizations and in assessing the extent to which the strong cultures that have emerged in the more successful enterprises have contributed to the successes of those organizations.

Deal and Kennedy have examined the process of corporate culture.[14] They point to very strong cultures as significant contributors to the success of such companies as GE, DuPont, Tandem, National Cash Register, and IBM. Deal and Kennedy define business culture in the same terms used above for medicine, including descriptions of the cognitive elements, value systems, beliefs, and the signs and symbols of the corporations. They point out, incidentally, that heroes are a particularly important type of organizational symbol, a point that relates dramatically to the need for charismatic leaders in certain stages of the development of all organizations.

Reviewing the nature of the cultures that have developed and the functional requirements for the success of each of the organizations indicates that the cultures of the successful organizations are quite different from one another, but that each is particularly apposite for dealing with the special problems faced by each company. The success of the existing large nonprofit staff and group model HMOs can be attributed in part to the development of a corporate culture that enhances the ability of the organization to deal with its most central problems.

---

[13] Fred Wasserman, interview, *Hospitals* **60**(22):84–86(1986).
[14] T. E. Deal and A. A. Kennedy, *Corporate Culture: The Rites and Rituals of Corporate Life*, Addison-Wesley Publishing Co., Boston, 1981.

In order to understand the possible consequences of the decision-making process within managed health care systems, we need to examine how the clash between the cultures of medicine and business can be worked out with regard to the critical questions involved in the organization and equitable delivery of personal health care services. The success of the voluntary health care institution requires continued attention to the development and management of the corporate culture and, especially, to the three sets of problems discussed above: the diverse nature of the business and medical cultures, the special problems of managing physicians in a complex organization, and the need to instill a normative structure that provides the necessary social control to protect the interests of the patients.

The stronger the corporate culture, the more the clash of the diverse cultures can be mediated. The development of a new shared set of norms, joint knowledge base, and language can foster the necessary cohesion between the professionals and managers. When business managers and physician managers speak the same language, internalize the same set of norms, express the same values and beliefs, and make their shared culture obvious at important organizational moments, the divisive effects of their different background cultures can be reduced. This process, known as acculturation, is the same process by which immigrants come to accept — and be accepted in — the new culture in which they have chosen to live.

An example of this shared culture can be found in the dual management perspective embedded in the culture of the Kaiser Permanente HMO system. A basic concept is that the management power is shared between a physician manager and a manager from the health plan or hospital side of the organization at every key level of the program. Around this partnership form of management, which has become a key component of the culture of Kaiser Permanente, a normative structure has developed. Symbols, language, and a complex belief system based on this structure now define the behavior of individuals within the system.

Significant Differences

The creation and management of the corporate culture is the business —perhaps the main business — of management, and the nature of the organization makes a significant difference on the content of the culture and how the culture is managed. If the organization is profit-making, the board is elected to represent the owners of the organization. The board transmits the concept that the function of management is to produce profits or at least to increase the equity value of the organization. This is not necessarily to be translated as an order to maximize profits in the short run, because profit-making organizations do not generally maximize short-term profit. But management must definitely make decisions based on the profit potential of the organization. A great deal of evidence suggests that profit-making organizations in the health care field do respond to this orientation.[15]

On the other hand, the boards of nonprofit corporations, particularly charitable nonprofit organizations, are formed to serve or otherwise represent the interests of society at large, or at least some significant position of society. They convey the message that the organization has a much broader range of social interests than producing returns on owners' investments. For example, among the purposes of charitable nonprofit organizations are the relief of poverty, advancement of education, advancement of religion, promotion of health, and other purposes beneficial to the community. The set of constraints placed upon management within this much broader set of goals is very different and produces both a very different milieu and very different types of outcomes.

This different milieu has important consequences.[16] Several studies, for example, document the different case mixes in nonprofit and profit-making hospitals. These differences are real and significant, but perhaps the most important difference is the social control in *pro bono publico* organizations. The environment exists within which the rights and interests of individuals, communities, and society at large can be assessed and protected. Critical decisions that affect patients and communities need not be made within the context of promoting the interests of stockholders. The public interest is much more salient.

Medical care has multiple goals, some of which are excellence, equity, and efficiency. The profit motive may disproportionately emphasize the third at the expense of the first two. This is particularly a potential problem in the case of the profit-making HMO, where the intersection between organization and professional medical practice is so much at issue in everyday decisions. Many technical processes that contribute to quality at the margin are not efficient. If resources are not allocated for a function because the allocation could affect the "bottom-line" (and hence reduce the stock price, which impairs raising new equity for expansion), quality may suffer.

[15] G. Stevenson, "Laws of Motion in the For-Profit Health Industry: A Theory and Three Examples," *International Journal of Health Services* **8**(2):235–256(1978).

[16] W. A. Rushing, "Profit and Nonprofit Orientations and the Differentiations-Coordination Hypothesis for Organizations: A Study of Small General Hospitals," *American Sociological Review* **41**:676–691(August 1976).

For example, reports are emerging from apparently successful for-profit IPA model HMOs that physicians are dismissed from the HMO if their utilization profile exceeds a preset limit, regardless of the quality of their medical practice. Similar reports are coming from for-profit hospital chains regarding staff physicians who do not produce "sufficient" business volume for the hospital. These cultural elements are much less likely to develop in a nonprofit organization, where the board of trustees espouses quality of care objectives as a matter of social value.

On the issue of equity, the deleterious effect of the profit-making HMO can be even more pronounced. Under profit-making constraints the culture reinforces the desirability of avoiding actuarial "bad-risks." Groups could be split by perceived risk, leaving uninsurable residues. Those groups with subnormal payment mechanisms or no adequate entitlement could be avoided by profit-making organizations. It would be very difficult to increase profits predictably if risks were truly mutualized. These attitudes, if they prevailed, could distort the social purpose of the health care system.

The critical decision nexus in an HMO is the competing interest between physician concerns (for their individual patients and for their own self-interest) and the concerns of larger societal groups, such as overall HMO memberships or the community generally. The balancing of these interests and of the relative power positions that affect decision-making is most problematic. Physicians have their professional responsibility to individual patients, a responsibility that is not always easy to discharge in a complex organized setting. Individual patient interests are not the same as the interests of the overall population. This produces conflict that can be best mediated within the context of a culture defined within a social purpose. An example of this problem comes again from the issue of controlling hospital utilization. Often, individual patients could benefit, on a social level, from an extra day or two in the hospital or from a social admission to a home care program. The overall population, paying for those admissions through premiums, is benefited from the application of an explicit set of criteria for hospital discharge or home care admission that limits utilization to that which is medically required.

Decision-making is very difficult in an HMO, as in other complex health care institutions, and the decision-making process is not always clear and explicit. Consequently, the decisions produced are not always perfect. In fact, remembering California's early Medi-Cal disaster, one can easily point to some clear-cut cases where the nonprofit form specifically was used for exploitation. The point is that when the decision-making process is complex, and when a social purpose culture is not strongly enforced, the public's interest can easily get lost. When stockholder interest is formally thrust into the situation in the medical care segment of society, there is great reason to believe the public interest, by definition, suffers significantly.

Whether, in practice, the public interest actually influences decision-making within a specific nonprofit organization is, of course, a separate question and one that depends in part on the values of those in leadership positions and in part on the ability to communicate those values throughout the organization. The question that concerns us here is which type of organization is inherently more likely to do this.

The impact of boards of directors or trustees can be seen to be relatively limited in most organizations. But where they really affect the management is in the questions they ask and in the information they seek. When board members understand that they represent a broader constituency than just the stockholders of a corporation, they tend to ask different questions and to lead the managers to work within a different normative structure. While they are required by their role to keep an eye on business elements of the organization, they are also required to keep an eye on the social function — the "mission." They need, by the nature of their responsibility, to add ingredients into the culture that provide the social leavening. And the management of any organization responds, to a greater or lesser degree, to the directions provided by its board. It then becomes top management's responsibility to transmit the "cultural imperatives" down through the levels of their organization.

CONCLUSION: THERE IS A DIFFERENCE

All of this suggests that, from a social perspective, profit-making organizations do not possess the appropriate characteristics required for the social control function in the health care system. This is so mainly because the decision-making mechanism in profit-making organizations is inherently at cross purposes with the unique characteristics of the health care segment of society — namely, the unusual and personal nature of the physician – patient relationship and the centrality of health and disease to individuals and to society.

Nonprofit organizations, on the other hand, do seem to possess — at least potentially — the social control mechanisms required to protect individual patients and society. This is especially true as more of the critical personal health care decisions are made in complex institutions and organized medical practice settings. Moreover, the success of the nonprofit approach in such organizations as Kaiser Permanente is prima facie evidence of the ability of nonprofit organizations to mediate the conflict between the two subcultures of professionals and managers and to bureaucratize professionals with a minimum of friction.

These conclusions, of course, deserve further scrutiny as the debate on this important public policy issue continues. The critical point is that any discussion of the relative roles of profit-seeking and nonprofit organizations must include careful attention to the functional requirements of the health care system discussed in this chapter. Finally, the exclusion of governmental organizations from this discussion was not meant to suggest that the federal role in this debate is inconsequential, but only to acknowledge a political reality in which public support for an expanded governmental role in the provision of personal health services has only just begun to reemerge. Given the cyclical nature of public policy debates, the pendulum may very well swing back toward new demands for more governmental solutions to the problems of organizing and delivering health care with excellence, equity, and efficiency.

ACKNOWLEDGMENTS

The author gratefully acknowledges the valuable suggestions of Donald Freeborn, Sara Lamb, and Clyde Pope at critical times in the development of this work. Martie Sucec's editorial assistance in the early versions of the document was extremely useful. The editorial efforts of Gary Miranda exceeded the usual contributions of a technical editor in the last two drafts of the work. Gary's insightful suggestions on form, order, and content significantly improved the finished product. Thanks to all.

CHAPTER 7

HOSPITAL STRATEGY AND PUBLIC POLICY: SEEKING THE "JUST RIGHT" BALANCE

James J. McCormack, Ph.D., M.P.H.

AN IDENTITY CRISIS

Contemporary literature on management defines the business environment with a fresh analytic framework. It calls upon organizations to analyze internal and external factors to assess present and future strengths, weaknesses, threats, and opportunities with respect to the production of goods and services in a competitive environment. Managers are exhorted to assess key factors in the external world, to forecast the relevance of historic forces and the direction of salient new trends and to identify those that have the greatest significance in assuring the future survival and well-being of their organizations.[1]

In this new approach to business planning, public, legislative, regulatory, and judicial policy are explicitly recognized as powerful environmental forces. Policy making in the governmental arena is greatly affected by the values and beliefs of elected and appointed officials. The clearly ideological assumptions of the current administration in Washington and the relatively vigorous policy debates of the 1980s have shaped

---

[1] David Muller "Planning, Strategic Managerial," in Lester R. Bittel and Jackson E. Ramsey (eds.), *Handbook for Professional Managers*, McGraw-Hill, New York, 1985, pp. 684–689.

a different value context for policy-making than was the case throughout the 1960s and early 1970s.

There is a long history in America of participation by private groups in public decisions. The American political decision-making process often has been described as one that produces outcomes or policies from a vortex of contentious interaction between private parties and public officials. Specific matters of policy are of interest mostly to those directly affected, and historically, these persons have been most active in shaping decisions.

Policy struggles occur however, within the constraints of broad principles or values that limit the extent of change and impart a recognizable American character to domestic public policy. Robert Morris has described five norms that shape the overall direction and continuity of social policy in the United States: (1) preference for private marketplace decision-making; (2) belief in government aid to the weak and helpless; (3) continued belief in the saving virtue of work; (4) continued optimistic view of progress through science; and (5) preference for shared responsibility.[2] The relative influence of these values on public policy varies over time, as the priority accorded each changes with the ideological emphasis of current elected leaders.

The contemporary environment is replete with assertions that two of these values should be emphasized to achieve efficient and economic results in public policy, i.e., private market decision-making and shared responsibility. The latter principle underlies a nostalgic wish to return to simpler times when local government and the family carried responsibility for the weak and helpless, and the former supports a variety of attempts to reduce the scope and functioning of government while extolling the virtues of private organization and market mechanisms over public structures and government programs.

How to Cope

The preference for private market-oriented solutions to meet social needs has emerged as an environmental force of unusual significance for hospitals and other health care institutions. This long-standing societal norm has arisen with fresh vigor and pointed relevance for hospital management and health care policy in the United States.[3] In this context,

---

[2] Robert Morris, *Social Policy of the American Welfare State*, 2d ed., Longman, New York, 1985.

[3] Geoffrey R. Weller and Pronal Manga, "The Push for Reprivatization of Health Care Services in Canada, Britain, and the United States," *Journal of Health Politics, Policy, and Law* **8**(3):495–517.

the growth of investor-owned health care enterprises was celebrated by much of the political, academic, business, and popular press in recent years. This public applause of private entrepreneurship in health care was accompanied by fervent statements about how investor-responsive organizations would be delivering the best product for the lowest possible price.

The hospital industry, comprised mainly of nonprofit, voluntary hospitals, appears to have reacted to this new ideological climate and associated realities in a twofold manner. On the one hand, hospitals have seen in the reaffirmation of this value the likelihood of less interference from governmental planning constraints and enhancement of a climate for growth and expansion. On the other hand, the apparent concomitant public judgment that market solutions should favor proprietary investor-owned entities was perceived as a threat to the dominance — and even survival — of the nonprofit hospital.

In retrospect, while the new strategic approach to planning was sweeping through American business during the 1970s it seems that it also was being absorbed by scattered voluntary hospitals, some allied together in the rapidly growing multihospital systems. This new approach seemed superbly suited for some voluntary hospitals as they began to think about how to respond to the aggressive activities of expanding for-profit hospital companies and shifting assumptions governing the direction of national health policy. Hospitals became quite conscious of their auspice identity as debate on Medicare reimbursement policies was conducted amid increasing media attention to the stock market performance of publicly held hospital companies. Voluntary hospitals, with a history of seeking after businesslike behavior, were encouraged again to learn from private companies and to imitate further their structure and behavior.

Does Form Really Matter?

Debate has heated up on the question of whether and to what extent there should be differences in the regulatory and reimbursement treatment of for-profit and nonprofit hospitals. Sharp questions are raised as to whether auspice is important in predicting hospital performance in terms of quality, efficiency, and provision of community care. Efforts to demonstrate superior efficiency or effectiveness of one form over the other mostly have concluded with statements of no difference.[4] On the

[4] Bradford H. Gray and Walter F. McNerney, "Special Report: For Profit Enterprise in Health Care," *New England Journal of Medicine* **314**(23):1523–1528(1986).

question of relationship between organizational form and the provision of free care, it seems that some of such care is delivered by all hospitals, at least to the extent it must and can be provided under local economic, social, and political conditions.[5] However, government and voluntary hospitals, more often than for-profit institutions, are likely to be located in areas where access for poor and lower income people is convenient, and the free-care burden concommitantly higher.

The national environment of hospitals is characterized by rapidly accelerating change. Initially viewed as regional or state phenomena, a wide array of trends have become an interrelated set of diverse challenges for hospitals across the nation, including

• declining admissions and lengths of stay
• medical advances which lead to removal of procedures from inpatient settings
• rising malpractice insurance costs
• increased pressure from insurers and businesses on cost and utilization controls
• state regulatory programs for rate control and subsidies for the uninsured
• public policy action to minimize outlays for public programs, without regard to secondary effects on the location, organization, financing, or supply of health care and hospital services.

To cope with these trends, many voluntary hospitals have plunged into commercially oriented strategic planning behavior and have responded aggressively to exhortatory rhetoric on the virtues of competitiveness. They now identify their "preferred markets," refer to the need for "competitive intelligence," and talk of actions desirable to establish a "sustainable advantage" in various types of service or "product lines."

Hospital behaviors that derive logically from use of the business strategic-planning model have resulted in unexpected confusion and hostility. Questions are raised by public officials concerning the "rightness" of these actions by nonprofit, tax-exempt organizations. The experience of Intermountain Health Care, Inc. in Utah may be seen in this light.[6] Businessmen who perceive nonprofit hospitals as competing with them have complained that voluntary hospitals should come under increasing public scrutiny, as perceptions grow that their behavior reflects more

---

[5]Toby Citrin, "Trustees at the Focal Point," *New England Journal of Medicine* **313**(19):1223–1226(1985).

[6]See report in Law section, American Hospital Association, *Hospitals*, April 5, 1987, p.66.

concern for revenue generation than for community service.[7] Trustee concerns about obligations inherent in tax-exempt status have been identified,[8,9] and hospitals are accused of commercialism and asked to defend their actions in light of the special privileges traditionally granted to nonprofit entities.

Today voluntary hospitals are challenged to clarify their identity and to declare their intentions for the future. The commercial behavior of many voluntary hospitals is a new concern in public policy. There is even ambivalence among some nonprofit managers about the desirability of maintaining the nonprofit status altogether. Both without and within the voluntary health care institutions there are many who are ready for a reconsideration of the very idea of the voluntary institution and exploration of its essential identity. This chapter examines this question, points to commercialism as a principal threat to continued maintenance of voluntary health care institutions and offers some advice about hospital and public behavior in an effort to enable the voluntary institution to reflect its nature even in these changing times.

THE VOLUNTARY ORGANIZATION

The history of the nonprofit form as applied to hospitals and other health care institutions has its roots in the social traditions of the Middle Ages in Europe, when distinctions between government and church were less clear than today, and when the assignment of private means to meet public needs was common. This history parallels, in part, the history of social welfare as a societal institution.[10] From these medieval roots came the nonprofit voluntary structure of the modern day hospital. It was a time when government and the church were the principal structures beyond the family to meet personal health and welfare needs. Modern economic interpretations of the rationale for the nonprofit form appear narrow and somewhat suspect in the broader context of the history of the hospital and its organizational antecedents.[11] While such interpreta-

[7]M. M. Dana, "Businessmen Protest Hospital Competition," *The Knickerbocker News*, Schenectady, New York, July 1, 1986.

[8]Catholic Health Association of the United States, "No Room in the Marketplace: Health Care of the Poor," Final Report of the Catholic Health Association, Task Force on Health Care of the Poor, CHA, St. Louis, Missouri, April 1986.

[9]Walter Trattner, *A History of Social Welfare*, 3d ed. The Free Press, New York, 1984.

[10]In this regard, see Rosemary Stevens, "A Poor Sort of Memory: Voluntary Hospitals and Government Before the Depression," in *Milbank Memorial Fund Quarterly*, "Health in Society," **60**(4):551–584(1982).

[11]Dennis R. Young, *If Not For Profit—For What?* Lexington Books, D. C. Heath Co., Lexington, Massachusetts, 1983, pp. 13–15.

tions are interesting and assist in economic analysis of contemporary events, they contribute little to an understanding of the real meaning of the organizational form itself. There well may be more to the essential character and original purpose of hospitals than such analysis can fully account for.

In narrow legal and financial terms, a voluntary nonprofit entity is defined by the nondistribution constraint: it may not distribute earnings to those who govern it. While this defines a nonprofit organization it does not explain the origin and purpose of the organizational form. Another view of the voluntary health care institution focuses upon the decision to associate of individuals who come together to pool their knowledge or activities with a goal other than the sharing of profits. Such participation is explained by a desire for self-expression and to influence events affecting the community. The origin, then, of nonprofit entities is in response to a call to perceived duty. Social scientists see participation in voluntary associations as demanding time, loyalty, and activity, the latter tending over time to assume an obligatory dimension.[12] This social enterprise view of the voluntary organizational form represents the reality of the voluntary hospital. The essence of a nonprofit voluntary structure is not to be found in its tax exemption, but in the essential characteristic of responding to the duty to serve. This is the rationale for the privileged position this form has been granted in our society.

In the Northeast, nonprofit hospitals were often organized jointly by persons in and out of government.[13] In other parts of the United States, religious groups provided the initiative, and in still other areas, civic minded persons chose the nonprofit form in establishing hospitals. The apparent motive in this history of organization creation was nonobligatory joining together of individuals to accomplish a communal good. In all these instances a choice was made to assume a responsibility, not for the risks of a commercial concern, but for acts of service. These positive acts of service can be seen as defining the essential character of nonprofit voluntary hospitals in the United States.

The conscious act to fulfill the needs of others is the foundation of the voluntary health care institution — its essence and rationale for existence. That this is a simple and unselfish idea should not obscure the uncomplicated reality. Out of shared feelings of responsibility for community members, in a long line of decisions going back in time to seventeenth century America, the nonprofit form has been chosen by

---

[12] Albert Meister, in John C. Ross (ed., trans.), *Participation, Associations, Development, and Change*, Transaction Books, New Brunswick, New Jersey, 1984.
[13] See Stevens, p. 568.

founding trustees to meet the needs of those requiring protection and care.

While the nonprofit, voluntary organizational form for hospitals and other health care organizations has been predominant in this country for two centuries, the for-profit form has coexisted for many decades, though more recently with distinctive regional concentrations in the South and Far West.

Some observers suggest that recent market share growth of for-profit hospital chains will slow because of changing public and business practices in payment arrangements for hospital services, and because of defensive planning, management, and political strategies by voluntary hospitals. As the early dramatic earnings fade into history, some believe that investor dollars, once attracted to hospital companies, will move toward other opportunities in health care, or elsewhere.

Since the media has drawn such attention to proprietary health care companies, many opinion leaders and policy makers have become preoccupied with them. The long-term importance of this peculiar fascination with for-profit hospitals in this decade, lies not in the market performance of such companies, but in the potential effect that this small group of organizations may have on the thinking of such leaders and hence, public policy.

Disquieting questions may be raised: will public officials, mesmerized by the societal norm of market preference and a public mood for minimalist government, be drawn to the view that auspice is of little consequence in hospital service? Will social commentators be attracted to analyses which argue that continuance of the tax exemption of the nonprofit voluntary institutions must be justified solely by the failure of proprietary businesses to satisfy a market demand?

Bob Sigmond has expressed concern that voluntary hospital leaders, influenced by the perceived "spectacular success at doing well" by the for-profit institutions, will concentrate their efforts too much toward that end also and not give sufficient attention to "doing good."[14] Reconsideration of the historic identity and motives behind voluntary hospitals may help to shape discussion of their basic rationale. Beyond that is the matter of how the internal and external forces have left many of these hospitals so vulnerable to criticism.

SEEKING THE "JUST RIGHT" BALANCE

All organizations, including hospitals, react to external and internal pressures and adapt to changing conditions as best they can without losing

[14]Robert Sigmond, "A Community Perspective on Hospital Ownership," *Frontiers of Health Services Management* **1**(1):33–39(1984).

sight of their purpose. Government policy for payments to hospitals has been traditional in the United States since colonial days. At different times in different localities, arrangements shifted from direct lump sum subsidies to discrete payments for services to individuals eligible for various public programs, and hospitals adapted to these changes. This adaptation has been virtually continuous, as government seems endlessly fascinated with inventing new means to continue a centuries-old partnership. Rosemary Stevens has observed that by the 1920s, the community hospital had ceased in many respects to be a charity and had become much like a business. She points out that before 1900, voluntary hospitals were public service institutions (generally receiving a lump sum appropriation from state or local government or both), but that after 1900, hospitals were being perceived as private nonprofit entities with which government might contract. This period saw a gradual shift to formal agreements for per diem payment and contractual arrangements specifying expectations and conditions of performance.

There also has been continuous change in other aspects of hospital operations. Medical education has changed, as has medical practice, and with it the type and variety of equipment, facilities, and supporting personnel required for the care of patients. Community expectations have changed as well, and many hospitals have adapted to them to one degree or another. Indeed for many hospitals, especially those in large urban centers, their service communities have changed. They now serve and respond to populations that differ in one way or another from the populations in whose service they were originally established.

Through the decades of change and adaptation, popular notions of the broader society always have had some influence on the behavior of hospitals, since the hospital must adapt to changing circumstances to survive. However, the critical question is always whether the adaptation can be accomplished without altering the purpose or the essence of the institution.

The ultimate test of the appropriateness of adaptive actions by the voluntary hospital to changing circumstances is assessment of the extent to which such actions are congruent with the essence of its identity: to act in service of the community. Application of such a test may be simple or quite complex depending on specification of the concepts of service and community. Whenever each of these is simple, unambiguous, and without contradiction, then judgment may be rendered with ease and confidence. Unfortunately, these conditions are not often found in the everyday world.

While there may be broad agreement that a choice to serve is the distinguishing characteristic of the nonprofit hospital it may reasonably be asked if it is appropriate to expect pursuit of this pledge to be so honored as to risk the survival of the institution. Obviously, some practical notion of moderation must be applied, since the voluntary hospital cannot be expected to act as a dutiful servant at the price of its own existence. The hospital is thus obliged to avoid excessive zeal in service and to adapt its actions to a middle ground expending energy and resources to do good while at the same time conserving capacity for doing good in the future or for other beneficiaries. A state of tension between resource expenditure and conservation is thus established as the natural order in the existence and behavior of nonprofit hospital and other health care organizations. In a revised test, then, the hospital must serve, not to a level of prodigality; and conserve, but not to the extent of indifference or miserliness.

With the service essence, and the tension between giving and holding viewed as crucial to an understanding of the nature of the voluntary hospital, then adaptive actions in search of "just right" plans and policies will often be regarded negatively by the various parties in any community who have interests in what hospitals decide. Among the hospital's constituencies there will be differences of opinion about what should be done or not done and when. Given variation in communities and in hospital resources, there probably cannot be a universally precise measure of the point of this "just right" balance.[15] However, holding out this explicit *intent* and demonstrating evidence, search for such is wise behavior for nonprofit hospitals who hold themselves out as serving their communities.

THE THREAT OF COMMERCIALISM

Initiation of new services and diversification beyond acute care into nursing homes, hospices, ambulatory surgery, home care, and other activities, have become common features of nonprofit hospitals looking for ways to meet community needs. More recently, nonprofit hospitals have sought to structure entrepreneurial commercial enterprises as new organizational means for conducting some of these activities. This has disturbed many observers, not because an entrepreneurial spirit is unfamiliar among nonprofit enterprises, but because the nature of commerce is so different from the traditions of voluntary health care and the ethic of

---

[15] For this notion of a just right balance, a debt is owed Abraham Edel, *Aristotle and His Philosophy*, University of North Carolina Press, Chapel Hill, 1982; especially Part 5 "The Theory of Practice," pp. 247–317.

service. Entrepreneurial behavior that is commercial in intent is now attractive to many voluntary hospitals and has become the source of a potentially damaging threat.

Commercialism means pursuit of the sale of goods and service to those willing to purchase them, and has little to do with any duty to meet the needs of others. The sale of goods is not really concerned with assumptions about needs or requirements for health care, but about demand, and the fact that people often will buy what can be sold to them. The emphasis shifts easily from need to want and thence to creating desires for purchase techniques of marketing and advertising.

The pursuit of businesslike behavior by nonprofit institutions of all kinds is a long-standing tradition in the culture of voluntary organizations in the United States. Hospitals by their size, complexity, and employee work force are highly visible in the mainstream of this trend. In past times, it was widely applauded; of late there has been criticism. Today, hospital concern for increased efficiency and economy has been transformed to a concern for increasing net revenue, and businesslike behavior has been transformed into behaving like a business; the latter cannot fairly be viewed as exactly similar to the former.

Among some hospital trustees, managers, and public officials, there is a growing discomfort that thoughtless introduction of ideas and techniques from the commercial sector will lead to excessive acquisitiveness by nonprofit hospitals. Many question the appropriateness of ideas and practices that appear suitable in the world of commerce but not in settings devoted to service and charity. Will there emerge a conflict of ideologies in administering the hospital organization? Can the separate corporate cultures of charity and commerce coexist in a single unified structure? If so, will not one have to be subordinate to the other? Will structural safeguards and programs of corporate socialization to original mission suffice to retain focus on the essential motive of service to the community? Is the current attractiveness of commercial proposals for revenue-raising of long-term significance or will this tactic result only in marginal benefits and be discarded in favor of a return to community fund appeals and other traditional efforts? Will the commercial flirtations strengthen the hand of those wishing to limit or remove tax exemption for voluntary organizations?

Behind these questions lies concern about a fundamental incompatibility of ends between the commercial and voluntary sectors of society. Two questions may be derived from this concern. Is the ultimate effect of commercial ideas and practices to cultivate attitudes of self-orientation rather than other-oriented cooperative attitudes? Is the effect to heighten a concern with private interest over social justice? To the extent that the answers to these two questions lead away from cooperative institutional attitudes and toward enhancement of private interests, there must be conflict between commercialism and the nature of the voluntary institution.

Some Feelings of Discomfort

In much of the country, nonprofit voluntary hospitals do not face competition from investor-owned hospitals. Tactics adopted from the competitive models of commerce are employed in a context that includes only other voluntary and public institutions. Nonprofit voluntary hospitals, of course, have some history of competition in relation to each other, but the new commercial ideology and changed business environment have created an entirely new quality of competitiveness. A condition of declining demand and utilization of acute care services now prevails. Hospitals compete with each other for physicians and for the patients they admit or refer for special services. Hospitals are developing new and different services, sometimes in competition with nonhospital voluntary or proprietary entities. For many hospital leaders, this more intense competitiveness is conducted with some discomfort on the question of the effect it must have on maintaining a pattern of behavior true to the central value of service to the community.

The commercial model induces a hospital to transform its essential character from duty and service to autonomy and financial return. Concern for the private interest of the hospital and those of its business network then succeeds concern for the community, whose needs led to the very existence of the hospital. These uneasy feelings may well be appropriate, for when the secondary economic attributes of the hospital become the principal concerns for policy-making, a fundamental change in the definition and character of voluntary hospitals occurs.

The Effect on Planning

To illustrate what it means to value private interest over social justice, let us ask how a city with several voluntary hospitals proceeds to reduce hospital capacity as inpatient demand falls. Will the busiest hospital in the "market" take a position that strengthens its own individual circumstances? Or, will that hospital's position reflect a decision process designed to seek the most socially responsible outcome? Will not an individual institution's decision in this situation reveal the extent to which commercialism and market-guided decision making alters the character of that voluntary hospital?

Stevens notes that early in this century, with the growing expectation by hospitals that public payment for poor patients ought to be available, a certain modification of the historic voluntary ideal occurred.[16] The previous close visible link between voluntary hospitals and local and state government began to blur in the 1920s, and by the 1930s, the hospitals were entering into a market-oriented environment.[17] While hospitals have been in a market-oriented environment for some time, particular attention must be accorded the intensity and pervasiveness of competitive ideology in the 1980s. The level of explicit discussion and widespread approbation of competitive management and marketing found today in hospital leadership circles is unprecedented. Evidence of the transformation of voluntary hospitals to mirror the structure and behavior of American business is now observed in all parts of the country, and in hospitals of nearly every size and character.

Hospitals have become fascinated by planning and management designs based on the notion of strategic business units (SBUs), and the specification of such units in terms of their relations with submarkets and with similar units under the control of rivals. Managers talk now of lines of business (LOBs) which are identified as "stars" or "dogs," or something in between. Such categorization schemes classify services of the hospital in terms of their significance to financial outcomes.

Never has there been more attractiveness, glamour, and color accorded the tools and artifacts of business planing than we can now find in hospitals as they seek new principles to guide their responses to changing circumstances. The fundamental principles behind these new planning tools are market-oriented, and they are specific to the assessment of performance by measures of short-run financial return. Furthermore, all of them assume a relatively hostile competitive environment within which operations must be conducted. Use of planning techniques based on these principles should cause grave concern for their effect on the integrity of voluntary hospitals who employ them without caution and moderation. Careless employment of these techniques will have potentially negative impacts on perspective, motivation, and mission of voluntary health care institutions. In the long run, they may not benefit the community all that much, either.

[16] See Stevens, p. 568.
[17] Rosemary A. Stevens, "Voluntary and Governmental Activity," *Health Matrix* **3**(1):26–31 (Spring 1985).

Fragile Status

These adaptive behaviors of the hospital have confused its several publics: citizens, patients, health professionals, financial supporters, and governmental leaders; for the voluntary institution is obliged to seek the "just right" balance between service and caring, which is their purpose, and the conservation of resources, which is their survival.

Several observers have pointed to this commercial behavior by voluntary hospitals as the origin of difficulties many have with public officials about reconciling hospitals' stated fidelity to a service mission with the underlying exchange relationship between voluntary institutions and government. This exchange relationship, of course, is the basis of voluntary hospitals' privileged position in the social and legal framework.[18] The perception is spreading that voluntary hospitals have responded to the opportunity — or threat — arising from the apparent success of their commercial cousins by seeking to imitate them. In response, many have urged that the community has a legitimate right, and arguably a responsibility, to question the appropriate discharge of the hospitals' service role, and civil authorities have called hospital leadership to task on the question of acting as "community service organizations" or becoming "competitive business entities."

The contemporary question is a simple one: will focus on "means" interfere with pursuit of purpose? Recognition of the need for a harmonious balance may be absent in some hospitals as they clamor to respond to pressures of the day or get caught up in the commercial ethos accompanying the use of competitive models and business techniques.

Rededicating the Hospital to Traditional Obligations

As hospitals identify and plan new activities, explicit reasons for these actions must be examined. As the means of revenue production is practiced, it easily, though not naturally, may become an end. With the potential for revenue-generation to succeed community service as a goal, an important element of the delicate balance which characterizes the special position of the voluntary hospital may disappear. An institutional decision-making process to link the contributions of new activities to unmet needs of the community may be required to protect the achievement of a "just right" balance between the twin obligations of service and survival.

[18] See Edel, Part 5, p. 181.

Expectations of appropriate behavior for voluntary hospitals should be reasserted and clearly communicated to counter the weight of negative viewpoints regarding current motives, interests, and intents of modern voluntary hospitals. Trustees, medical staff, and administrators ought to consider initiating formal processes within their institutions to discuss the extent to which their new planning efforts have compromised attention to the service mission.[19] The service mission should be considered with reference both to patients of the hospital and to the population or area from which these patients come. In addition to these two reference points, the several obligations of the hospital to internal constituents — employees, physicians, and trustees — must be examined. This process of dialogue and choice regarding appropriate behavior for the voluntary hospital should be anchored by the tests suggested earlier, to cultivate cooperative institutional attitudes over self-orientation, and to advance a concern for social justice over private interest.

An important issue is the concept of shared institutional moral responsibility: Who holds the greatest share of responsibility for keeping the hospital true to the service mission? In the corporate form it would seem to be the trustees. They are led or aided in this responsibility by their senior administrative staff. They are enabled in this task by their medical and other professional associates to whom they have accorded access to the resources under their governance. While a general restatement of the mission of the voluntary hospital would be of assistance in the contemporary environment, more specific statements are also needed to specify desirable institutional behavior.

Six areas of behavior are central to the rededication of voluntary health care institutions to their promise to perform community service: (1) raising revenue for charitable purposes; (2) sponsoring professional education and training; (3) providing service for the poor; (4) being responsive to community needs; (5) strengthening community integration; and (6) participating public policy.

Revenues and Charity

There exists today a complex array of public payments to hospitals, including direct grants, contracts for specific purposes, and payments for service to eligible individuals. In the case of voluntary hospitals, these payments are, each and all of them, payments into the revenue stream of charities, not businesses.

---

[19]Robert Stenrod, "Corporate Strategies for Catholic Hospitals," *Health Progress*, pp. 30–34 (June 1985).

Over the last two decades the introduction of payment schemes that pay only specified elements of all costs, after taking account of other hospital revenues, has reduced hospital incentives to raise charitable gifts as regular income. Payment practices of this type have weakened the identity and ability of hospitals for presenting themselves to the public for charitable contributions. The idea of the voluntary hospital as a community institution dependent upon, maintained by, and responsive to the community, is in peril.

It should be expected of hospitals that they organize and vigorously pursue fund-raising efforts to permit them to undertake necessary but difficult and financially unrewarding programs of service. A related expectation is that voluntary hospitals will clearly explain their process for allocating funds to community service projects.

Hospital behavior in fund-rasing — as well as in generating revenues from Medicare, Medicaid, insurance, and "other income" sources — should be carefully reviewed in the public policy arena. Perhaps some form of revenue protection could be offered hospitals in exchange for explicit reporting on both fund-raising and disbursement activities. An important element of such a public dialogue would be a mutual statement of assumptions and criteria regarding the role of the hospital as a community service institution.

The practice of raising revenue for charitable purposes by charging higher rates for those who can afford them, to subsidize care to others less well off, has a long tradition and should not be abandoned without careful scrutiny. Also, the operation of some voluntary enterprises according to the principles of commerce is not unusual. Hospitals and other voluntary health care agencies should be comfortable with strategies that build upon this history. However, difficulty arises when there is no internal system to defend against potential conflicts between service and revenue generation. Revenue generation from commercial enterprises is not wholly inappropriate to the role of the hospital. However, a balance must be struck on when to press a competitive advantage and when to refrain from an action in the interest of the institution's essential identity — that is, in recognition of its obligations as well as its opportunities.

Given the general financial and market circumstances of many voluntary institutions, it is questionable if they should expect substantial funds from commercial efforts. If the infusion of funds will be minor relative to other sources, then some effort by hospital leadership to dampen the rhetorical excitement and preoccupation with this topic in the media and trade press could be beneficial. Issues of more immediate relevance to the long-term financial stability and progress of institutions might then receive more attention. Interested audiences might focus on questions of health care delivery from the perspective of "persons to be served" rather than the current "savings for large payers" viewpoint often used now as the criterion of what ought to be desirable policy for the future of voluntary hospitals.

Professional Education and Training

Medical professionals learn the traditional arts and new techniques of health care in the hospital — where the action takes place. Medical schools and other schools for health professionals rely on hospitals as settings for imparting practice skills, and the voluntary hospital, especially, is a historic partner of these schools. However, the hospitals have always faced the task of balancing care with training. The education and training role also has required of the hospital a search for a "just right" balance, this time between patient rights to competent care and the maintenance and extension of a supply of skilled professionals.

Partially hidden behind the recent cloud of promotional rhetoric and the growing commercial aura in health care is the need for continuance of the expensive and unprofitable function of professional training. Financial support for this activity often has been submerged within patient care accounting and subsidized through that income stream. However, questions are asked, in an increasingly strident tone, about the isolation of such costs and possible relief from them for third-party payers. An alternative is sought to shift these expenses from health to education cost centers and to find "education" sources to support them. Separation of these costs from health expenditure accounts, however, would not alter the fundamental need for integration of their function within service delivery settings.

Accounting efforts might be directed toward identifying education and training costs to explain and rationalize subsidies for this activity on an equitable basis. However, allowing certain payers, who benefit from the hospital, to avoid their share of these costs would reflect a short-sighted social policy toward stability in the supply of health care practitioners. This is not to defend maintenance of training programs that are poorly run or of inadequate quality or size. It is to argue that short-term responses to immediate fiscal pressures, acceptable for commercial enterprises in adapting to changing market circumstances, are not behaviors desired of permanent institutions whose contract with the community includes long-term resource maintenance through periods both good and bad. Medicare, Medicaid, and all health insurers should shoulder their share of support for training health professionals.

Serving the Poor

The earliest understanding of the hospital was as a place of service and rest for poor, disabled, and vulnerable persons. The voluntary hospital in the United States is identified with a tradition of last resort and final refuge. This remains prominent today, as serving the poor continues as the most symbolic and sensitive test of whether a voluntary hospital is meeting its obligation to the society that granted its special charter.

Service to the poor requires care for individuals unable to pay. Voluntary hospitals must admit, at the least, to a duty to fulfill this promise of service arising from their nonprofit status. However, simple service to the poor, by itself, is a weak and minimalist response, not in the deep charitable tradition of hospital voluntarism.

An aggressive and robust dynamism in serving groups in need characterized our voluntary hospitals in the past, and that history should be renewed and used to challenge today's too-common tendency toward a guarded commitment for poor and undesirable groups: the uninsured, the chronically mentally ill, victims of diseases such as AIDS, and other groups not deemed "suitable" targets for today's strategies of marketing for short-term financial performance.

The record of voluntary hospitals on the whole, still shows a continuing commitment to serve people unable to pay. Charity care is still a prominent feature of voluntary hospital behavior, but there is reason for concern that the new commercial criteria of success will divert resources from the charitable aspects of the hospital mission.

The Catholic Health Association (CHA) recently suggested to its members that specific attention be given to the poor in their annual budget and program planning. They propose that official hospital plans and budgets include objectives for care of the poor and that explicit mechanisms be established for processing free or reduced fee care. Members of CHA were exhorted also to make care of the poor a permanent item on their public policy agendas at both the state and federal levels.[20]

Responsiveness to Community Needs

The premise of commerce is that goods and services are to be sold in a marketplace where all parties communicate their individual wishes to sell and to purchase — at a price. The result is an alternating rhythm of demand and supply. The market place organizes itself to match the

[20]Catholic Health Association of the United States, op.cit.

different innumerable demands of a consumer public. But in contrast to these private wants and wishes, there are recognized common human needs for which every community of people must provide. Over time, communities establish minimum acceptable standards in various aspects of life, housing, income, health care, that are to be available to all of its members, as a common expectation or right of entitlement. Such standards may change as the circumstances of the community change, but all societies define such common human needs to be met through some mutual effort. The satisfaction of such distinguishable minimum requirements is assumed by community institutions both governmental and nongovernmental. They endure their own complicated environment often without the comfort of a predictable alternating rhythm. Needs of persons and groups are perceived and met by hospitals often without the presence of a willing buyer or payer.

While occupying uncertain places in commerce, notions of public need and social justice are in comfortable surroundings in the tradition of voluntary health care institutions. Ideas of fulfilling a basic standard of adequacy in provisions to treat illness and disease are at the root of the origin of voluntary health care, warmed by impulses of decency, human caring, and public protection on the part of persons closely associated with both elected government and community leadership.

The market organizes its producing capacity to fulfill wants and desires, whereas nonmarket institutions organize their producing capacity on a different basis — at least that has been the historical assumption. However, at this time, nonprofit institutions, organized to fulfill community needs, are being distracted toward satisfying solely private preferences. Such behavior does not strengthen confidence in their future recognition of a more public-regarding ordering of their priorities. Responsiveness to community needs is difficult for institutions not truly committed to value public interests above private. And, for those seeking some balance among the many demands of modern administrative life, it is easy to fall into political outcomes instead of facing the hard decisions often required to address community needs.

It is sometimes convenient to confuse politically acceptable decisions with community responsiveness, especially where hospitals are not encouraged to distinguish private interest constituencies from community and public interest. The community interest or need is that which is most likely to affect more rather than fewer persons; more rather than fewer hospitals; more rather than fewer alternatives of different type and style; and to admit to more rather than fewer serious conflicts with preferences of small private groups in the hospital network.

Assuming specific responsibility for serving unpopular people with unpopular problems is one example of being responsive to need. The mission requirement of service is often pro-active in such instances. Should not the expectation be that the voluntary institution look for opportunities to be of service as a community institution focused upon producing public, not private, benefits?

Responsiveness to community may motivate some hospitals to reject competition as unnatural and to act in concert with others to specify and address local needs. If voluntary health care organizations do not respond to AIDS, drug addiction, or teen pregnancy, for example, just what institution is expected to do so? These are not marketing questions, they are issues of responsiveness to every-day realities in countless American localities. Hospitals should again adopt a perspective that is community wide rather than institution specific; identifying groups that are un-served, leading the public dialogue about local health service require-ments, and acting in the tradition of service, not commerce. Expecting that only one local hospital will perform this role while others act within the commercial guidelines of the marketplace would be unfair. All volun-tary hospitals should be expected to be responsive and to work in some shared arena about individual roles to be undertaken to meet needs. Community responsiveness cannot be seen as a sole requirement for government hospitals, or programs, especially in the current environ-ment. The exchange relationship underlying the status of nonprofit health care organizations demands that public hospital responsibility be balanced by attention and initiative from the voluntary sector.

Community Integration

In earlier and easier times, organized philanthropic efforts served to integrate and coordinate the intentions of local hospitals through assur-ance of support for capital fund raising. This integrating force is barely present today, as business philanthropy plays a much smaller role in hospital capital financing. Community fund drives no longer function as a force to encourage voluntary integration by hospitals. Even the public health planning apparatus of the country, once intended to provide an integrative impetus, is weakened to the point of virtual nonexistence, and perhaps was never properly structured for such an effort.

Once, hospitals were expected to work together for a community, now they are not. Integrative behavior, such as actions that bring hospi-tals together to strengthen each other, to enhance and develop each other as parts of a unified whole fabric of people and things to cure illness and protect community health, now depends solely on institutional hospital leadership — for no other source of influence is present to do this task.

The current atmosphere of unbridled self-realization and economic Darwinism has supplanted an earlier focus on integrative strategies to achieve a health care system ideal of adequacy, equity, and equality. Competitiveness is not recognized as a counter to the ideal of community integration; and yet it is close to a full ideological triumph in the hospital world. An accelerating commercial evolution encourages isolated specific behaviors that obscure common interests and possibilities for joint endeavor, and justifies and glorifies individualism and competitive behavior *for its own sake* — not because of any discernible outcome of superior effectiveness or efficiency in curing illness, protecting health or serving *all* of the community.

Hospital leaders who continue to specify in their mission statements a set of behaviors that focus on community service and integration should speak clearly and often of their institutions' present and future plans and programs: about all of the why's, how's, when's and by whom to be paid for — inviting public dialogue on the contribution their approach makes to interests in the community at large, as well as to those of their internal constituencies, patients, physicians, and employees.

Public Policy Participation

Hospital and other voluntary health care organizations are well informed of public policy proposals that affect them. Public policy issues of high interest include the availability of financial and professional resources, and the definition of what is acceptable quality of care. The hospital public policy agenda seems increasingly to be self-oriented and to have protection of the institution as the primary goal.

Hospitals are organized for their disparate self-interest in an ever-expanding number of national and state groups dedicated to representing viewpoints through lenses of increasing specificity — public, proprietary, voluntary, religious affiliated, medical center, community, multi-institutional, independent, or serving only the uninsured and poor. Each separate group contains many members of other groups; hospitals will be members of several if an institutional characteristic matches the narrow condition used as the distinguishing mark of their special interest, obligation, or purpose.

The effect of much of this associational effort may be implicit approval for setting aside definitions of need and service in favor of studies of market segments for solicitation of desires, wants, and preferences in setting the future course of hospitals. Without cohesiveness, decisions will be made, not on standards of "need," but on the basis of success in achieving a "sustainable advantage over the competition" for a specific hospital, and public policy will be encouraged that will permit each hospital's institutional vision to be pursued without the traditional concern for how these separate futures might combine in any given locality to assure that health needs of all in the community are met.

Hard Times and Hard Choices

This self-oriented public policy strikes at the core of the voluntary–government relationship underlying the special status of voluntary health care institutions. The "social contract" of collaboration implicit in the historic subsidies to the voluntary sector would be torn asunder if commercial behavior were fully adopted by voluntary institutions.

Will the voluntary hospital lose its birthright as it becomes a commercial enterprise? Cannot a more thoughtful position on, the middle ground, be articulated as the better public policy approach? Hospitals could work to initiate anew the old dialogue with government to restate their special position, but do they want to do so? Have the expectations and rewards for those who control hospital policy developments been so closely modeled on the commercial sector that the current direction is impossible to reverse without bitter internal conflict?

A separate inquiry about public policy participation of hospitals and other health institutions concerns their interest and support for programs that extend the accessibility of services to those who cannot pay or are otherwise unserved. Do voluntary hospitals care any longer about the poor in their communities? Has net revenue supplanted service as the yardstick of accomplishment for administrators and trustees? Are the public hospitals to be the only choice for the truly poor? While it may seem to some that these questions are of only rhetorical relevance, they are more than that. Not all community hospitals have been comfortable with past notions of service to unpopular and disadvantaged groups. Not always and everywhere is there local support for care of these unserved groups.

Hard times are normal circumstances for institutions that serve substantial numbers of poor and uninsured people. Elected officials must be exhorted, cajoled, and often shamed into supporting adequate care and protection for the poor and disadvantaged. Public authorities should be encouraged to expect all hospitals to share in caring for the unserved in each community. Hospital activism for public funds to care for the poor is consistent with the history and essential nature of institutions actively committed to the duty and obligation of service. Service requires existence and public officials must expect to help sustain the hospital. This expectation should be used in forging a political view of the mutual nature of the voluntary – public alliance to care for health needs through the mechanism of the community hospital. The most credible voice to renew the dialogues on how best to refresh and adapt this old arrangement to current circumstances must be the hospital trustees, with their very singular characteristic of service by voluntary commitment.

Credibility depends heavily on actions, and the hospital community should take the initiative in public policy debates by clear and repeated enunciation of their good deeds and of their support for public policies, which extend access to care. Often, the local government is responsible for persons most in need, but not eligible for organized payment programs, and many issues affecting care of the poorest are squarely before local officials. Fostering a mutual dialogue and link with local officials may be a too infrequently traveled route to more equitable sharing of responsibility for the care of the disadvantaged.

Within the public policy framework are embedded unspoken — and perhaps forgotten — understandings of what communities are supposed to receive in exchange for granting tax exemptions and other subsidies to voluntary institutions. A revitalized participation by hospitals in public policy must include efforts to engage officials on the practical aspects of this historical relationship in contemporary circumstances. The unspoken understandings or misunderstandings should be unearthed, dusted off, and examined in light of present hospital and local circumstances and the common ground between voluntarism and government ought to be rediscovered.

AT THE CROSSROADS OR BEYOND?

Adoption of business strategic planning in the voluntary health care services field has contributed to the separation of institutions from each other and the communities they were originally established to serve. Service, to all too many voluntary institutions, has lost its meaning, and the notion of community of interest has given way to a concept of corporate survival. In many cases, the traditional view that charitable nonprofit corporations were meant to cooperate to help build community togetherness and common resources for confronting local human needs, has been lost. As voluntary institutions behave more as businesses, their self-description as community service institutions becomes less and less credible.

As government has adopted mechanisms for payment of voluntary social and health care agencies that are similar to arrangements with commercial enterprises, the historical clarity of mutual interest and shared objectives between charitable institutions and government has become clouded. Behavior by hospitals and governments in the most recent decade has created a commercial environment for hospital operations—an environment that now threatens the continued existence of the voluntary community hospital.

Across most of the United States, community-oriented planning to determine the amount and character of necessary institutional health services is no longer viable. A policy of survival of the most competitive has become normal. The service essence of voluntary organizations is endangered by the new environment, and it may be that the special exchange relationship with the community that is the rationale for the privileged position of the voluntary institution in public policy will be dissolved. Expectations of hospitals by government officials and of government by hospital trustees and administrators are confused and in need of orderly examination.

A crisis of values has arisen for hospitals and other voluntary health care institutions. The guiding principles of the voluntary institution must be restated, and the behavioral meaning of these values must be redefined. Expectations for voluntary institutions in these times ought to be discussed widely by trustees, administrators, physicians, employers, insurance organizations, public officials, and local citizens. The social contract between localities and these organizations requires clarification on all sides. Who is to do what for whom in exchange for what?

Six areas of policy making were identified in this chapter for reexamination. It was proposed that hospitals be expected to plan and initiate programs to raise charitable funds. Further, government policy should be restructured to encourage such activity and to ensure that hospitals engage the community on the subject of mission and goals.

The role of the hospital and other voluntary institutions in training health care professionals should be reaffirmed, and a collaborative process with the professions and government should be established to accomplish their different goals in renewing the supply of skilled personnel. Financing this training should continue to involve payments by third-party sources to assure skilled care for future beneficiaries and patients.

Action to care for the poor must become a legitimate character test for all voluntary hospitals. But, this cannot be the only test. There is a lot more to community service than just charity care. The now absent and forgotten expectation that hospitals will not needlessly duplicate expensive medical capability requires reconsideration. Competition within the market has supplanted system integration as an object of trustee attention. Trustees should revisit their history, and their common sense, and seek to rededicate their institutions to goals of cooperation and collaboration with the other hospitals and medical staffs of their communities. Some process of interinstitutional planning must be returned to health policy decision making in local communities. A view of health care resources as a unified system to serve the whole group is not a strange idea for a service supported through a combination of tax dollars and virtually compulsory occupational welfare benefits.

Responsiveness to community needs requires that trustees, employers, government, media, and local citizens come together to reject the mantle of commercialism for their voluntary service institutions. Needs of the general population, and of subgroups within, were once the focus of decision making by hospital leaders. Responding to market demand has pushed aside interest in responding to needs. Only when hospitals act in concert can an ideal of community integration be pursued. This ideal holds that as a population works together to solve one mutual need, it learns the skills to confront others and grows into something greater than its separate subparts. Competitiveness as a motivating ideology is inappropriate to the historical tradition, philosophical subtlety, and practical complexity of the uniquely American interpretation of the voluntary health care organization. Rededication of the voluntary hospital must mean reexamination of the meaning of equality, equity, and adequacy of health care service in local communities. Competitiveness as a concept is an insufficient principle for organizing a just health care system, and unnecessary for most of the behavior integral to achieving such a goal.

Accomplishing a modern reinterpretation of the voluntary health care institution should occur in a partnership among government, trustees, physicians, other health professionals, employers, and insurers. This has been — and can be — a unique hallmark of the voluntary health care institution.

8

WHAT DISTINGUISHES THE VOLUNTARY HOSPITAL IN AN INCREASINGLY COMMERCIAL HEALTH CARE ENVIRONMENT?*

Stanley B. Jones
Merlin K. Du Val, M.D.

PROFOUND ADJUSTMENTS

Twenty years ago, the American public supported federal Medicare and Medicaid programs to assure that all citizens would have reasonable access to the same class of quality health care at a cost each could afford to pay. The nation did not realize that as it worked to make care afford-able to the individual, it would create a health care system that neither government nor private industry could afford. But this has, in fact, been the case. The 1970s saw intense federal and state activity to control these rising costs through regulation. After almost a decade of effort, the failure of the regulatory approach is more and more widely acknowledged.

The causes of these high costs of medical care are complex. The lessons have yet to be fully learned. More and more argue, however, that three steps taken by society seem to have contributed greatly. First, public debate and promises converted a human aspiration for unlimited effort to cure disease into an expectation of unlimited health care for

---

*This chapter was adapted from a paper prepared by the authors for the American Healthcare Institute, with the collaboration of Dan Zwick and Health Policy Alternatives, Inc. Beyond the articles cited, input and ideas for the chapter were provided by interviews with executives in the American Healthcare System and other experts on voluntary hospitals in the United States.

each individual. Second, through public and private insurance we insulated the individual from directly paying the full cost for the services received. Third, we paid institutional providers and professional practitioners on a cost reimbursement basis for the services they provided. Whether a result of these or other factors, the demand for services, and the volume and prices of services rose rapidly — and the costs of federal and private insurance programs skyrocketed.

As a result, American businesses have taken matters into their own hands. More and more are insisting that competitive market forces must operate in health care, and that insuring and payment practices must change to encourage this. Today, businesses are negotiating directly with providers over price. Simultaneously, the largest public purchaser of health care services, Medicare, has begun to price its benefits prospectively. State Medicaid programs are following suit. The impact of these new purchasing and insuring tactics has brought health care into the commercial marketplace in a rapid and indeed precipitous fashion. This shift to a competitive market environment from a cost-reimbursement environment is demanding profound adjustments in our nation's voluntary hospitals.

Many voluntary hospital trustees, who accepted their responsibilities as an act of community service, today find themselves surprised and sometimes uneasy at the extent to which business objectives influence their hospital's actions and their board decisions. Voluntary hospital managers, in turn, find themselves hiring more staff with training and skills in business management, and are increasingly being forced to analyze, plan, and make decisions in business terms that place greater emphasis on the market for and profitability of various health care products.

The uneasiness of trustees and managers is often an indication that they have not found ways to satisfactorily integrate the increasingly important business missions and values in hospital care today with the traditional community service voluntary status. The result is a legitimate fear that, in pursuing the business mission, they will lose their identity, their soul, and perhaps their tax-exempt status. In fact, since managers and trustees sense they are dealing with two value systems that often conflict, they ask themselves what voluntary hospitals should stand for —what can and should distinguish them from other hospitals?

It is clearly urgent that voluntary hospital managers and trustees understand such conflicts and consider how to balance or integrate these two value systems. Peters and Waterman, in *In Search of Excellence*, point out that "the real role of the chief executive is to manage the values of the organization."[1] Managing the several value systems that pertain to health care delivery may be today's most critical challenge to voluntary hospital leaders.

This chapter attempts to address these issues from the points of view of (1) the trustees and managers of individual hospitals; (2) the trustees and management of hospital systems; and (3) other hospital leaders and policymakers. Trustees and managers bear the major responsibility for defining voluntary hospitals' historic community services mission, and must undertake serious reconsideration of the practicality of this mission in today's commercial health care environment.

COMMUNITY SERVICES AND BUSINESS MISSIONS: THE CONTEXT FOR THEIR CONFLICT

The Flourishing of the Modern Voluntary Hospital

The voluntary hospital began in this country during an era when there was, at best, a very limited market for hospital services, and hospital care was considered a public service. Medical care was based on a very limited science, and hospital care was regarded as a last resort for the most seriously ill and injured. While even the early voluntary hospitals charged patients who had the means to pay, they were chartered to serve the entire community; indeed, they were of greatest importance to the poor because many higher income patients generally received care in their homes. These "public" institutions, as voluntary hospitals were then called, were seen by the community as the only alternative to government-funded and operated hospitals, and often received start-up funds from local or state governments to help finance their work.

Many of these voluntary hospitals were operated by religious organizations that emphasized service to the poor and were staffed extensively by volunteers or religious groups whose incomes were raised through philanthropy. Others were started and supported largely by ethnic groups as a way of taking care of people with common cultural heritages, including many poor immigrants. These early voluntary hospitals were perceived as community institutions in that they usually served a population defined in geographic, ethnic, or cultural terms and were both supported and held accountable by the leaders of their communities.

From these humble beginnings, hospitals have developed services of great value to people of all incomes, are compensated for the vast

[1] T. J. Peters and R. H. Waterman, *In Search of Excellence*, Harper and Row, New York, 1982.

majority of their services, serve almost every community, and produce a substantial share of the gross national product. This flourishing of hospitals can be attributed to a number of factors. First, improved aseptic, surgical, and anesthesiological techniques that required a controlled institutional environment vastly improved the value of hospital services to the public. Later, affiliations with medical schools, for the education of health professionals and research, also enhanced hospitals' reputations for scientifically advanced care and tapped into rising public hopes that science could produce cures and treatments for more and more diseases and injuries.

Second, beginning in the 1930s, partly in response to the effect of the Great Depression on voluntary hospitals' revenues, a system of third-party payment was developed to cover the costs of hospital care. Blue Cross plans were established as voluntary organizations to assure that more individuals would be able to afford, and hospitals would be able to collect for, hospital care. Following World War II, federal tax and wage policy and enthusiastic support from labor unions prompted employers to rapidly expand the purchase of hospital insurance for their employees. Hospital insurance soon became as important as hospital care had become. The success of Blue Cross ultimately attracted many commercial insurance companies into health insurance as a business opportunity. Then, in the 1960s, the federal government moved to complete this third-party payment system by enacting Medicare and Medicaid to pay for care to the elderly and to the poor who could not afford or obtain coverage from these private insurance plans. For a time, the federal government even gave consideration to enacting a program of national health insurance that would have made health insurance coverage more comprehensive and extended it to the 30 million or so who still had not been reached with adequate health insurance.

Third, increased public demand for care led to public and private efforts to bring the miracles of modern hospital care into every community. Early on, some state governments became major benefactors of hospitals, offering to finance start-up costs as well as making contributions toward the costs of care for the poor. In the 1940s and 1950s, the federal Hill-Burton program and private foundations invested heavily in hospital construction. The federal government further reflected the enthusiasm of the public for science and health care by making heavy investments in biomedical research, in programs to expedite the dissemination of new technologies into clinical practice, and in programs to expand vastly the number of physicians and other health professionals.

In terms of government and private attitudes toward hospitals, this period of remarkable development was driven by rising public hopeful-ness about biomedical research and hospital care, the willingness of private corporations to pay rising health insurance premiums, and by government's willingness to invest more and more public funds to assure access to care. The goal of the government and private institutions alike was to develop the most clinically advanced and highest quality care possible, and to assure that there would be enough providers and other resources to make it available in every community. At the local level, private corporations placed their chief executive officers on hospital boards to assure the development of the best care for the community; they also participated actively in government-funded health services and planning organizations working to assure hospital cooperation in provid-ing needed services in their communities.

Attitudes Toward the Hospital in the 1980s

Even as government, corporations, hospitals, and physicians were coop-erating to expand health care, a radically new and different set of atti-tudes about health care and hospitals began to emerge. By the 1980s, these new attitudes were expressed in actions of federal and state gov-ernment and private corporations.

Even in the beginning, some were predicting Medicare would be far more costly than anticipated. By the mid 1970s, the costs were clear. Indeed, the rapidly rising cost of both public and private insurance programs had become a major national issue.

The federal government responded with actions intended to hold down costs for the entire country and for its own programs. Health planning legislation to head off a growing oversupply of hospital beds, refinements in Medicare and Medicaid law and regulations to tighten payments under these programs, and grant funding for the start-up of health maintenance organizations (HMOs) were enacted. During the inflationary mid-1970s, the federal government even continued manda-tory wage and price controls on hospitals after they had been lifted for other areas of the economy. But the height of the government's efforts to control costs for the entire nation came several years later when Presi-dent Carter proposed that hospital price controls be reinstituted on an ongoing basis. The proposal was defeated in Congress with the promise by hospitals that a "voluntary effort" would be undertaken to hold down rising hospital costs for the nation.

By the late 1970s, confidence had fallen to near zero that the federal government could legislate and implement an acceptable regulatory program to control health care costs for the entire country. However, as confidence in regulation decreased, concern over the costs of public programs continued to rise. Today, concerns with expenditures for health care dominate government policy to the near exclusion of the concerns with access and quality that dominated policy just a few years ago. While some state governments, including a few "all-payer" states, have continued a regulatory approach, for the most part state and federal governments now limit their efforts almost exclusively to controlling the costs of their own health benefit programs. The implementation of the massive diagnostic related groups (DRGs) reforms in Medicare, for example, has been aimed at reducing federal costs above all.

A similar history might be traced for private corporations. Today, many are redoubling their efforts to purchase care for their own employees at whatever savings they can achieve with little hope or intent of controlling costs for their entire community, state, or nation.

In the early days of the voluntary hospital as a public institution that served as an alternative to government, the hospital and the care it provided were not thought of in marketplace terms. But the hospital market looks different to purchasers today. Due partly to their success, hospitals are seen as offering a valued service that most consumers are willing and able to pay for (through their insurers) at levels that allow an attractive profit or margin. There is a strong commercial market in hospital care—a far cry from the early days of the voluntary hospital. Indeed, the "monetarization" of the health care industry, which has created a market where services can be sold at a profit, "has set the stage for the explosive growth of for-profit medicine."[2]

Also, the hospitals themselves are seen differently. They are seen as a business for the following reasons:

• Their staffs have been professionalized and the role of volunteers and religious groups has been vastly reduced.
• Their identification with specific ethnic communities or their original neighborhoods has been eroded.
• Their dependence on philanthropy and support has been weakened by a policy of setting patient charges at levels to cover all costs.
• For-profit hospitals are operating successfully and finding willing investors.

Since hospitals are perceived as businesses, they are treated more and more like businesses by big purchasers of care and are expected to

[2] E. Ginzberg, "The Monetarization of Medical Care," *New England Journal of Medicine* **310:**1162–1165 (1984).

respond in businesslike ways. In fact, many seem to believe there is a great deal of "fat" in hospitals dating from the free-spending era of the 1960s and 1970s that can be squeezed out by more businesslike practices. Protests from hospitals that such practices will compromise quality and squeeze out charity care and community services are often suspected as attempts to avoid being businesslike and to protect the comfortable fat in the system.

Today's established hospital market has become hotly competitive. Hospitals are competing for patients, diversifying into new services, and taking other businesslike steps designed to assure that they maintain or increase their market share of health services. These signs of a mature, no longer expansive, hospital market are widely attributed to

• an oversupply of inpatient hospital capacity due to changes in technology that allow more care to be given on an ambulatory basis, and to third-party payer pressures to hold down inpatient services
• an increasing supply of physicians often competing with the hospital for patients
• growing efforts by government and corporate purchasers to buy health and hospital care in ways that encourage providers to compete for their subscribers or beneficiaries by offering lower cost care
• an increasing willingness of the consumer/patient to change physicians and hospitals, and generally to regard health care as a service to be carefully purchased and
• a spreading deregulation of hospital care that permits easier entry into the market and eliminates protections (franchises) of existing institutions

This mature buyers' market for health care prompts purchasers to ask for better value and lower costs from hospitals as conditions for doing business with them.

Government and private purchasers seem convinced that hospitals could offer a package of services to their patients that is less costly. Per-case payment systems (e.g., DRGs) are intended to offer hospitals the incentives to do just that. Hospitals responding to these incentives are, in fact, reducing lengths of stay and services. Today, they are providing a different hospital care product to Medicare, one that has the beneficiary going home from the hospital earlier, somewhat less completely recovered, and in need of more intensive care and support outside of the hospital than previously.

Per-case payments to hospitals are only the first step toward much broader and more inclusive products where the buyer can purchase most of the health care services needed for a full year from a single, vertically integrated provider. Capitated payments to HMOs are a case in point.

By purchasing such broad, integrated products, government and private corporations shift to the providers the responsibility of regulating the costs of a broad range of services, and the risk of setting a price that covers the costs of integrated services.

Government and corporate attitudes toward the hospital are now much more consistent in that they believe that competition can control health care costs. This philosophy calls for hospitals to compete for patients based on the price and quality of their services. It assumes that hospitals will act like businesses in a competitive marketplace in the long-term best interests of all concerned.[3] In such an environment, government and private purchasers of hospital services not only see themselves as justified in seeking the lowest possible prices for their beneficiaries and employees, but as deterring unnecessary hospital expansion and perhaps forcing a needed reduction in hospital capacity.

As part of this philosophy, the federal government has pursued antitrust regulation to induce more effective hospital competition. With greater reliance on market forces, the government has greatly reduced the funding of community health planning activities. Some would further purify competition by removing from the price paid to hospitals for patient care all costs of education, indigent care, public health, social services, research, and other traditional community service activities. These costs seem outside the commercial marketplace for services, and vary from hospital to hospital. Including them in health services prices makes it difficult for the purchaser to compare service costs at different institutions.

Finally, this philosophy suggests that excessively comprehensive health insurance has insulated the consumer from the high costs of health care. It created a market in which anything seemed affordable to the patient, even as costs rose, but became less affordable to the government and employers who purchased the insurance. Efforts by government and corporations to increase cost-sharing of insurance, and proposals to lessen the favorable tax treatment that encourages the purchase of insurance are intended to reduce the extent of insurance coverage and to increase the consumer's pressure on insurers and providers to hold down costs.

---

[3] D. Light, "Is Competition Bad?" *New England Journal of Medicine* **309**(21):1315–1318 (1983).

Community Services and Business Missions

The aforementioned events have had the effect of giving greater prominence to the voluntary hospitals' historical business mission as opposed to their community services mission. Rosemary Stevens writes that "We have always had a very entrepreneurial voluntary sector in this country with respect to the attractions of private patients." She further points out that some religious hospitals in particular "went out of their way to build up a very large number of paying patients from the beginning," and cites a 1904 census of nonproprietary hospitals that showed as much as 43 percent of hospital income came from paying patients and 30 percent from government.[4] In fact, for much of their history, voluntary hospitals have had to strive to be businesslike in order to survive and prosper.

In addition, voluntary hospital managers and trustees have long been forced to balance and integrate the disparate values of practicing clinicians, educators, and researchers with the hospital's need to meet expenses and to produce a viable operating margin.[5,6] They have also balanced their zeal for clinical and scientific leadership with the community's need for less dramatic services and the institution's need for a balanced budget.

These differing objectives sometimes coincide, but more often remain in constructive tension, leaving the manager and trustee to balance them on a day-to-day, issue-by-issue basis. In the past, voluntary hospitals have managed these several missions and generally worked out any conflicts between them to a degree that has allowed most to thrive. However, this task has become much more difficult in the 1980s because a greater emphasis is being put on the business mission by voluntary hospitals *as a matter of survival* in response to the demands of purchasers and changes in the marketplace for hospital services.

In general, the basic elements of the community services and business missions can be outlined as follows:

The Community Services Mission These objectives and values are commonly found in the mission statements of many voluntary hospitals. They also are implicit in much of the recent literature which describes their potential conflicts with business values. They include

- identifying the community's health care needs (in terms of improv-

---

[4] R. Stevens, "Voluntary and Governmental Activity," *Health Matrix* **III**(1):26–31 (Spring 1985).

[5] A. Reading, "Involvement in Proprietary Chains in Academic Health Centers," *New England Journal of Medicine* **313**(3):194–197 (1985).

[6] B. Culliton, "University Hospitals for Sale," *Science* **223**:909–911 (1984).

ing health status) and offering hospital and related services that meet these needs

• providing the highest quality clinical care possible to patients

• making health and health-related services accessible to all members of the community who need them

• cooperating with other hospitals and other providers of care to assure quality, access, continuity, and responsiveness to community needs while avoiding duplication of services and unnecessary costs

• contributing to the training of health professionals and to the conduct of research for the long-term improvement of health care

• supporting the professional practice of medicine, and working with and through physicians in the community to assure that the hospital mission is met

• participating with local community leaders and institutions to prompt them to take responsibility for assuring health care to all members of the community, and to offer philanthropic and political support for this mission

The Business Mission   The business mission active in many hospitals today seems to include

• offering such health and health-related *services* as can be charged for at prices high enough to cover all economic costs and produce an operating margin sufficient to assure the hospital's continuing viability as an institution, or which attract patients who use other profitable services in sufficient quantity to offset a low return or any losses, or which are required as part of a marketing effort to attract patients for a range of services whose overall operating margins meet the hospital's needs

• offering services to those *patients* whose insurer, or who themselves, can pay sufficiently high prices to support the hospital's costs plus the needed level of operating or profit margin, or who are served as part of a community relations/marketing effort to attract patients whose payments in total meet the hospital's needs

• increasing the hospital's *share* of patients and health services in its market area by competing successfully with other hospitals

• forming joint ventures with physicians, other providers, and insurers to *vertically integrate* and better market their services in competition with other providers in the area

• affiliating with a regional or national hospital chain or system to obtain economies of scale, opportunities for *horizontal* and *vertical integration*, or capital to finance competitive activities

• conducting *education* and *research* to the extent such investments produce a competitive edge in new technologies, or help attract patients by enhancing a reputation for quality care

• working as a *good corporate citizen* with community leaders on projects that contribute to the long-range standing of the hospital in the community, and advocating additional government or private programs to finance care for the poor

• entering other *nonhealth services enterprises* to the extent they generate needed profits or operating margins

The public's willingness to spend steadily increasing amounts of money for health care in the past obviated the need to pursue business missions in voluntary hospitals strongly enough to seriously threaten either the community services mission or the voluntary hospital's sense of identity. That is, society made enough money available to hospitals, in one form or another, that hard choices were not demanded of most. Hard choices are being forced today, and the conflicts between missions are being surfaced and intensified by the increasingly commercial health care marketplace.

WHERE MISSION AND BUSINESS ARE NOT EASILY BALANCED

Some actions support both the community services and business missions in a hospital, but often these missions pull in different directions. The fundamental characteristic of a voluntary hospital in the contemporary commercial health care environment is its effort to balance or integrate its diverse missions while, at the margin, maintaining and protecting its community services mission.

This chapter tries to answer the following questions about decisions in the key areas of hospital activity: (1) what services to offer; (2) what patients to serve; (3) how much to compete with other hospitals; (4) how to divide hospital revenues among the hospital, its system, and its community services; (5) how to relate to the medical profession; and (6) how to raise needed revenues.

For each area, the potential limits to integrating the two missions are examined in order to find the margins where community services are most likely to be abandoned by a highly or primarily business mission oriented hospital.

What Services to Offer

Hospital leaders routinely review the mix of services offered in light of new technologies, changing opportunities or needs, and new sites or formats for services. They might decide, for example, to add new diagnostic equipment, open or close a pediatric service, purchase or open an ambulatory care center, or offer health promotion programs. To identify the values guiding these decisions, hospital leaders might ask themselves:

• In deciding what *types* of services to offer, how do you balance the community's health needs with the hospital's need to offer services that produce higher operating margins or profits?

• In deciding what *volumes* of services to offer, how do you balance the volume required by the community to meet health needs at affordable costs with the volumes that your hospital can sell profitably?

Most health services are needed both for the health of the community and for profitability. Other needed services may be unprofitable in themselves, but their existence attracts patients who use other services that are profitable to a sufficient degree to offset the loss. Still other unprofitable services, such as health education programs, may be consistent with the business mission if they pay off in improved public relations and contribute to the long-term acceptance and use of the hospital by the community.

Some community services, however, may never, by themselves, be profitable, bring in profitable patients, or improve community relations. Others may be risky in that their profitability is uncertain, require long-term subsidy, or have a low chance of ever contributing enough to the operating margin needed to assure survival and success as a competitor in the marketplace. One voluntary hospital official calls these risky community services "mission risks," that is, financial risks that voluntary hospitals take in pursuit of their community services mission. Such services may be good community service, but they are bad business. Many of these risky, unprofitable, or low profit services are likely to be lost if more and more voluntary hospitals come to favor a business mission over their community services mission.

In addition, favoring the business mission might lead to hospitals offering services that are of lower priority in terms of community health needs at the expense of other, more necessary services; or simply offering more services than are needed at greater expense and even risk to the community.[7,8] For example, higher margins or profits may result from greater use than is medically necessary of a service such as CAT scan-

[7] E. Pellegrino, "Catholic Hospitals: Survival Without Moral Compromise," *Hospital Progress*, pp. 42–49 (May 1985).

[8] D. Wikler, "Forming an Ethical Response," *Business and Health* **2**(3):25–29 (1985).

ning. Similarly, cosmetic surgery may prove more profitable than operating an emergency room or maternity clinic.

Which Patients to Serve

Hospitals are faced with the need to develop sources of patients to reverse falling inpatient occupancies brought about by changing technology and patterns of health care. This is leading to the development of networks of referring physician groups, primary care centers, and satellite hospitals, and of HMOs or other arrangements that sell the hospital's services to employers or insurers. To identify the values guiding these developments, one might ask:

• How does one's decisions to seek out and serve particular groups of patients in the community balance the interest of those who most need care with those who can pay the most for services?
• In offering particular types and volumes of services to a selected group of patients, how does one balance the groups's need for the service with their (or their insurer's) willingness to make higher payments for services?

Usually, a hospital is able to collect enough from most patients (or their insurers) in a community to generate an adequate profit or operating margin. At the same time, it may be "good business" to offer care to a limited number of additional patients, whose low payment levels erode operating margin, in the interest of good public relations and assuring long-term acceptance of the hospital in the community.[9] For high-paying patients and the limited number of low-paying patients, the community services and business missions motivate similar decisions.

For many low-paying patients, however, business considerations pull against the community services mission. Too many patients who have no insurance at all (public or private) or who are covered by very skimpy Medicaid programs, or who are covered by private insurance with very high cost-sharing or low payment schedules, can erode profits or operating margins too greatly to be consistent with the business mission. Such patients may be neglected or avoided in favor of patients whose payments are higher by hospitals pursuing their business mission.

By careful market segmentation, a hospital can work to capture a greater proportion of patients from groups who pay more generously for services. By carefully locating the hospital or its satellites in areas with

[9]R. Johnson, "Competition Presents Opportunities for Not-for-Profit Systems," *Health Progress*, pp. 31–35 (November 1984).

high insurance coverage, and carefully targeting groups for marketing through their Preferred Provider Organization (PPO) or HMO, and by restricting or expanding hospital services based on whether they draw paying patients or not (often restricting emergency room or clinic services), hospitals can increase the proportion of paying patients in their payer mix, thereby increasing their profit or operating margin. A hospital can also offer enhanced levels of services/amenities, such as "upscale" maternity services, to better-paying patients as a way of attracting them and selling more services. As business-oriented hospitals emphasize these marketing practices, multiple levels of care result for individuals of different abilities to pay, and needed care may become less accessible to the poor and uninsured.[10]

How Much to Compete

Shrinking patient volumes are forcing hospitals to consider either downsizing or reaching out to capture more patients from other hospitals, particularly paying patients. In fact, most hospitals in multihospital communities seem to have concluded that they must compete to increase their share of the total patient services provided in the community, i.e., their market share, if they are to survive or be successful. In seeking market share, one might ask

• How do decisions to offer particular types of services balance the need for stronger net patient revenues with the needs and capabilities of other hospitals/providers in the community?
• How do decisions to offer services to particular groups balance the hospital's revenue needs with concerns for the overall quality, accessibility, and affordability of care for the community?

Historically, hospitals have always both competed and cooperated. The present intense competition for patients and higher net patient revenues, however, seems to be leaving less and less room for the type of cooperation envisioned in the community services mission.[11]

Nevertheless, a strong case can be made that many competitive actions by hospitals are consistent with both community service and business missions. In establishing new sites of care, new types of services, and new health care/insurance products, hospitals are attempting to give

---

[10]Q. Young, "The Danger of Making Serious Problems Worse," *Business and Health* **2**(3):32–33 (1985).

[11]R. Sigmond, "A Community Perspective on Hospital Ownership." *Frontiers in Health Services Management* **1**(1):33–39 (1984).

consumers what they most want and need — often at a lower price. In fact, competitive motives may require providers to be even more responsive to the needs and desires of patients than community services motives. For example, in our buyer's market for health services, elderly Americans, who have more and more purchasing power and constitute a growing market for care, might find providers finally offering them the types of services they have always wanted.

There are instances, however, where decisions to compete with other hospitals may adversely affect service quality and patient accessibility and may even raise the costs of care in the community. For example, several hospitals in the same geographic area may offer a service, such as bypass surgery or helicopter evacuation, because they fear the loss of medical staff or patients if they don't. They may do this even when there are not enough patients in the area to cover the fixed costs associated with this service, or to keep clinical teams busy enough in multiple hospitals to offer highest quality care. There are even cases where voluntary hospitals have initiated a service they thought would prove unprofitable, only to find it subsequently profitable — until several other hospitals added it.

Again, hospital competition can, in the long term, downsize unneeded hospital capacity, thereby reducing the costs of care in the community. This result would be consistent with both the community services and business missions. However, in the short run, until closures take place, the tactic is likely to produce decreased margins and increased prices in hospitals whose occupancy is reduced, temporarily raising health care costs for the community. Moreover, competition may put hospitals out of business that are best located to assure access to care to a portion of the community. For example, hospitals serving areas of lower paying, inner-city neighborhoods often find other hospitals today increasing their marketing to doctors or patients in the closer-in suburbs from which they have traditionally drawn their better paying patients. If the inner-city hospital cannot effectively compete for these paying patients, its payer mix will deteriorate and its net revenues will fall. Its quality of care can be affected, and ultimately, if it closes, the poorer neighborhoods may find it necessary to travel many miles farther to seek care from the surviving hospitals.[12]

Finally, some would argue that hospitals that use tough admissions and collections policies are acting in a way consistent with both the business and community services missions because they reduce costs of bad debt shifted to other patients. It can be further argued that referring

---

[12] Young, op.cit.

to public hospitals patients who cannot pay simply forces government to assume its appropriate role of paying for services for the poor. However, when public hospitals or funds are either not available or are insufficient to absorb such shifts, patients may be deprived of needed care.

Voluntary hospitals might be unwise to go too far with such competitive strategies. Competitive tactics that obviously damage other providers needed by the community could be "bad business," leading to poor public relations and lower long-term acceptability of the hospital and its services. This may be true even for proprietary hospitals in some communities. However, there is clear potential for the overall accessibility, quality, and cost of care in a community to be compromised by hospitals competing for better paying patients without regard for the role of other providers in meeting the overall needs of the community.

How to Allocate Hospital Revenues

All hospitals today must accumulate reserves and improve operating margins or profits to generate capital.[13] This is prompting systems of hospitals to look for ways to shift revenues from some of their constituent hospitals to finance competitive ventures (or even operating losses) at other member hospitals. Both of these uses of available revenue can reduce the hospital's reinvestment of its operating margins in particular communities. In making decisions in this area, it might be asked

• In deciding how much operating margin or profit to generate, how are the needs of the community balanced against the need of the institution to survive or grow? The need of other hospitals in the system or chain to survive or grow? The system or chain's need to survive or grow?

• In deciding how to set prices (or what services to encourage) in the hospital, what kind of balance is struck between maximizing revenues and limiting charges in the interest of keeping health care more affordable for the community?

Both community services and business missions induce hospitals to raise revenues to support improved services to the community. Both missions also prompt hospitals to set prices or aim at restraining revenues per patient, either to be price-competitive (per the business mission), or responsive to what the community can afford (per the community services mission).

There are cases, however, where the two missions can lead to diver-

---

[13] F. Sloan and R. Vraciu, "Investor-Owned and Not-for-Profit Hospitals: Addressing Some Issues," *Health Affairs* **2**(1):25–37 (1983).

gent actions. In some markets, a hospital can increase its prices or revenues per patient well above its costs and still attract patients. For example, many hospitals, particularly those that are investor owned, have been found to charge higher prices on ancillary services as a means of raising maximum revenue.[14] This situation may occur because the hospital has worked to establish a profitable mix of payers (i.e., a high proportion of well-insured patients) or a profitable mix of services, or, because it faces relatively weak price competition on less visible hospital services — such as ancillary services. By taking advantage of such markets, a hospital can generate higher revenues, thereby increasing costs to the community while investing its improved revenues in its own expansion or outside the community in its system. It seems clear that a hospital or system favoring the business mission is likely to be more ambitious in pursuing and exploiting markets to increase revenues for its own purposes.[15]

The transfer of community-produced resources outside of the community is inconsistent with the community services mission, especially if there is a judgment that there are health or health-related needs remaining unmet in the community. The transfer of earnings out of the community to pay investors in proprietary chains, for example, has been criticized as an example of misuse of community resources.[16] There is an equally difficult question for voluntary hospital systems regarding the extent to which the community services mission justifies a hospital in one community raising hospital revenues over and above its community needs in order to subsidize or invest in a less affluent community.

How to Relate to Physicians

Hospitals are increasingly working with physicians to influence their practice patterns, to engage them in joint business ventures, and, in some cases, to selectively include them in hospital activities based on economic considerations. These practices can conflict with the hospital's traditional role of support for quality in the practice of medicine and can create conflicts of interest for physicians. In making decisions in this area, one might ask

- In deciding which physicians to work with, how does one balance

---

[14] J. Michael Watt et al., "The Comparative Economic Performance of Investor-Owned Chain and Not-for-Profit Hospitals," *New England Journal of Medicine* **314**(2):89–96 (1986).

[15] M. Schlesinger, "The Rise of Proprietary Health Care," *Business and Health* **2**(3):7–12 (1985).

[16] K. O'Rourke, "An Ethical Perspective on Investor-Owned Medical Care Corporations," *Frontiers in Health Services Management* **1**(1):10–26 (1984).

the quality, types, and volumes of services needed by the community with the need for practice patterns that produce the greatest operating margins or profits?

• In deciding how to involve physicians in hospital management, how does one balance the need to support their professional judgment on quality with the need to give them economic incentives that support those of the hospital?

• In deciding what level of medical education and research activity to support, how does one balance activities that promise financial return for the hospital with those that support and improve the future practice of medicine generally?

Both the community services and business missions support many hospital/physician relationships. Offering more economical care in less costly settings (and shortening hospital lengths of stay) are usually consistent with both ideals. So also is choosing physicians whose reputation for quality care among peers and patients reassures the community about the quality of the hospital's services. In addition, to the extent that "quality" services are demanded by the health care consumer, business objectives support physicians and hospitals striving to offer such services in their regular activities and through joint ventures. Indeed, as competition for patients among physicians and between physicians and hospitals increases, new opportunities and needs for closer medical staff/hospital cooperation are evident. More jointly managed activities may ease long-standing tensions in these areas and, in fact, improve both quality and economy of care.

Similarly, both missions support some educational, and research activities.[17] In addition to the market advantages that derive from a reputation for quality, there may be business advantages in training health professionals in the hospital, PPO, or HMO environment in which they will practice, to better assure the compatibility of their practice patterns with the philosophy of the institution, or to attract a quality medical staff that wishes such programs. Research activities may also produce clinical capabilities that open business opportunities for the hospital. To be preeminent in new experimental transplant techniques, for example, can bring great publicity and reputation for quality to a hospital, and enhance its competition for patients. On the other hand, both missions might argue for a reduction in the levels of educational activity, to the extent it is unprofitable (from the perspective of the business mission), or to the

---

[17] J. Moxley, "On Being Courted by the For-Profits: Conferees Voice Anxieties, Hopes," *Health Progress*, pp. 30–31 (May 1985).

extent it is widely acknowledged to be producing an oversupply of physicians and other health care practitioners (from the perspective of the community services mission).

However, there are also areas where the two missions may conflict. First, the types of educational and research activity supportable under the two missions are likely to vary. Training in specialties whose residents improve the hospital's operating margin, and research that promises to lower costs of treatment, are more likely to be favored under the business mission.[18] On the other hand, the community and nation may need more primary care physicians, for example, or development of a new diagnostic technology for certain illnesses. Such programs may not be undertaken if they increase hospital costs without commensurately increasing hospital revenues. Of course, an affiliation with a medical school, or a reputation for supporting research, may prove to be good business in terms of long-range marketing; in the short run, however, strong business incentives are likely to cause hospitals to favor particular specialty training programs and certain research and equipment acquisitions.

Further, the two missions may produce different results in markets where the consumer's impressions of quality are poorly developed. Some have argued that because consumers are often poor judges of quality, the judgment or consensus of the medical profession is usually relied on as the best protection. In their competition for patients, hospitals are likely to put pressure on organized medical staffs and physicians generally to agree to different practice patterns and arrangements. To the extent that these pressures and joint ventures between hospitals and physicians may give physicians economic incentives to compromise their judgments for financial gain, so also may they undermine the professions' role as guardian of quality.[19] In fact, strong pressures from either the hospital or its physicians to release patients earlier, or to reduce utilization of expensive resources, can quickly undermine the physicians' guardianship.

For a hospital to select physicians for collaboration based on low resource use practice patterns alone holds similar hazards. Quality may require different levels or types of care from what the consumer understands, or from what is described by the averages of practice for various DRGs or capitated populations. The community services mission seems to call for a more professionally determined and less market-determined standard of quality.

---

[18]J. Stein, "From the Editor," *Business and Health* **2**(3):1 (1985).
[19]A. Relman, "The Future of Medical Practice," *Health Affairs* **2**(2):5–19 (1983).

Finally, there are still communities with many insured patients and weak price competition where a hospital can raise revenues by unnecessary admissions and outpatient visits, and by encouraging physicians to offer as many billable services as possible to patients.[20] In such communities, the business mission may encourage over-utilization of services. However, Medicare, Medicaid, and private prospective payment arrangements are making these practices more difficult for some services.

Best to Raise Revenues

The hospital must decide to what extent to seek community philanthropic support, to what extent to advocate community responsibility for adequate health services in the community, and to what degree to share control over hospital activities with other community groups. In making these decisions, one might ask

• How does one balance the hospital's need for financial and governance autonomy to compete in the marketplace with the community's responsibility to assure needed care to all its citizens through philanthropy and local governance of the hospital?
• How does one balance responsibility to the system, with responsibility to the community?

Good business and community service both require good relationships with community leaders and efforts to be responsive to community needs. Advocacy of federal, state, or local government programs to provide or pay for needed services that cannot be offered in the marketplace is also consistent with both missions.

However, a community service orientation may allow community leaders an opportunity to veto or require actions by the hospital that are not always in the hospital's best business interests. While the business mission recognizes that good community relations are important, excessive community control can force a hospital into making poor business judgments or taking unprofitable actions.

Conflicts also may occur between hospital systems and the community. To the extent that a system or chain levies overhead costs, profits, and/or shares of operating margins on specific hospitals, it may make demands that conflict with what the community expects from the hospital. The system may impose financial requirements on the hospital for purposes from which the community does not believe it derives commensurate benefits.[21]

---

[20] H. Luft, "For-Profit Hospitals: A Cost Problem or Solution?" *Business and Health* 2(3):13–16 (1985).

[21] *Utah County v. Intermountain Health Care, Inc.*, No. 17699, June, 1985.

WHAT DISTINGUISHES A VOLUNTARY HOSPITAL?

The health care marketplace today is in a period of rapid and fundamental change. The voluntary hospital distinguishes itself in this marketplace by its struggle to give priority to its community services mission against a business mission that is critical to successful competition. At the margin, the voluntary hospital that gives priority to its community services mission is likely to strive to meet community needs that are beyond what good business alone would suggest.

Voluntary hospitals carry on this struggle through governance structures and management processes that are distinctive and consistent with their strong community orientation. The management structures and processes described here are ideals. Consequently, they are stated in starker or less ambiguous form than are found in practice. Moreover, while they include examples identified in specific hospitals, there is probably no voluntary hospital that presents all the described features. Nevertheless, the ideals suggest a standard against which a hospital's faithfulness to the voluntary tradition can be reviewed.

Beyond the Requirements of the Business Mission

The voluntary hospital affirms both its own responsibility to meet its community's priority health care needs and the community's responsibility to help meet these needs, through the hospital's board membership and authority. The voluntary hospital board should be representative of the community and be expected to review and approve hospital activities in terms of both their importance to the hospital and how they respond to the community's needs. If the critical decisions of the hospital were made by the management and staff of the hospital without the review of a strong board that is clear on its community responsibilities, the decisions would be likely to favor more and more the survival and growth needs — and the business mission — of the institution over the needs of the community.

The voluntary hospital board ideally would have fiduciary responsibility not only for the finances of the voluntary hospital, but also for assuring survival of its community services values. In other words, the board should manage the hospital's values as well as its finances. It would be obliged, therefore, to honor and implement the community services mission's primary focus on the needs of the community. By subjecting itself to this type of community authority, the voluntary hospital assures its responsibility to the community over and above what good business and the demands of the marketplace advise.

The voluntary hospital might also maintain ongoing and close working relations with other public and private agencies that express community needs and consensus. These agencies include community coalitions, planning agencies, health professional organizations, United Fund organizations, and local governments.

The voluntary hospital would work through its board and affiliations to educate other community institutions concerning the health needs of its members and to encourage these institutions to assume a share of the responsibility for the hospital and its efforts to meet these needs. The board and other organizations might advocate community responsibility for health activities to government and private corporations and support philanthropy and fund raising as a means to this end.

The hospital might also relate to its own employees in a way that exemplifies responsible health-related employment policies for other employers in the community. Some voluntary hospitals have interpreted this to include, in addition to comprehensive health insurance, child and elderly dependent day care services for their own employees.[22]

Finally, the voluntary hospital would also take a leadership role with physicians and other providers to involve them in fulfilling the community services mission. This effort includes arranging contributions of time and service by physicians on the hospital's staff to serve poor patients without charge, and to help in the overall assessment of community needs and development of plans to respond.

Methods of Raising Revenues

In a voluntary hospital, pursuit of the business mission is a means of containing costs and raising hospital revenues in order that its community services mission can be pursued. Philanthropy and advocacy of government support are further affirmations of the community's ultimate responsibility for meeting health care needs. The voluntary hospital, therefore, would raise revenues through both active marketing and other businesslike practices and through vigorous fund-raising efforts.

Strong business skills and rigorous pursuit of the business mission are necessary to produce operating margins adequate to assure the hospital's survival as an entity. The capacity to support activities that increase costs without raising revenues to cover them depends more and more on the hospital's success at building a strong operating margin in the competitive marketplace. Thus, strong business management has emerged for many voluntary hospitals as a means to achieving community service ends.

However, hospitals are more constrained in today's price-competitive

[22]P. Henroit, "Catholic Health Care: Competing and Complementary Models," Center of Concern, Washington, D.C., 1985.

marketplace from raising large amounts of revenue from higher-than-cost health care prices. This condition has led hospitals to enter a variety of non-health-related businesses, ranging from parking lots to consulting services, as a means of raising extra revenues. Many voluntary hospitals weigh very carefully the reasons and motivations for such business ventures and consider whether these ventures conflict with their community service mission. Some restrict their ventures to health and related activities for fear of moving so far from the scope of their community services mission that it no longer offers guidance to their activities.

Voluntary hospitals also would encourage philanthropy and use such funds for community services that are beyond what the business mission supports (i.e., "missions risks"). Some hospitals have established foundations, with local corporate and public support, into which both contributions and hospital revenues derived from their business ventures are placed.

Management for Both Missions

By placing business-oriented staff in constructive tension with staff whose mission and values are community services oriented, a voluntary hospital would assure that both orientations are heard out more fully by hospital trustees and managers. Unless a conscious effort is made to be certain that these varied perspectives and values are represented in decisions, it is reasonable to expect, in our competitive marketplace, that decisions will increasingly reflect the hospital managers business efforts on behalf of the institution's survival and growth. Only a hospital that manages both sets of values and gives each a chance to be heard in decision-making may achieve the "best of both worlds," i.e., a community services oriented hospital that is businesslike in efficiency and in raising revenues in the marketplace to help support its community services. In this way, a hospital can compete in most commercial health care markets without being entirely commercialized. For example, a Catholic hospital that places its business managers in tension with its religious managers is establishing the kind of constructive tension that could produce this result.

This management philosophy argues for affirming strong management roles for physicians and other professionals and ties to other health professional groups in the community. In this way, their values can be heard on decisions affecting the quality of care, such as acquisition of new technology, educational and research programs, and evaluation of the clinical and/or health needs of the community.

Joint ventures raise special risks along with the opportunities they offer. Voluntary hospitals would shop carefully for the right partners. To maintain and balance countervailing values requires that joint venture partners either share the hospital's community services values or be bound by very specific contractual agreements or corporate bylaws and governance agreements that preserve appropriate influence for both business and community services values in the joint venture.[23,24] Similarly, joint ventures between voluntary hospitals and physicians should be structured to ensure that practicing physicians and nurses are not faced with economic incentives that may overpower professional values concerning clinical practice.

Similarly, management within chains or systems of voluntary hospitals would be sufficiently decentralized to provide the local hospital or clinic enough autonomy to be accountable to community leaders and to represent a countervailing force, on behalf of the community, in negotiations with the system's corporate headquarters.

Balancing Plans

The voluntary hospital's plans for the future would include analyses of both market opportunities and community needs, as well as strategies that respond to both. While most planned actions probably fit both missions, some actions may be planned for community service reasons alone because there is no adequate business justification for them. These actions constitute financial risks that are intentionally taken by the hospital in the name of its community services mission — its "mission risks."

One type of mission risk involves offering various types of needed services that have little or no likelihood of maintaining or improving the hospital's operating or profit margin. Such services may range from social services to pediatric intensive care, depending on the needs of the community. Or they may involve keeping an emergency room open in spite of its tendency to attract patients who are unable to pay for their care, or operating burn centers whose costs exceed what they can collect. A mission risk in one community, of course, may prove to be good business in another community.

A second type of mission risk involves foregoing opportunities to increase revenues because the actions involved would not be consistent with assuring the community-wide accessibility and quality of care or with containing the total cost of care in the community. For example, a

[23] Light, op.cit.
[24] R. O'Brien and M. Haller, "Investor-Owned or Nonprofit?" *New England Journal of Medicine* **303**(3):198–201 (1985).

voluntary hospital may decide not to offer a specialty service that is already being offered by another hospital, even though it believes it could attract more patients by doing so.

Indeed, there may be circumstances when a voluntary hospital should decide that its community services mission would be best served if it were to greatly downsize, radically change its services (such as becoming a long-term care facility), or go out of business. In a community that is seriously overbedded, and where a particular voluntary hospital is a logical candidate for closure, and where other community-oriented hospitals are present and working to meet the community's needs, is there a point where the voluntary hospital should withdraw from the competition? In most cases, "no margin, no mission" is a call to pursue the business mission and compete, but there are times when the community's needs should take precedence over those of the institution.

To guide them through these difficult decisions, some voluntary hospital trustees and managers evaluate requests or opportunities for changes in services, new business ventures, or other actions using criteria carefully developed to assure that they consider *both* the business mission and the community services mission. Some hospitals have written criteria specifically for acquiring satellite hospitals and clinics, for example, that require weighing the community's overall need for the activity along with the business opportunity involved.

In addition, the voluntary hospital must plan how much patient and other revenues are needed to support mission risks and how they will be developed. It would also plan how revenues will be allocated between local community and system activities, considering all the activities of the hospital in light of the needs of the community. A hospital would weigh the advantages of system involvement against local investments pursuant to both its business and community services missions.

Plans to meet revenue needs should not be limited to patient revenues but should include programs to produce philanthropic contributions and government support. To the extent that projected revenues require limits on needed services (such as limits on charity or uncompensated care) or affect the development of needed services in the future, hospital plans would reflect these restrictions. The plan might also suggest how revenue raising steps might allow this condition to be improved in the future. For needed services for which no source of support is foreseeable, plans might include appropriate advocacy efforts.

Distinctive Voluntary Hospital Services

While all communities share a common need for a wide range of health services, many communities need special services from their hospitals responsive to their population's special problems or the hospital's special role in the community. Such special services may range from school health programs to teen-age pregnancy clinics to operation of burn units. Similarly, while the market for health services is similar for a wide range of services in most communities, it varies from community to community in terms of what special services can be supported on a business basis, how much competition there is with regard to various services, and how much revenue can be raised to subsidize unprofitable services.

In some communities, where public opinion censures hospitals that do not treat all who come to their doors — good business may require a hospital to offer some level of uncompensated care lest its reputation be hurt in ways that ultimately may drive away paying patients. In other communities, hospitals are able to make public announcements of restrictions in treatment, and how they will be enforced, with little business loss. Single-hospital communities usually place far stronger expectations on their hospital in terms of meeting community needs than do large multihospital communities.[25]

Further, what services constitute mission risks depends on what payers for services do in each community. As the hospital market changes, will major insurers, corporations, and state and local government continue to push down the hospital's prices, or will they come to support the need for community services, either in the prices they are willing to pay or through corporate philanthropy and government appropriations?

Finally, and perhaps more importantly, how will payers and each community react to the type of mission risk a hospital takes when it foregoes potential new revenues by deciding not to compete for the patients of another hospital that is needed by the community? Can and will voluntary hospitals be able to downsize or change their services rapidly enough to be able to survive as institutions without taking patients from such other needed hospitals? And to what extent will the community and purchasers understand and pay higher prices or provide philanthropy to cover the costs of this forebearance, or even refuse to deal with a hospital that chooses to victimize a needed hospital?

The distinctiveness of a voluntary hospital must, therefore, be judged *relative to its own immediate market* — and the mission risks it succeeds in taking in that environment. In general, however, such services would be those that, in a specific community

1 lose money (i.e., require a significant and continuous subsidy from

---

[25] Sigmond, op.cit.

other services); *or* are very risky in terms of their ultimate profitability; *or* are likely to produce a return on investment that is lower than other possible services or lower than needed to support competitive success; *or* are likely to take a very long time to pay off, if at all; and,

2 provide little or no other business advantage, e.g., in terms of public relations — *or* do not contribute to the use of other more profitable services.

Any given service or activity may be on or off the mission risk list depending on the community. Frequent candidates for the list include trauma and burn units, emergency room services, rehabilitation services, pediatric intensive care, health promotion and education services, meals-on-wheels services, hospice services, graduate medical education in some specialties, and research. In addition, services to certain populations are frequent candidates for the mission risk list, including services to the uninsured poor, individuals and employer groups with limited insurance, the unemployed whose insurance benefits have run out, rural communities in depressed economies, inner-city, low-income populations, adolescent mothers and their children, handicapped, frail/chronically ill elderly, alcoholics and drug abusers, and AIDS patients.

THE VALUE OF VOLUNTARY HOSPITALS

What would be lost to our society if voluntary hospitals were to deemphasize or abandon their community services missions and pursue primarily or solely their business mission? Would we lose enough that it is worth the cost to society of tax and other government policies to encourage voluntary hospitals to continue to pursue their community services mission?

As discussed in earlier sections, most types of services, and services to most types of populations, can be offered for *both* business and community service reasons. That is, a relatively complete integration of the business and community service missions is possible for these services. However, the hospital care market does not permit *all* needed services to be offered to *all* members of the community for business reasons alone.

A strong case can be made for encouraging and supporting voluntary hospitals during their present period of accommodation to a competitive marketplace. Policy makers need to give voluntary hospitals an opportunity to demonstrate their capacities to integrate and balance their community service and business missions, so that they can both deliver the health care that public and private purchasers want at a cost that is appropriate and meet community needs beyond what the business mission alone would require. Some insist that it is too late — that voluntary hospitals are so constrained by the market that they can do little beyond what their business mission supports. But, if voluntary hospitals are counted out before they can demonstrate this capacity, it will be a great loss to the nation.

The Paradigm

While it is too early in the current period of change to quantify the present or future value to society of voluntary hospitals, some bases of their value are clear. First, the efforts that voluntary hospitals undertake to pursue the community services mission undoubtedly have been critical in shaping the paradigm of what a hospital is and does. They have shaped hospital manager and trustee expectations that all hospitals should take mission risks to some degree. Voluntary hospitals, of course, are not the only hospitals that pursue community services missions or take mission risks. As mentioned earlier, hospitals that are the only provider in rural communities seem to offer similar community services regardless of their ownership. Historically, however, the voluntary hospital is the primary force behind the current hospital paradigm. If voluntary hospitals ceased to nourish and support it, and managers and trustees were to come to expect hospitals to be businesses like any other, hospitals generally might well feel that it is no longer their responsibility to offer the less than maximally profitable services that are part of the community services mission. It is impossible to know how much this would influence hospitals' actions and the value of the mission risks they take for their communities until it is gone, and government is asked to step in to provide the services it once inspired.

Indeed, voluntary hospitals historically have shaped the paradigm not only for hospital care, but for health care generally, and for many other activities in our society. The hospitals' pursuit of the community services mission has influenced public expectations of all health care institutions. It has served a particularly important role with community physicians, serving to awaken them to the community's expectations and needs, and to organize their efforts to this end.

The voluntary hospital paradigm also reinforces private community responsibility in education, housing, and nutrition, as well as in theater, fine arts, and other areas. In American society, voluntary institutions historically have nurtured individual, community, and institutional responsibility for meeting a variety of social and cultural needs by private action, outside of government. This tradition is critical to a society that believes in maximizing private individual and community responsibility and limiting the role of government. Also, loss of the voluntary hospital is likely to diminish the role and respect accorded to voluntarism generally and could encourage a dualistic view of health care and other activities such that only government and business exist as valid alternatives.

Expectations

Second, the voluntary paradigm influences public expectations of hospitals, and helps determine what hospital activities constitute good business. Many hospital managers and trustees are doubtless prompted to offer unprofitable services to their community in order not to violate the community's expectations of them. To violate what the community (i.e., the hospital's customers) believes is the appropriate responsibility of the hospital is not in the long-term business interest of the institution — especially if there is a competitor nearby who behaves in ways the community judges more responsible. Thus, the voluntary tradition currently leavens the competitive marketplace in ways that make many things good business. If it were to disappear, public expectations would change in time — perhaps to the point where hospitals are seen as businesses like any other. At that point, many unprofitable services that it is now good business to offer could and would be dropped, or left to government to pay for. The volume of such services is also impossible to estimate — until the voluntaries are gone!

Relief of Burden

Third, if voluntary hospitals were to abandon their community services mission, it would increase the costs to federal, state, and local governments. There are millions of Americans with no public or private insurance coverage and limited means to pay hospital bills. In addition, many clinically desirable services are not adequately paid for by public or private insurance. Further, we know that many specific services to particular populations will never be good business, nor will they ever be profitable. We also know that many education and research programs are being conducted at levels beyond what good business dictates. A substantial portion of the costs of these services and activities is being financed in voluntary hospitals through their charge structures, business activities, and philanthropy. If these subsidies and the hospitals that support them were lost, the total burden, which is substantial, could fall on government.

A Lid on Costs

Fourth, loss of voluntary hospitals could increase the total public and private costs of hospital care to the nation. Ordinarily, competition reduces costs by reducing prices. But when it leads to building redundant facilities and services, competition can have the opposite effect. Some might argue that, in time, the market will cause the less competitive of these redundant facilities to close, and result in the survival of only the more efficient. With health care and hospitals, however, this is not ordinarily what happens. Hospitals that are the principal source of care in poor inner city or rural areas are often kept open by increased government or private voluntary funds, even though their occupancy rates fall drastically due to the loss of their paying patients to competitors with lower operating costs — and lower indigent care loads. Other hospitals stay in operation by raising their charges to cover their rising overhead costs *even when* their occupancy levels drop very low. And in many cases, hospitals offer duplicate high-cost services to compete for patients — even though there are not enough patients to go around, and charges for other services must be increased to cover them. In other words, in an environment of weak price competition, but strong competition for patients on bases other than price, duplication of services and excess facilities is encouraged. This can increase costs to public and private payers for a long time — perhaps indefinitely. The willingness of the voluntary hospital to forego revenue in such situations as a "mission risk" is a countervailing force to this type of cost-increasing behavior.

Values and Vision

Fifth, the voluntary hospital embodies a set of values in health care that helps quicken the conscience of the community concerning the sick and poor and inspires a vision of what medicine and health care can accomplish for mankind, beyond what the marketplace demands. Voluntary hospitals have traditionally striven to offer the best care possible to people who are sick and injured out of concern for the persons involved — regardless of their ability to pay. This primary focus on human need, rather than on a business opportunity to sell services, serves to direct the conscience of the community to these needs. Many improvements in medicine and health care technology have limited or no potential for return as business investments — at least in the short term. Indeed, some result in a decrease in hospital revenues (e.g., ambulatory surgery), while others may require large investments to treat only a few patients. Current payment practices under many payment programs (including the DRG system) strongly discourage research on and clinical use of new technologies that could help the patient. To lose the voluntary hospitals' ideal of first meeting human need, and its capacity to go beyond what the consumer and purchaser currently demand in the commercial marketplace, would greatly diminish the vision and drive of the health care system toward improved health care.

Pluralism and Preference

Sixth, voluntary hospitals are particularly visible expressions of the pluralism of our society and its belief that the interplay of institutions and individuals of varying ideals and practices will produce a better life for all in the long run. Many social agencies and religious institutions exist for the purpose of providing an outlet for individual citizens who are interested in pursuing social goals that are altruistic and that go beyond their expectations of government. Indeed, those involved pursue their activities and offer their services with greater enthusiasm and satisfaction simply because they are doing so in a voluntary setting. These individuals are the heart of the voluntary hospital and the values it stands for. In a pluralistic society, there is every reason why a voluntary locus for such people should be maintained.

Stability and Permanence

Finally, there is the issue of stability and permanence in the distribution of a critical social good such as health care. Historically, hospital care in the United States began with a voluntary system. It was later followed by the development of a public system created to achieve limited governmental purposes. Voluntary hospitals became and remained the mainstay of our health care system. Their capacity to accommodate the changing needs of the public they have served is evidenced by the fact that they have persisted and provided stability to our hospital system as the single most important element over a history when both public and proprietary institutions have cyclically expanded and contracted. The recent resurgence of proprietary hospitals, and the reconsideration of the roles of public, voluntary, and proprietary institutions marks an important new period for hospitals. The history of voluntary hospitals indicates they will make responsible adjustments to public needs during this period and continue as the dominant and stabilizing force in our hospital system now and in the future. The loss of our voluntary hospital system would represent, in an historical context, an unconscionable threat to the permanence and stability of our system.

Need for Federal Restraint

This is a time of great and fundamental challenge to the voluntary health care system. This chapter has advanced arguments as to why it is essential that America retain its voluntary hospital system as a critical element of a competitive marketplace, at least until we can determine how successful voluntary hospitals can be in balancing the competitive pressures they are facing with the demands of their traditional missions, how large the unmet need would turn out to be if such missions were abandoned, and how it might otherwise be met.

Faced with increased competition for market share, there is strong pressure on many such institutions to pursue business missions so singularly that their community services missions are all but abandoned. Voluntary hospitals will make important decisions in the next few years concerning the extent of the mission risks they can take. Society and government have a very high stake in the outcome of these decisions. Changes in government policies toward voluntary hospitals could have a major impact on these institutions' decisions in an era when hospital executives and trustees are struggling to manage their changing values.

The process of balancing and integrating values in an institution during a period of change is a difficult and sensitive one. Some trustees and managers might be relieved if laws were enacted, or the public judgment otherwise expressed, that labels them a "business like any other." It would simplify their problems and allow them to proceed with a clearer sense of what constitutes success, unencumbered by the fuzzier, more difficult-to-interpret community services values—and the sometimes difficult relationships to various community groups and leaders that are entailed. Such a judgment might prompt other trustees and managers (such as those from religious orders) to conclude that they should get out of health care and express their sense of community services mission in other fields, such as housing or education. Actions by the federal government that express such judgment, in tax and Medicare law for example, could drastically affect the will and capacity of these institutions to continue the struggle. In other words, premature legislative actions based on the idea that hospitals are turning into businesses like any other will become self-fulfilling prophecies—they will help assure that outcome, and could cost our society dearly.

The competitive marketplace for hospitals is strong and working. Government should wait and watch how hospitals adjust. By such restraint, government can allow the voluntary alternative an opportunity to prove its continued value to our society, in the years ahead in this new era of our history, as it has proven itself in the past. In addition, government policy makers should review proposed and existing policies aimed at other objectives to assure that they do not worsen the voluntary hospitals' chances of continuing their historic mission.